The Cult of the Revolutionary Tradition

PATRICK H. HUTTON

UNIVERSITY OF CALIFORNIA PRESS

BERKELEY · LOS ANGELES · LONDON

The Cult of the Revolutionary Tradition
THE BLANQUISTS IN
FRENCH POLITICS, 1864-1893

University of California Press
Berkeley and Los Angeles, California
University of California Press, Ltd.
London, England
© 1981 by
The Regents of the University of California
Printed in the United States of America

1 2 3 4 5 6 7 8 9

Library of Congress Cataloging in Publication Data

Hutton, Patrick H.
  The cult of the revolutionary tradition.
  Bibliography: p.
  Includes index.
  1. Blanqui, Louis Auguste, 1805-1881.
2. Socialism in France—History.   3. France—
Politics and government—19th century.   I. Title.
HX263.B56H87   322.4'2'0944   80-28850
ISBN 0-520-04114-3

  Portions of chapters VI and VII were published in the *Journal of Modern History* and are reprinted here by permission of the University of Chicago Press.

FOR LINDA
and her love of France

Contents

Illustrations

Preface

In tracing the thirty-year journey of the Blanquists through the revolutionary politics of late nineteenth-century France, I have made a journey one-third as long. In the course of gathering material for this book during the past ten years, I have traveled to France several times. Although I did not begin by studying the Blanquists, they were the group upon which my interest in the French Left finally coalesced. I first became acquainted with the Blanquists while doing research for my doctoral dissertation on the Boulangist movement. Whereas I found the Boulangists interesting for political methods which pointed toward the future, I found the Blanquists equally so for their dedication to traditions rooted deep in their revolutionary heritage. The Boulangists are often identified with the Right, yet their political campaigns were highly experimental. The Blanquists are thought of as a left-wing faction, but their political conceptions were based upon a strict reading of fading rhetorical formulas coined during the French Revolution. Sorting out the relationship between these two groups marked my point of departure and served as the basis of an article which appeared in the *Journal of Modern History* in 1974.

But the study of the Blanquists themselves launched me on a more extended journey. Having probed the politics of Blanquism, I decided to consider its intellectual sources in the thought of the Blanquist youth movement of the 1860s. I was surprised by what I found. I discovered that the core of Blanquist ideology was neither socialist nor nationalist, but atheist, and that the Blanquists' efforts to give their cause a political expression were derived from their atheist convictions. I discovered as well a certain intellectual depth in their arguments, at least in the writings of their most intelligent spokesmen—Henri Place, Albert Regnard, and especially Gustave Tridon. Their cause went deeper than the anticlericalism of the day, that is, the political protest against the public role of a Church which obstucted social and educational reform. Their quarrel was with the idea of religion itself, which they saw as a barrier to positive action in the world.

The Blanquists argued that the first task of revolutionaries in the modern world is to dispel myth—myth being equated with illusion. But the history of the Blanquists is full of the irony of a group which made revolution to combat myth only to discover the deeply mythological sources of their own conception of revolution. The Blanquist myth of revolution is best understood through the study of the rites and rituals they constructed over the three decades of their political activity. This process of building a liturgy of revolution began simply, even peripherally, but eventually it became their all-consuming passion. That passion I have labeled the politics of anniversary remembrance.

Among the most characteristic rites of the politics of anniversary remembrance were the pilgrimages which the Blanquists and other veterans of the French revolutionary movement made to Paris's eastern cemetery, Père-Lachaise. This is the graveyard not only of the Commune's heroes, but also of the Commune's last stand. In the era before the first world war, hundreds, sometimes thousands, of left-wing militants gathered there each year to manifest their revolutionary solidarity by paying tribute to the dead of the Commune. Like other historians who have studied Blanqui and his followers, I have traced their ritual steps across Paris to that old cemetery. On my first visit, it was with some difficulty that I found Blanqui's grave. The gatekeeper told me, "He is not here." But I had heard that sort of refrain from French officialdom often enough not to take the remark seriously, and I continued my search among the walkways and tombstones until I happened upon it, not far from the "wall of the *fédérés*," the hallowed ground where the Commune's last defenders were gunned down. Dalou's sculptured effigy of Blanqui still invites meditation. But I also sensed the degree to which it was a relic of a form of witness which has since disappeared. Blanqui's monument has ceased to serve as a symbol for a vital ideology to become an artifact of a system of thought closed in upon itself.

If my interest as I began this project was in the nature of the Blanquists' convictions as revolutionaries, my interest as I concluded was increasingly bound up with the techniques through which they held fast to these convictions as their conception of revolution became outmoded. In this respect, I have profited greatly from the work of *Annales* historians and others who have investigated the problem of collective mentalities. These historians have shifted the focus of attention from the stimuli of new ideas to the lethargy of habitual ways of thinking about things. Their emphasis upon the structures of thought rather than upon specific ideologies enabled me to grasp the full significance of the history I had been writing. I came to realize that the ideas of revolutionaries could be viewed in terms of changelessness as well as change, and that the Blanquists' emphasis upon precedent and repetition was deeply rooted in an archaic mentality which understood revolution as a resurrection of an unchanging primal state of mind. Such revolutionaries, by making their conceptions concrete in the ritual reenactment of past revolutionary experience, could continue to shape the minds of followers and sympathizers, even though the forms of thought they employed bore little relationship to the realities of the present age. In this respect, I have learned a great deal from the classic study by Johan Huizinga, *The Waning of the Middle Ages*, which shows how the forms through which a set of values command respect and convey beauty can remain powerful long after they have ceased to serve the specific needs of the cause for which they were created.

Writing this book has often been a lonely journey, but it has been made easier by the kind help of others along the way. The first draft was composed in Soubès, a tiny village in the foothills beneath the Causse du Larzac, where I lived with my family during a sabbatical year in 1974-75. I often felt the incongruity of writing about a Parisian movement in that remote corner of the Languedoc. But Paris, a city I love, was by then one in which I could no longer afford to live. During the year I interspersed research in Paris with reading microfilms and writing in the countryside. The strategy worked well and permitted me to learn about a side of French life which few Americans have the privilege to see. I am especially grateful to Jane and Julian Archer, who lodged me during my trips to Paris. Their zest for life in that city, their knowledge of its byways, and their ingenuity in dealing with the problems of living there made my trips comfortable and enjoyable.

I am grateful to the librarians and employees of the Bibliothèque Nationale, especially for their photographic services. All but one of the illustrations in this book are drawn from the collections of the Cabinet des Estampes at the Bibliothèque Nationale, and I appreciate the permission to reproduce them. In studying the Blanqui papers in the Salle des Manuscrits at the

Bibliothèque Nationale, I was aided by Maurice Paz, a scholar who analyzed the collection for his doctoral dissertation. His willingness to share his profound knowledge enabled me to see the connections between many documents which I might otherwise have overlooked.

I also thank Hélène Tulard and her staff at the Archives de la Préfecture de Police, in Paris, who have aided me on each visit over the past decade. In their new quarters near the Place Maubert, they display the same unfailing goodwill as when the archives were located on the Quai des Orfèvres. Although I miss the charm of the old reading room, the availability of holdings at the new location is a decided improvement over the old days. Denise Fauvel-Rouif, directress of the Institut Français d'Histoire Sociale, kindly made the Eudes papers available. Pierre Pagneaux, librarian at the Institut Universitaire de Hautes Etudes Internationales in Geneva, placed the Granger papers at my disposal.

Portions of Chapters VI and VII have previously appeared in the *Journal of Modern History* and the *Journal of Contemporary History*. I thank the editors of these periodicals for permission to publish material from the articles in somewhat altered form.

I am especially grateful to the National Endowment for the Humanities and to the American Council of Learned Societies for grants which made possible my research trips to France.

My colleagues in the History Department at the University of Vermont have given me solid encouragement in this project and have offered thoughtful criticism of the interpretation underpinning it. I owe special thanks to my colleagues Wolfe Schmokel and Robert V. Daniels, who read and criticized portions of the manuscript. My friend Carolyn Perry prepared the typescript with superb skill.

My deepest gratitude goes to my wife, Linda, who has shared all my travels to France. When I completed my doctoral dissertation in 1969, she presented me with a wax turtle in recognition of my perseverance. She may have hoped the gift would prod me to accelerate my pace on future projects, but it has served rather as a reminder of the customary speed at which I work. Nevertheless, she has read each of the many drafts of this book with careful attention. She remains my most insightful critic.

There are, of course, deeper, less tangible sources to this study. They stretch back to my years of graduate study at the University of Wisconsin. The inspired teaching and dedication to scholarship of my professors there launched me on this venture. I am grateful to Henry Bertram Hill for his sustained personal support and confidence in my work and to George L. Mosse, whose scholarship I greatly admire and from whom I have learned so much.

P.H.H.

Burlington, Vermont
1 July 1980

CHAPTER I

The Blanquists in the French Revolutionary Tradition

This is a study of the use of myth and ritual in French revolutionary politics. It focuses upon the disciples of Louis-Auguste Blanqui, the legendary hero of the French revolutionary movement in the nineteenth century. The Blanquists were a sect of professional revolutionaries, bound by personal ties and by loyalty to Blanqui. Successively a student society during the Second Empire, a political faction in the Paris Commune of 1871, a band of exiles in England in the 1870s, and a committee of Communard veterans in Paris during the 1880s, the Blanquists enjoyed a sustained reputation for being the most zealous defenders of the French revolutionary tradition. Because of this reputation, they exercised far-reaching influence in left-wing politics in the early years of the Third Republic.

Throughout the nineteenth century, the revolutionary movement in France had placed its faith in a conception of the French Revolution of 1789-1794 as a formative experience providing precedents for future action. The experiments with political and social reform attempted during these years provided touchstones against which revolutionaries measured their efforts. Political discourse was phrased in a terminology coined during the revolutionary era. Contemporary events were interpreted in light of the revolution's patterns. The leading personalities as well as the anonymous participants in the revolution were in turn idealized in historical writing, in journalism, and ultimately in the popular imagination. This formative experience was, moreover, one which offered a seedbed of new political and social theories. Although nineteenth-century revolutionaries could arrive at no consensus about the relative merits of these theories, they nonetheless agreed that it was to this seminal experience that they must return for inspiration and guidance. Through these efforts to revisit the French Revolution in some comprehensive perspective, the myth of an eighteenth-century event became a nineteenth-century tradition.[1]

For an appreciation of this revolutionary tradition, the Blanquists provide the richest source of all. For they were inspired by the sentiment that they were completing the unfinished agenda of the French Revolution. In their efforts to renew the enthusiasm which had animated the popular insurrections of 1792, of 1848, and especially of 1871, they commemorated these events and eulogized their martyrs. What distinguished the Blanquists was their rituals. More than any other revolutionary group in late nineteenth-century France, they celebrated their heritage with symbols, rites, and festivals. In effect, they became the liturgists of the French revolutionary tradition.

The Blanquists spoke for a conception of revolution best characterized as Jacobin. The term had been invented during the French Revolution three-quarters of a century before and had in the intervening years been variously defined. Its original meaning was derived from the name of a club in Paris where many of the leading politicians caucused during the early days of the French Revolution. In the following years, the Jacobin club established contact with similar societies throughout the country, and these in turn played a key role in organizing support for the revolution and in sustaining revolutionary fervor. In the process, the term Jacobin came to characterize the political elite of a variety of republican factions (Girondin, Montagnard, Dantonist, Maratist) which rivaled one another for leadership in the revolutionary assemblies. The term is sometimes applied more precisely to the revolutionary faction led by Maximilien Robespierre which wrested leadership from the others by advocating a strong, centralized revolutionary government empowered to carry out the vital tasks of the revolution. This identification of Jacobinism with state power found its fullest expression in the work of the Committee of Public Safety, which exercised broad discretionary authority to prosecute warfare abroad and internal subversion at home from 1792 to 1794. Whether broadly or narrowly defined, the term was usually reserved for the revolution's elite of political radicals, as distinguished from its popular cadres—notably the *sans culottes* of Paris, who advocated a more significant role for the ordinary citizen in monitoring and carrying forward the work of the revolution.[2]

In the nineteenth century, however, Jacobinism came to be more loosely construed. Those hostile to the revolutionary movement employed the term in a pejorative sense, that is, as a catch-all phrase to describe anyone whose ideas or activities seemed a threat to constituted authority.[3] But even among revolutionaries themselves, the meaning of Jacobinism acquired broader connotations, for the term expressed the common ground of their aspirations. In short, Jacobinism became a term which denoted political attitudes rather than political factions. It was, moreover, a reformulation which put the accent upon the solidarity of revolutionary elites and their popular followers rather than upon their differences.[4] In this study, Jacobinism will be employed in the nineteenth-century sense: as a set of fundamental conceptions about the political ideals of the revolutionary movement shared by a wide spectrum of the French Left. Militants who joined rival revolutionary factions, who preferred different party labels, and who disagreed about specific policies nonetheless were at one in accepting certain underlying assumptions about the nature and meaning of the revolutionary movement. These assumptions, in turn, shaped the political vocabulary, the modes of parlance, and even the styles of behavior which enabled them to relate to one another even when they disagreed. In this sense, Jacobinism marked the conceptual boundaries which framed the mental universe of those revolutionary militants within the French tradition who were committed to political action. It was these Jacobin attitudes which in their repeated restatement through the nineteenth century provided the revolutionary movement in France with its essential political conceptions.[5]

In the first instance, Jacobins were nationalists. Their nationalism stressed the sovereign power of the people to oversee matters of state. Their political slogans preached solidarity among the oppressed and called for a revolution of national liberation. In the nineteenth century, the oppressors were ordinarily identified as the newly privileged aristocracy of wealth, the lawyers, businessmen, property owners, and other notables who had used the French Revolution to install themselves as the new political elite. Accordingly, Jacobins drew a distinction between the "legal" and the "real" countries, entities which might coincide geographically but which represented different conceptions of the national interest. The legal country was composed of the civil elite, men whose wealth and property provided them with the right to vote and to hold public office. The real country was composed of the "people," a grouping vague enough to include artisans, shopkeepers, skilled craftsmen, domestic employees, and the honest poor. Their productivity, integrity, and good

sense, the Jacobins claimed, made them the rightful heirs to the
political power for which they had fought in a succession of
Parisian insurrections but which they had been repeatedly denied. The Jacobins were French patriots, but they were not chau-
vinists. They expressed a strong sense of solidarity with oppressed peoples of other nations. They believed that the various
peoples of Europe shared a common struggle against the cosmo-
politan aristocracies which dominated their respective countries.
This emphasis upon national liberation gave to Jacobinism a combative edge. For the Jacobins, the idea of nationalism grew out of
feelings of revolutionary comradeship which, they believed,
would radiate their influence as the revolution gathered
momentum.[6]

Second, Jacobins were democrats. They believed that politics
implied participation, and they committed themselves to varied
forms of direct political action. Jacobins stressed the importance
of involvement in political clubs and societies. Regular participation at political meetings, formal and informal, was for the Jacobin politician of the nineteenth century a way of life. At the
same time, Jacobins were suspicious of parliaments as institutions in which the common interest was often sacrificed amid
the bargaining of elites. While the necessity of parliaments was
conceded, the Jacobins reserved the right of the people to monitor
parliamentary deliberations. Their watchword was vigilance over
the legislative use of power. When such power was misused, they
invoked the right of popular intervention. In this way, the "revolutionary days" of 1789, 1792, 1830, and 1848 received theoretical justification. The suspicion of parliaments was balanced by
sympathy for strong executive, even personal, leadership. The
ideal political leader stood above party, embodied the national
interest, and, by a combination of example and persuasion,
evoked from the people a commitment to seek the national interest. From 1789 to 1871 a number of Jacobin tribunes aspired
to fill this role: Danton, Robespierre, Hébert, Napoleon, Ledru-
Rollin, Gambetta, and of course Blanqui. The task was to inspire
without dictating to the people. It was a balance never achieved,
often perverted, yet continually appealing in its call for high-
minded simplicity amidst the complex, sometimes venal dealings
of ordinary politicians.

The Jacobin ideal of democracy also had its social implications.
Jacobins believed that a sense of social responsibility could only
be fostered in a society which set limits upon the wealth and

poverty of its citizens. In the Jacobin mind, the capacity for self-sufficiency was to be combined with an acceptance of social responsibility, an ideal which could only be achieved in a community from which extreme affluence and extreme indigence had been banished. While the Jacobins were not socialists, they were committed to a certain measure of social equality. They tended, moreover, to see the little people of the cities as their primary constituency, and to display a corresponding mistrust not only of the bourgeoisie but of the rural world as well.[7]

Third, Jacobins were republicans. The meaning of republicanism in the Jacobin perspective must be understood in terms of the political struggles of the French Left in the nineteenth century, struggles which perpetuated a fundamental quarrel among the leaders of the French Revolution. The revolution had begun with a consolidated front of opposition to the institutions of the Old Regime. But as the old order collapsed, this revolutionary phalanx divided into liberal and democratic movements. The liberals, identified especially with the interests of the middle class, quickly consolidated their power and proceeded to create a regime based upon constitutional law, parliamentary supremacy, administrative uniformity, and special political privileges for the propertied classes. This model of revolution, with its accent upon juridical reconstruction, served as the foundation for the Constitutional Monarchy of 1791, the Constitutional Republic of 1795, and the July Monarchy of 1830.

Liberalism shaped not only a succession of political regimes, but also a style of political behavior sometimes labeled Orleanism. Orleanism, as it was exercised by the middle-class political dynasties of the nineteenth century, eventually shaped the governments of opposing regimes—the Second Republic, the last years of the Second Empire, and the early years of the Third Republic. It was as a liberal movement, therefore, that the French Revolution bequeathed its most enduring legacy to the nineteenth century. Yet the liberal revolution was to a large extent made possible by the democratic one with which Jacobins identified. This cause, for which the popular classes of the cities (especially the sans culottes of Paris) provided the cadres, inspired the political insurrections, the revolutionary days of July and October 1789 and of August 1792, which enabled the liberal revolution to survive. Only from 1792 to 1794 did this democratic movement briefly rival the liberal elite for direction of the revolutionary cause. During those years, the Jacobins succeeded in creating a republic based upon universal suffrage, strong executive leadership, and a commitment to experiment with economic and social reforms. This more egalitarian revolution failed to survive but nonetheless served as a precedent to inspire the revolutionary days of July 1830, February 1848, and September 1870.

The revolutionary politics of nineteenth-century France, therefore, can be read as a rivalry between these two movements, at times united against more conservative forces, but at odds once their common cause was about to succeed. In 1830, 1848, and again in 1870, liberal and Jacobin interests acted in concert to topple constituted authority. Yet in each instance, the liberal politicians consolidated the victory and denied the Jacobins the implementation of their vision of popular democracy. Out of this protracted struggle, republicanism became the motto of the Jacobin opposition. Republicanism came to be identified not only with an alternative conception of government to that fashioned by liberal politicians, but also with political methods which historically had identified democracy with popular insurrection.[8]

It is at this juncture that the ideological solidarity of nineteenth-century Jacobins begins to unravel. For Jacobins quarreled among themselves over the question of how revolutionary authority should be exercised: through formal direction or inspired example. It was a debate which dated from 1793, when Montagnards, favoring the former approach, and Hébertists, favoring the latter, had been rivals for leadership of the popular revolution at Paris. In interpreting their own role as leaders, the Blanquists looked to the Hébertists for their self-conceptions. The Hébertists had been prominent figures in the Revolutionary Commune of Paris of 1793. They presented themselves as the most egalitarian of the revolutionary factions. Deeply involved in the municipal politics of Paris, sensitive to the interests of the sans culottes, the Hébertists opposed Robespierre and his Montagnards for their dictatorial style. The latter insisted upon the right of the revolutionary elite to pose goals and to exercise broad discretionary power to accomplish them. For the Hébertists, however, the role of the revolutionary elite was instrumental only. Ultimate authority for shaping the revolution rested with its popular cadres. The revolutionary might be a teacher, an agitator, or a moral authority, but never a commander. In challenging the authoritarian approach of Robespierre, the Hébertists created the enemy who was to become their executioner in the

spring of 1794. Still, the Blanquists preferred the Hébertist conception of inspirational leadership, which taught that the authentic leader must share the suffering of oppressed people. In this
respect, the Blanquists especially admired the Hébertists for the
revolutionary festivals they sponsored, festivals in which the
sans culottes could see their virtues made concrete in ceremonial
pageantry. The revolutionary festival, by obliterating distinctions between leaders and followers, placed the accent upon the
collective identity of the revolutionary party as a confraternity
unified by a common struggle.[9]

Yet the Blanquists recognized that more than ritual would have
been needed to sustain the popular revolution in 1793. The inability of the Hébertists to promote successfully their democratic ideal led the Blanquists to emphasize the importance of the
professional revolutionary who could ensure that the revolutionary cause would survive even after popular enthusiasm had
waned. The professional revolutionary was a secular monk—
totally committed to revolutionary action, totally adapted to its
ordeal, and totally given to the personal asceticism which such
activism entailed. The revolutionary's secret society was the asylum in which the revolutionary ideal was guarded until conditions permitted it to inspire a larger following once again.

Partisans of Hébert by preference, the Blanquists became followers of "Gracchus" Babeuf, known as the first professional
revolutionary, by necessity.[10] With the fall of the Jacobins and
the return to moderate liberal rule in 1794, Babeuf organized a
conspiracy and plotted a coup d'etat. He was captured, tried, and
executed in 1797. At his trial, he bravely defended his actions
and spoke eloquently of the immortality of the ideals he had
championed.[11] In this way, Babeuf implanted the notion that
others would succeed him to carry on his struggle. The story of
his conspiracy and martyrdom thus became an inspiring legend
for the revolutionary underground of nineteenth-century
France. There were moral attachments, if not real links, between
the followers of Babeuf in the 1790s, the secret societies of Blanqui in the 1830s, and the Blanquist youth groups in the 1860s.
For the Blanquists, the failure of the popular uprisings of 1830
and 1848 appeared to confirm the necessity of the professional
revolutionary's ongoing role. It had been the professional revolutionary who, since the fall of the Hébertists, had sustained the
hopes of the revolutionary cause. Across all the defeats which
the revolutionary movement had experienced in the intervening

century, the Blanquists continued to hear echoes of Babeuf's defiant cry.[12]

Despite the immersion of the Blanquists in memories of revolutions past, Marxist historians have ascribed to them an important preparatory role in the rise of the socialist movement in France, conceived as the wave of the future. In this respect, they are praised for their revolutionary activism rather than for their social theories. Marxist scholars usually present the Blanquists as unreflective precursors of the Marxists, as militants who espoused a doctrine of revolution more noteworthy for its enthusiasm than for its content. Eduard Bernstein, for example, analyzing the French revolutionary movement in its waning days, praises the Blanquists for their commitment to "creative revolution," but he chides them for their inability to grasp theoretically the economic foundations of historical change.[13] Roger Garaudy likewise argues that neither Blanqui nor his followers ever understood how economic processes shape historical development.[14] For André Marty, the Blanquists were simply activists who shared Marxist goals but who proved unable to formulate them adequately.[15] From the Marxist vantage point, it is clear, the willfulness and spontaneity of the Blanquists were viewed as sorry substitutes for a more patient understanding of the laws of history

But the differences between Blanquists and Marxists amounted to more than different degrees of intellectual sophistication in interpreting the same social reality. Marxism was not just a scientific statement of Jacobin revolutionary theory. It spoke to the new realities of an industrial, mass society, realities which had little to do with the preindustrial world of artisans and shopkeepers in which Jacobin thought had first been honed. Marxism introduced a vocabulary of economics, a conception of the social structure, and a theory of political change which forced the revolutionaries of late nineteenth-century France to rethink their basic commitments. Some militants, notably Jules Guesde and his followers, gave themselves totally to the new doctrine and became vigorous proselytizers for it. But for the Blanquists and many other veterans of the revolutionary cause in France, Marxism threatened to cut the revolutionary movement adrift from its historical moorings.

In fact, Marxists and Blanquists in late nineteenth-century France conceived of revolution in opposing ways. The Marxists described the good society with metaphors of the future and spoke of economic processes preparing the way for a new kind of revolution which would free man from the burdens which had been his lot throughout history. Participation in the revolutionary cause represented a quest to fulfill a historical process which was creating a new social world from which there would be no return. The Blanquists, however, were clearly trying to recapture an ideal of social harmony lost in the past. The revolution to which they committed themselves was an intellectual one, based upon a conception of the good society which they believed had been briefly implemented during the Revolutionary Commune of 1793. It was, moreover, a social ideal which they believed had still earlier precedents, one which had been discovered and forgotten repeatedly through the ages. If the Marxists contended that ideas were but a reflection of underlying economic processes, the Blanquists affirmed the primary importance of ideas and were continually preoccupied with the aesthetic images in which their ideas could be more effectively conveyed.

The nature of this intellectual confrontation between French Marxists, espousing a new socialism for the industrial age, and the Blanquists, steeped in the heritage of the revolutionary tradition, has long been obscured by the hagiographic interpretation of the rise of the socialist movement in France offered by its first historians. Some, such as Alexandre Zévaès, Paul Louis, and Maurice Dommanget, read into the origins of the movement their own aspirations for a gathering unity of the socialist cause. Hence they characterize socialist ideology in late nineteenth-century France as an eclectic doctrine which assimilated the various currents of French social thought into a new, collectivist blend.[16] In this view, Blanquists and Marxists contributed to a common philosophy. It is not surprising, therefore, that in studying the Blanquists these historians have focused on the intellectual formation of Edouard Vaillant, the Blanquist militant whose efforts to marry Blanquism and Marxism epitomized their conception of French socialist thought.[17] Vaillant had prepared the way for their interpretation by describing the ideological evolution of the Blanquists in terms which follow closely his own personal development toward a "revisionist" Marxist social philosophy.[18]

For these historians, the rise of socialism provides the essential frame of reference for discussion of the nature of the revolutionary movement in the latter half of the nineteenth century. In the transition from the neo-Hébertist doctrine of the Blanquists to the modified Marxist ideology of the nascent Socialist party, they explain, the intellectual continuity of the revolutionary tradition was preserved, the revolutionary movement was renewed, and revolutionary theorizing was elevated to a more scientific plane. The argument is typified in Dommanget's tableau of the aging Blanqui graciously declining Paul Lafargue's invitation to participate with his celebrated father-in-law, Karl Marx, in the drafting of the inaugural program of the French Socialist party in 1880, thereby quietly passing the baton of revolutionary leadership to the young Jules Guesde, the most ardent apostle of the new collectivist doctrine.[19]

But the arrival of Marxism upon the French political scene during the 1870s, far from providing a new basis for revolutionary unity, prompted the Blanquists to draw deeper into the old forms of revolutionary practice. They had risen to prominence in the Second Empire (the 1860s) by identifying themselves with the cutting edge of Jacobin revolutionary ideology. But their role in the Third Republic (the 1880s) had less to do with the radicalism of their doctrine than with their determination that it should endure. Throughout the 1870s in exile and the 1880s in Paris once more, the Blanquists provided leadership for that element of the revolutionary movement which preferred to cherish its heritage rather than to seek out a new direction. They had become the guardians of the revolutionary tradition. The task, they believed, was to reaffirm its value as a basis for future change in opposition to the newfangled notions derived from collectivist doctrine. This concern drew diverse revolutionary factions together by evoking the deep convictions which united them. As the realities of earlier insurrections receded into the past, so too did the quarrels which had once divided them.

By the 1880s, the meaning of the revolutionary tradition, shorn of the issues and controversies of an earlier age, revealed the simpler, underlying imperatives described above as the common ground of Jacobin thought: comradeship in political struggle as the foundation of patriotism, social virtue as the basis of popular democracy, republicanism as a prerequisite for social reform, and the French Revolution as the experiment in which these ideals were first tested. Such principles commanded broad assent among left-wing militants in the early years of the Third Republic and provided a basis for ceremonial solidarity designed to rekindle the enthusiasm which had inspired earlier insurrections. Rather than gathering into a common fold, the revolutionary movement in late nineteenth-century France remained deeply divided over whether the good society was a past or a future ideal.

It is in this context that the Blanquists' preoccupation with myth and ritual must be appreciated. They practiced what is best characterized as a politics of anniversary remembrance. It became their task to make the revolutionary tradition concrete through rites of commemoration designed to glorify the martyrs and dramatize the events of the revolutionary movement since 1789. Herein the Blanquists partook of a wide array of activities: ritual walks among the places in Paris sacred to the revolutionary movement, pilgrimages to the cemeteries where fallen heroes of the revolutionary cause were buried, the erection of monuments to honor the most celebrated martyrs of their cause, and literary reminiscences in their newspapers of the heroes and villains of the revolutionary saga. The anniversaries of the revolutionary days of a century of insurrection punctuated a calendar of liturgical celebration. These activities, moreover, placed an accent upon the aesthetics of the revolutionary experience. The Blanquists devoted much imagination to the creation of tableaux of remembrance in which the beauty and harmony of the ceremony transfigured the original event by lending it a wholeness it had never possessed. Busts of revolutionary leaders, often cast by well-known sculptors, dotted the cemeteries of Paris, especially the eastern cemetery of Père-Lachaise. In the cult of the dead, the contradictions and enigmas of the personalities of departed revolutionary leaders were overcome in images of them which personified only their revolutionary virtues.

In planning and organizing these ceremonial activities, the Blanquists, though a small sect, proved able to mobilize large demonstrations of revolutionary solidarity in the 1880s. Such ceremonies revealed that the ideals of the revolutionary tradition continued to convey power long after the realities they were designed to meet had disappeared. For this reason, the Blanquist cult of the revolutionary tradition can be likened to a code of chivalry for the revolutionary movement. The cult evoked allegiance to Jacobin ideals deeply embedded in the mental habits of a wide spectrum of the Left and fulfilled in fantasy their expectations about the future of the revolutionary movement.

If the Blanquists and other like-minded revolutionaries held fast to Jacobin conceptions, the political world around them was fast changing. The years 1864 to 1893, in which Blanquist activ-

ities were concentrated, mark a crucial era of transformation for
the political process, an era which witnessed the advent of mass
politics. Mass politics signifies the efforts of political leaders to
integrate vast numbers of people into political parties by providing them with a fuller sense of participation in the political
process. Earlier, parties across the political spectrum had been
small, informal, and generally elitist in character. Structures
grouping people with similar political leanings were few. The
world of politics was for the most part limited to the caucuses of
parliamentary deputies and municipal councillors or to the news-
rooms of journalists. The parties of the Left appealed to popular
constituencies but only occasionally sought to mobilize them and
rarely drew them into their councils. Even the secret societies of
the revolutionary movement were content to remain small and
sectarian. The new mass politics depended upon strategies designed to sustain popular political involvement in an age in which
the franchise had been significantly extended.

In the Third Republic, members of the Chamber of Deputies,
as well as a host of departmental and municipal officials, were
elected by universal male suffrage. To exploit these possibilities,
the modern political party, with its national organizational structure, its syndicated press, its hierarchies of officials, its demand
for electoral discipline, and its increasingly sophisticated techniques of propaganda, was born.[20] The participation to which
the new electorate was invited was more vicarious than real, but
no party was immune to the changes that were occurring. The
Blanquists, like other political groups, were faced with a need to
democratize their organization. Subtly, the ceremonies they had
designed to recall old traditions began to serve the ends of the
new politics. The politics of anniversary remembrance had been
intended to reawaken slumbering revolutionary fervor. But as
the prospect of a popular insurrection appeared unlikely in the
1880s, the demonstrative displays provided by the festivals of
the revolutionary tradition contributed to the momentum of
electoral campaigns.

A measure of the change taking place is revealed through a
comparison of the two great political crises in which the Blanquists participated, the Paris Commune of 1871 and the Boulangist movement of 1886-1889. The Paris Commune fitted easily
into the historical pattern of popular insurrection in the nineteenth century. The insurrection in which the Commune was
born contained many of the ingredients present in earlier up-

heavals: Parisian economic and social unrest, a provisional government with tenuous loyalties, and a confrontation between liberals and democrats over the most appropriate form of government with which to replace the old order. But the Commune was too short-lived and harried by adversity to acquire clear definition. The meaning of this regime for those who viewed it in retrospect, therefore, was derived less from what it was than from their hopes for what it might have been.[21] For Marx, the Commune was a prelude to the long-awaited revolution that would usher in the classless society. For the Blanquists, in contrast, it was not only a revolutionary event but a conception of the good society derived from the experience of the Revolutionary Commune of Paris in 1793. Of this conception the Blanquists had become apostles well before the events of 1871 had actually transpired.

The idealized memory of the Commune, culled from its prophetic anticipation as much as from its actual manifestation, remained vital to Blanquist politics in the Third Republic. The myth of the Commune became a major component of their cult of the revolutionary tradition, as this myth reaffirmed earlier revolutionary experience in the process of absorbing it into present revolutionary practice. Presented literally by the Blanquists as an event which recapitulated a century of past revolutionary experience, the myth of the Commune soon exercised a wider, figurative appeal for those on the Left who had become disillusioned with the Third Republic during the 1870s. The moderate republican leadership of the new regime had set an "Opportunist" course, one which adapted republican objectives and values to the institutional machinery and parliamentary procedures which had served the constitutional monarchies of the nineteenth century, and in whose liberal image the Third Republic had initially been designed. The Blanquist myth of the Commune provided the Left with an emblem of some future, if as yet ill-defined, democratic republic which might eventually supplant the existing regime. Throughout the 1880s, the Blanquists were able to capitalize upon this conception of the Commune to reinforce their own image as the authentic bearers of the revolutionary tradition.

The Boulangist movement, too, was an expression of Jacobin discontent which drew together the constituent elements of the revolutionary tradition. Radicals, populists, and Blanquists were all enticed into General Boulanger's cause. The Boulangists were

committed to constitutional revision, and their propaganda about
creating a more open, democratic republic evoked longings similar to those which had perpetuated the myth of the Commune.
Yet Boulangist political rhetoric was constructed of high-blown
phrases about national reconciliation which did not draw upon
the specific political imagery of the revolutionary tradition. In
the Boulangist restatement of Jacobin values, Blanquist concerns
were lost from view. Yet Blanquists and Boulangists were attracted to one another out of a mutual understanding of the
power of political rituals.

The appeal of the Boulangist movement to the Left was in its
methods. It was the first popular opposition movement to deal
extensively in modern techniques of publicity, mass rallies, and
elaborate campaign organization.[22] Sensing that Boulangism
was a movement which might effectively undermine the political
establishment, the Blanquists hoped to use it as a basis for launch-
ing an insurrection in the midst of the chaos they believed Boulangism would promote. Rather, the effect of the Boulangist
adventure was to obscure Jacobin concerns and ultimately to
reveal the waning power of the cult of the revolutionary tradition. The Boulangist movement was soon scattered and its participants compromised in its ensuing scandals. With their revolutionary ideals trivialized in the ambiguous objectives of Boulangism, the Blanquists lost the esteem of the French Left. The
link between Blanquist-inspired ceremonies and the Left's recollection of its revolutionary heritage was thenceforth severed.

In one sense, the history of the Blanquists represents the attrition of their belief in a conception of revolution modeled upon
the popular insurrections of late eighteenth- and early nineteenth-century France. In their changing perception of their own
ideology through a generation of revolutionary activism, the
Blanquists exchanged a vision of revolution as a real possibility
for one of revolution as an ideal fantasy, to which some of them
clung despite their awareness that it would change nothing. In
the demise of the Blanquists in the 1890s, the cult of the revolutionary tradition as a factor in left-wing politics dissolved, soon
to be replaced by the rituals of the new socialism.

Yet the study of revolutionary thought is of interest not only
for its particular ideologies but also for its underlying mentalities. The point is that the revolutionary movement, like other
groupings on the political spectrum, had its modernizers and its
traditionalists. In late nineteenth-century France, the Marxists

were the modernizers, presenting a doctrine tailored to the changing needs of the revolutionary movement. Open toward the future, Marxism tended to be experimental, as its "revisionist" expression makes manifest. The Blanquists, however, were clearly in the traditionalist camp. If Marxist thought was noteworthy for its flexibility, Blanquist thought was conspicuous for its rigidity. It was the rigidity of the Blanquists' thought which underpinned their reputation as intransigent revolutionaries and which led them to untenable extremes. In this sense, Blanquism represented the expression of an archaic revolutionary mentality which interpreted present realities in light of images identified with a primordial golden age.

Most studies of revolutionary thought dramatize change, but this study of the archaic revolutionary mentality will underscore the inertial power of habits of mind which rendered difficult the acceptance of change. The Blanquists are remarkable for the tenacity with which they clung to their conceptions despite changing realities. It is as if they possessed a mindset which retained its forms even though its content was periodically drained and renewed. In this book that mindset will be considered in depth via an analysis of the myth of revolution through which it found expression—myth being understood not as a fiction to be exposed, but rather as an integral structure of thought out of which a comprehensive vision of the world, past and future, is formed. Briefly stated, that myth contained the following elements: allegiance to an archetypal hero, born incarnate in successive historical ages; the elaboration of a typology of revolutionary roles and virtues; the definition of revolutionary practice in terms of sacred times and places; the conception of revolution as a primordial event to be recreated; the formulation of a hermetic doctrine which reveals the hidden meaning of visible conflict; the division of the world into sharply drawn camps of good and evil; comradeship as the essential bond of the revolutionary movement; and internal subversion as the primary threat to the revolutionary cause. The terminology used to identify these elements was modified. But the elements themselves remained unchanged.

What endured for the Blanquists through thirty years of working in the revolutionary movement was their will to believe in this myth of revolution. Despite changing conditions, party labels, and leading personalities, the Blanquists remained faithful to this mythic paradigm. Historians have been interested in the Blanquists because they dealt directly with the problem of inciting a popular insurrection. But for the Blanquists themselves the event of revolution was never as important as the state of mind which made it possible. Especially in their mature years, they were more obviously concerned with the problem of sustaining revolutionary fervor in the absence of revolutionary situations. In their stress upon willfulness at every stage of their experience as revolutionaries, and in their persistent fear that they themselves would lose their willpower, the Blanquists drew deeper into their preoccupation with myth and ritual. Their rituals became more elaborate as their cause became more desperate. But the mythic paradigm to which they were committed remained the ultimate source of all their endeavor. What begins as a study of activism, therefore, ends as a study of faith. How the two are intertwined provides the substance of this book.

CHAPTER II

The Legend of Blanqui

Out of the secret revolutionary societies of early nineteenth-century France emerged a leader of such exceptional stature that the story of his life was destined to become a legend. Louis-Auguste Blanqui (1805-1881) is at once the best known and the most obscure of the militants identified with the French revolutionary tradition, for his life was a paradoxical interplay of publicity and secrecy. He is celebrated as the most unrelenting insurrectionist of his age, yet much of this reputation rests upon his involvement in a single scheme: an abortive attempt to overthrow the July Monarchy in 1839. Though active in the revolutionary underground for much of his career, he exercised wide influence through his momentary but highly visible role as journalist and orator during the revolutions of 1830, 1848, and 1870-71. Although he was reputed to rule his followers with dictatorial zeal, he professed that he wished no supervisory role, and he taught his disciples that a leader should be emulated rather than obeyed. Feared by conservatives as a sinister conspirator breeding discontent, he was revered by sympathizers as an unrelenting idealist, alone in his struggle against political oppression. To the outsider, he was stern and aloof. To his intimate acquaintances, he appeared genial and deeply humane. Extolled as a theorist of revolution, he never expressed his point of view systematically.

Most of Blanqui's early writings were destroyed, and the archives of his surviving correspondence, memoirs, and reflections (bequeathed by one of his disciples to the Bibliothèque Nationale) are a jumbled mass which historians have deciphered only with great patience.[1] At the time of his death, his life for his eulogists epitomized the adventure of the romantic revolutionary. Yet the somber reality of his existence was the dull routine of prison—the prisons of a monarchy, an empire, and two republics which buried him alive for more than forty years. But Blanqui held fast to his convictions through all his trials, and in brief but telling episodes he regained his freedom long enough to lend his personal leadership and moral authority to the revolutionary cause. Out of these intense, often contradictory images his legend was formed.

Blanqui's saga is worth recounting.[2] He was born in 1805 at Puget-Théniers, a town in the foothills of the Alps not far from Nice. His father, Jean Dominique Blanqui, had been a leading republican figure in Nice and served briefly as a delegate to the Convention, where he sat with the Girondins. Later, he rallied to the empire, for which he was awarded the post of subprefect at Puget-Théniers by Napoleon. The fortunes of the Blanqui family fell with the empire in 1814, and young Auguste was sent to Paris to live with his older brother Adolphe. At the lycée Charlemagne, Auguste quickly established a reputation as a brilliant student. So wide were his intellectual interests that, upon completing his secondary studies, he enrolled simultaneously in the Schools of Medicine and Law at the University of Paris.

Auguste had embarked upon what promised to be a distinguished professional career. His brother Adolphe, who likewise excelled in his studies, became a professor and a leading authority on liberal economic theory. But Auguste was destined to follow a less respectable route. From the early 1820s, he was lured from his studies to the Carbonari, the radical republican societies at Paris; and eventually he abandoned the university altogether for political journalism. As hostility toward the Bourbon regime mounted in the late 1820s, he took a post as reporter for *Le globe*, a leading opposition newspaper edited by the Saint-Simonian Pierre Leroux. During the "July days" of the Revolution of 1830, he found a place on the barricades for the first time. For his participation in the revolution, he was decorated by the new Orleanist monarch with the Order of July. It was the only accolade he ever received from French officialdom.

Blanqui, soon rejecting the July Monarchy as a mockery of the ideals of the French Revolution it claimed to have fulfilled, abandoned public protest for life in the political underground. The student agitator had become the revolutionary conspirator, a passage between estates dramatized in a famous courtroom profession of faith while standing trial in 1832 for conspiracy. When asked by the judge to state his profession, Blanqui identified himself as a "proletarian" and proceeded to excoriate the regime for its oppression of the thirty million peasants and workers of France. For this bravado he was sentenced to a year in prison.

1. The young Blanqui: a legend for radical youth during the Second Empire. Phot. Bibl. Nat.

Confinement did not dampen Blanqui's fervor. A veteran of Godefroy Cavaignac's Society of the Friends of the People, a secret society which had played a part in July days, Blanqui began to form secret societies of his own. With Armand Barbès, he launched the Society of Families in 1836. Dissolved by the police, the group was reconstituted as the Society of the Seasons in the following year. Labeled a dangerous subversive by the Orleanist government, Blanqui was frequently arrested and with each prosecution his prison sentence lengthened. His greatest gamble came in May 1839 when, together with his comrade Barbès, he led a contingent of five hundred rebels in an assault on City Hall at Paris in the hope of toppling the regime in a "revolutionary day" of popular insurrection. Blanqui's insurgents were success-ful in occupying the building but were beaten in two days of fighting. Spared an initial sentence of death for his part in the uprising, Blanqui was consigned instead to life imprisonment at Mont-Saint-Michel with the expectation that his cause would likewise suffer slow extinction.

Blanqui's only respite from revolutionary activity during these years of plotting against the July Monarchy was a love affair with Suzanne-Amélie Serre, whom he married in 1834 and with whom he spent a few happy years. But Suzanne-Amélie died soon after Blanqui was sent to Mont-Saint-Michel, and he was left to face his ordeal alone. In failing health, he was transferred to the prison hospital at Tours in 1844. Pardoned as terminally ill in December of that year, Blanqui spurned the favor and spent four more years in voluntary captivity.

With the uprising of "February days" 1848, Blanqui was freed. He hastened to Paris, where he assumed a leading role within the radical faction. He organized a club, the Central Republican Society, which sponsored nightly lectures, and soon became one of Paris's best-known orators. The club was a springboard for the organization of popular rallies.[3] On March 17, he led a crowd of a hundred thousand to demonstrate at City Hall in an effort to postpone elections for a constituent assembly which, he feared, if held too soon would choose a conservative majority. His fears were justified: with the April elections, the republic passed into the hands of more moderate leadership. But Blanqui and the Parisian radicals were undaunted. On May 15, they led another formidable demonstration, this time to the National Assembly, where Blanqui delivered an impromptu oration. Declaring the National Assembly dissolved, he and his companions proceeded to City Hall, where they vainly attempted to set up a new pro-visional government. Republican government officials had by this time become as uncomfortable with Blanqui as their Orle-anist predecessors had been.[4] Blanqui was rounded up with other radicals in May 1848, tried for sedition before the High Court at Bourges in 1849, and sentenced to ten more years in prison.

During these ten years of imprisonment, Blanqui's life became a legend. As the authorities of the Second Republic and then the Second Empire shunted him from one jail to another, stories of his exploits began to circulate. Composed of the mélange of accounts of his arrests, trials, and imprisonments over two decades, the earliest formulation of the legend of Blanqui carried dark connotations. Most people perceived him as a cunning agitator who plotted continuously to subvert the public order and who surfaced mysteriously at Paris each time a popular insurrection was in the making.[5] The stereotype ascribed to him unusual powers and unusually base intentions. Blanqui's reputation among his revolutionary comrades, moreover, was sullied by the charges of Jules Taschereau, a journalist and public official of the July Monarchy, who published a document suggesting that Blanqui had been a spy for the police during the 1830s and had furnished them with data on the secret societies.[6] Although the charges were never substantiated, Barbès chose to believe them and openly condemned Blanqui.

Calumniated by his enemies, abandoned by his friends, Blanqui was sent to ever more remote prisons. In 1849, he was incarcerated at Doullens in the department of the Somme. In 1850, he was transferred to Belle-Ile-en-Mer, off the coast of Brittany. From there he made a daring escape, only to be captured and transported to prison overseas. In 1857 he was sent to Corte in Corsica, in 1859 to Mascara in Algeria. Amnestied in August of that year, he had no sooner set foot on French soil than he was threatened with transport to a penal colony in Guiana. He weathered that harassment but was arrested in Paris in 1861 for conspiracy to overthrow the government and confined in that city's infamous political prison, Sainte-Pélagie. By that time, the somber hues of Blanqui's many prisons colored his very name. Thenceforth he was known in the popular imagination as "the imprisoned one."[7]

It was appropriate, therefore, that Blanqui's first admirers should have discovered him in this, his most characteristic setting. The Blanquist youth movement of the 1860s was formed out of a nucleus of student admirers who first became acquainted with Blanqui at Sainte-Pélagie.[8] It was their interest in the legends of the revolutionary tradition which first drew these students to him. Just as Filippo Buonarroti, the companion of Babeuf in the conspiracy of 1796, had once acquainted the young Blanqui with the traditions of the French Revolution, so Blanqui served these aspiring revolutionaries of a new generation, who were intent upon reestablishing lines of continuity with the revolutionary underground of the early nineteenth century. In the mythology of the young Blanqui, his admirers saw the model of a life they wished to imitate. They were moved by his rejection of a comfortable career in order to pursue a higher moral calling. His willing acceptance of the image of the political outlaw dramatized for them the direct relationship between values and action in authentic political behavior. Blanqui's legend was an emblem of revolutionary courage and his life a vital link with the secret history of the popular revolution of 1792-1794 which the political elites of the nineteenth century had tried to sever. Thus "the old one" (Le Vieux), as they came to call Blanqui affectionately, became a mentor for youth, as these students looked back upon his secret societies as asylums in which the values of the popular revolution had been preserved.

But Blanqui was for his disciples more than a living archive of past revolutionary glories. He was a model of revolutionary asceticism. His followers stood in awe of the patience with which he endured imprisonment for most of his adult life. Those who shared his confinement pointedly comment upon the quasi-monastic regimen of work, conversation, and exercise from which he never permitted himself the slightest departure. Even out of prison, whether in seclusion abroad or in hiding in Paris, Blanqui displayed the same steadfast self-discipline. In his dedication to the economy of experience in every aspect of his personal style of life, he conveyed a sense of the great style of simplicity and courage to which a revolutionary must commit himself. For this reason, he did not build an organization, but called a following. His appeal to the youth movement which assumed his name in the latter half of the nineteenth century was in the authenticity of a way of life grounded in moral passion.[9]

Blanqui seems to have possessed an intuitive sense of the power of ritual in enhancing his image as a political rebel. To a certain extent, he crafted his own legend. A story is told by Albert Callet, an admiring student, of a pilgrimage made with Blanqui one day toward the end of the Second Empire to the tomb of the four sergeants of La Rochelle, executed some fifty years before (1822) for their opposition to the restored Bourbon monarchy. There the aging insurrectionary hero confided that his witness to that atrocity had marked his conversion to the revolutionary cause.[10] Callet was not alone in his observations about his hero's love of commemorative acts. Paul Lafargue also commented upon Blanqui's reverence for rites of remembrance.[11] It should be noted that Blanqui's first public manifesto as a student leader in 1830 was a plea to the youth of the Medical and Law Schools of the University of Paris to mourn the death of Benjamin Constant, champion of the libertarian values of the French Revolution through the repressive years of Bourbon rule.[12] Some of Blanqui's personal eccentricities suggest his fondness for ceremonial gestures which gave concrete expression to his commitments. His tattered garb, described with loathing by Alexis de Tocqueville, was a self-conscious affirmation of his identification with the suffering of the oppressed.[13] He sometimes signed his newspaper articles "Suzamel" in honor of his late wife; and in his mature years he only rarely removed a black glove which masked the ring he wore in devotion to her memory.[14] In such ways, Blanqui wove images of his personal experience into the lore of a revolutionary heritage in which he sensed himself profoundly rooted.

Because of Blanqui's ability to identify his life with remembrance of the revolutionary tradition his legend assumed grand proportions. For his student followers of the Second Empire, the legend focused on his specific contribution to the revolutionary movement. For them, the name Blanqui inspired the awe of authority. To his rare commands, they were prepared to give unquestioning obedience. During the civil war of 1871, they lamented his absence as the loss of a lawgiver who might have provided the energy and direction needed to save the Commune of Paris from defeat by the national government at Versailles.[15] But as the legend of Blanqui was reformulated in grandiose images during the early years of the Third Republic, it lost its power to inspire commitment.

In the years following the Commune, respect for Blanqui broadened to include many sympathizers who had had no previous connection with him and who rejected his specific strategies for revolution. The image of the rebellious youth, the essence of the early legend, was gradually discarded in favor of one of the aging sage of the revolutionary tradition. By 1879, his name had become the emblem of republican unity in the campaign for the amnesty of the Communards. In that year, he even won election to the Chamber of Deputies as a candidate symbolizing that cause.[16] With heightened respectability came recognition for attributes thitherto unnoticed. Arthur Ranc, once Blanqui's comrade in the revolutionary days of 1848, now likened Blanqui to Léon Gambetta, the moderate republican spokesman, as one of the few genuine statesmen of the age.[17]

It was also in these years that Blanqui's talents as a theorist were for the first time appreciated. His writings on economic and political subjects were published in anthology by his faithful lieutenant Ernest Granger.[18] Benoît Malon, a well-known social critic, gleaned clippings of the newspaper articles Blanqui had written through the years in the hope of discovering traces of a socialist content.[19] Even his tract on cosmology received some recognition.[20] One might argue that by the time of his death in 1881 almost all republicans were Blanquists, although devotion to his memory hardly involved any special sacrifice. Blanqui had become the disembodied emblem for an extremely vague conception of the revolutionary cause, and his legend had acquired connotations of sentimentality altogether foreign to the studied pessimism with which he had accepted his ordeal. It was in this nostalgic vein that Gustave Geffroy, as a preparation for writing what was to be the first full-length biography of Blanqui, visited all the prisons in which he had been incarcerated so that he could vicariously share Blanqui's suffering.[21] The product was an unusually romantic portrait of a man who personally disdained romanticism.

The fact that the legend of Blanqui exhibited so many faces and exerted such a diverse appeal suggests why it is difficult to define the extent of the man's following. As a political movement, Blanquism was complex. Its influence was felt in different ways by different constituencies. Never a political party in the modern sense, it was something more than a coterie of professional revolutionaries. Its character has perhaps best been defined by Arthur Ranc, who drew a distinction between Blanquists of the first and second degree.[22] The first group was composed of a relatively small number of conspirators—militants dedicated to the overthrow of the existing political order. The second designated a much larger group of sympathizers—politicians who looked upon Blanqui as a symbol of the republican cause. The conspirators were sectarian, given to intrigue and clandestine agitation. But the sympathizers, while occasionally willing to be demonstrative, were reluctant to be subversive. That is why the Blanquist movement cannot be regarded as a single political party. It is better described as two networks of followers, each employing different methods, yet reinforcing one another in their common identification of the values of the revolutionary tradition with the legend of Blanqui. The distinction between these two elements of Blanquism endures throughout the thirty-year history of the movement.

The conspirators emerged out of a network of friends and acquaintances formed in the Latin Quarter in the 1860s. At its inception in 1864, this first Blanquist coterie numbered about fifteen.[23] Nearly all were students at the University of Paris. Hailing from middle-class backgrounds, graduates of provincial lycées, they were young men of talent, sometimes of wealth, who were preparing for careers in the liberal professions. Among the first disciples of Blanqui were several medical students: Emile Villeneuve, Victor Jaclard, Léonce Levraud, Paul Dubois, and Pierre Vaissier. The group also included a number of aspiring lawyers, among them Edouard Losson, Eugène Protot, and Gustave Tridon. Louis Marchand and Germain Casse were journalists, testing their talents in the ephemeral newspapers of the Latin Quarter, while Edmond Levraud, a wine dealer, was the sole representative of the world of commercial affairs. Most of them had come to the university with distinguished records of academic achievement; yet they found their formal studies stultifying and soon drifted from their classes to the bohemias of the Left Bank. Like many Parisian students in that era, they were caught up in the ferment of this intellectual underground, in which interest in the revolutionary tradition was being rekindled after a decade of silence. They were attracted as well to the positivist philosophy of Auguste Comte, which taught that religion was a myth to be dispelled in the modern age. Blanqui's future followers complained bitterly of the obscurantist influence of Catholic teaching on educational policies. The medical students, especially, regarded religious dogmas as an impediment to scientific research.[24]

Hostile to a clericalism they associated with the Napoleonic regime, inspired by the history of the revolutionary movement in France, these young men joined the republican opposition, a rising force in the early 1860s. For a time, political conversations in the cafés of the Latin Quarter, together with occasional forays into the streets to heckle the imperial family on its official outings, constituted their most dangerous pursuits.[25] Their encounter with Blanqui turned them toward a more serious style of political opposition. In following him, they chose to identify with the "damned of history," his phrase for those who chose to be pariahs for justice's sake. Was it not the choice, they argued, which Blanqui had made when he was a student some thirty-five years before?

With Blanqui as their mentor, these students began to think of themselves as an elite circle of the revolutionary avant-garde, a self-conception considerably enhanced once they had successfully arranged Blanqui's escape from the prison wing of the Necker hospital in 1865. Blanqui remained at liberty until the eve of the Commune. His followers, accepting conviction for political dissent as a badge of merit, passed in and out of Louis Napoleon's prisons for the remaining years of the Second Empire. Confinement, then, was both a rite of initiation into, and a training ground for, the Blanquist conspiracy of the 1860s.[26] During the decade, virtually all Blanqui's followers were imprisoned at least once, and a few, such as Casse, Humbert, and Rigault, compiled impressive records of prosecution and imprisonment.[27]

These initiated disciples, who had once honored Blanqui with their prison visits, were paid similar tribute by those who aspired to join their cause. Gaston Da Costa has left a charming sketch of his own first prosecution as a young man of seventeen. Arrested for having participated in a demonstration against the emperor in 1867, Da Costa was brought before the court. Concluding that the accused was politically naive, the judge was inclined to dismiss the charge. But the would-be political rebel rose to the occasion by delivering a speech so critical of the empire that the judge had no choice but to sentence him to prison. "Happily for my vanity," Da Costa reminisced many years later, "I was talented enough to earn my first two-week prison sentence and a fine of 200 francs through my polemic. I was happy, as was my father; my mother cried."[28] In his willingness to share Blanqui's prisons of political opposition, Da Costa, like Blanqui's other followers, affirmed that beneath the dark legend he had discovered a bright authenticity in Blanqui's quest.

The character of the Blanquist conspiracy was shaped as well by Blanqui's didactic yet distant relationship with his followers. A group of five or six young men enjoyed a privileged relationship with him and interceded for him with the rest of the entourage. In this way, the Blanquist coterie, while seeking recruits for a wider conspiracy, created an inner circle—a kind of elite within the elite Blanquist comradeship. Edmond Levraud, Edouard Losson, Victor Jaclard, Eugène Protot, Gustave Tridon, and Emile Villeneuve corresponded regularly with Blanqui and relied upon him heavily for advice and moral support.[29] Acting as their tutor in revolutionary politics, Blanqui asked them to prepare biographical sketches of prominent historical personalities so that they would better understand the nature of the contemporary struggle. Edouard Losson wrote an essay on Anacharsis Cloots (for whom the Blanquists showed surprising sympathy), and Emile Villeneuve composed a sketch describing the treachery of Louis XVI. Gustave Tridon prepared detailed studies of the historical origins of the neo-Girondin ideology of such contemporary republican politicians as Jules Simon and Emile Garnier.[30]

Such exercises were designed by Blanqui to provide his disciples with a theoretical grounding in the deep sources of the cause to which they had committed themselves; in moving from the theoretical to the practical plane, however, Blanqui played a more cautious role. His scrupulous attention to detail and his sensitivity to the timing of political strategies prompted him to restrain rather than encourage his disciples in their enthusiasm for direct action. Thus Blanqui expressed exasperation over Emile Villeneuve's premature and clumsy efforts to expand Blanquist activities in 1866.[31] His refusal to permit his disciples to intervene in the proceedings of the congress of the First Workingmen's International at Geneva in September 1866 provoked a confrontation between those who obeyed and those who defied his order.[32] It was with many reservations that he helped his followers plan the storming of the arsenal at La Villette in August 1870, an adventure conceived and executed in imitation of the uprising he had led in 1839 (and equally disastrous in its consequences). During the one demonstration of the Siege of Paris which might have taken an insurrectionary turn, that of October 31, 1870, he abandoned any design he might have had to overthrow the provisional government, once he had been reassured about its intentions to continue the war against the Prussians.[33]

Blanqui's directives, like his intellectual direction, were generally given from afar. During the late 1860s, he was rarely visible even to his favored disciples. Living for the most part in seclusion in Brussels at the home of his old friend Dr. Louis Watteau, he visited Paris only on rare occasions and always in disguise.[34] Some Blanquist militants claim never to have seen him at all, and within the inner circle only Tridon had frequent, direct contact with him.[35]

The role of Gustave Tridon (1841-1871) deserves special men-

tion, both because of the particular favor he enjoyed with Blanqui and because of the quintessential role he would play among
the Blanquists as their intellectual spokesman.[36] Tridon was a
young man of depth and sensitivity. The son of a prosperous
landowner from Dijon, he was independently wealthy and destined to inherit a substantial fortune, which he eventually bequeathed to his Blanquist comrades. Trained as a lawyer, Tridon
considered himself too timid for the adversary proceedings of
the courtroom. In one of his early letters to Blanqui, he confided
his fears about defending himself in a local court on a game
poaching charge.[37] But there was nothing timid about his ideas;
nor, when challenged, was he reluctant to defend them. Tridon
bore up courageously on trial and in prison under a series of
indictments for political subversion in the late 1860s.[38] All the
while, he wrote searching essays on political and philosophical
subjects in a complex, sometimes ornate prose, essays which
earned the respect of his comrades, who regarded him as their
leading theoretician. At the same time, he counted heavily upon
Blanqui—as much for emotional support as for intellectual criticism.[39] Tridon, moreover, displayed a capacity for synthesis
which Blanqui himself never acquired. His writings, therefore,
provide the more accessible statement of the Blanquist viewpoint on most issues.

The first group of Blanqui's disciples was composed of self-
conscious intellectuals. Subsequent adherents were more obviously activists. Typical of the latter were Ernest Granger and
Emile Eudes, who remained deeply committed members of the
Blanquist group throughout its history and who directed its fortunes in later years. Granger (1844-1914) belonged to a prominent family of the provincial bourgeoisie;[40] his father, a staunch
republican, was a lawyer and a gentleman farmer in the Orne
valley, north of Paris. An excellent student at the lycée at Versailles, Granger enrolled in the law school at Paris in 1862 at the
age of eighteen and soon entered the fray of radical republican
politics. Joining the Blanquist student group in 1866, he was
admired by all from the outset. In a letter of March 30, 1867,
Tridon described him to Blanqui as "a man of good sense and of
good faith whom I recommend to you with enthusiasm."[41] Granger was taciturn, capable, reliable, qualities which enabled him to
play a leading role in the formation of secret paramilitary units
in the late 1860s. Joining him in this enterprise was Emile Eudes
(1843-1888), a young pharmacy student from Saint-Lô in Nor-

mandy. A man of enormous vitality, Eudes was one of the group's leading advocates of a coup d'etat to be executed in imitation of Blanqui's historic raid on City Hall in 1839. He worked relentlessly to prepare for such an undertaking. Lacking talent as a political journalist, he was nonetheless willing to serve Blanquist-affiliated newspaper ventures as managing editor, a post which rendered him liable for statements made by others and in which he was in due course prosecuted.[42]

By the last years of the Second Empire, the inner circle of Blanquist militants was no longer composed exclusively of students. Certain skilled workers, such as the wood-carver Gustave Genton and the railroad engineer Edmond Mégy, were valued for their influence among workers and respected as reliable men of action.[43] Most acclaimed in this category was the iron worker Emile Duval (1840-1871), whose fame by the time of his death in battle as a general for the Commune was widely heralded. Duval was portrayed by his Blanquist comrades as the ideal type of worker—independent, resourceful, and energetic. He worked closely with Eudes and Granger in recruiting for the Blanquist paramilitary units. He earned the special admiration of his comrades for his role as organizer of the metallurgical workers' strike at Paris in the spring of 1870, to which employers were forced to capitulate after four months.[44] Out of the behavior of such stalwarts as Duval, Genton, and Mégy, the Blanquists conjured up a studied image of the ideal worker as a skilled professional with the independence of mind and resourcefulness to lead others. In its elitist connotations, it was a conception of the worker at odds with the Marxist one, which identified the growth of the worker's political consciousness with his professional degradation and pauperization.

But Marx's conception of the role of the worker had made little headway in the French labor movement during the Second Empire. Far more influential were the theories of Pierre-Joseph Proudhon, who urged workers to form cooperative labor organizations and to avoid politics. Proudhon's image of the ideal worker—skilled, self-reliant, and self-sustaining—was close to that of the Blanquists. But they rejected Proudhon's notion of the social autonomy and political independence of the worker and preferred to stress the importance of political and social rapport between workers and radical intellectuals. The watchword of Blanquism, after all, was not social cooperation but political struggle, and the Blanquists viewed the apolitical stance of the

Proudhonist-inspired labor movement as a capitulation to existing political authority.[45] At the same time, they were aware of
the appeal of Proudhon's ideas to the incipient French trade
union movement, and of the power of Proudhonist labor leaders
in the First Workingmen's International, organized in the mid-
1860s. Sensing the potential value of the International as a force
for revolution, and hoping to frustrate the efforts of the Proudhonists to dominate it, the Blanquists laid plans to intervene at
its congress in Geneva in 1866. Blanqui's last-minute order to
boycott the session had a divisive effect upon the Blanquist delegation, some of whose members decided to make a polemical
intervention anyway.[46]

The Blanquists abandoned further efforts to play an active
role in the International until after the Commune. But Blanqui
and his followers continued to monitor its annual congresses for
the remaining years of the decade. Blanqui made a point of attending the congress at Brussels in 1868 as an auditor, and over
several years he prepared detailed analyses of the organization's
changing policies.[47] He and his followers were especially intrigued by the role of Mikhail Bakunin and his anarchist faction,
which began to assume a more important role in the International
by 1868 and to give its policies a more combative edge.[48]

There were many similarities between Bakunin's anarchism
and Blanqui's Jacobinism. Both stressed the elemental, creative
power of the popular will to revolt, and both attached considerable importance to the role of secret societies in catalyzing it.
Their differences over the use of political power in the wake of a
popular revolt did not present themselves until the Paris Commune. As personalities, Blanqui and Bakunin provide a study in
contrasts. Blanqui was aloof, tiny in stature, and self-contained,
whereas Bakunin was gregarious, physically imposing, and ex-
uberant. Yet Bakunin, like Blanqui, was legendary for the adversity he had overcome in his single-minded commitment to revolution; hence he drew admirers for many of the same reasons
Blanqui did. It was their rivalry for the affections of radical
youth, as much as their ideological differences, which set them
at odds in the late 1860s and which prompted some Blanquist
youths to shift their allegiance.[49]

As early as 1868, Victor Jaclard, one of Blanqui's favored inner
circle, was touched by Bakunin's charisma. As delegates to the
Berne Congress of the League of Peace and Freedom, an international organization of reform-minded intellectuals who shared

many of the objectives of the International, Jaclard and his Blanquist companion, Aristide Rey, were persuaded by the genial
Russian émigré to follow him to Geneva to reconstitute the
dissident wing of the League as a section of the International.[50]
By 1870 they had abandoned the Blanquist conspiracy altogether
in order to work more actively in the International. In these
efforts, Jaclard managed to persuade Blanquist militant Emile
Duval, then leading a major strike of metallurgical workers at
Paris, to channel his strikers into sections of the International.
Jaclard's defection especially was considered a serious blow to
the secret organization that the Blanquists had constructed by
that date. Emile Eudes, in his commentary on these years, casti-
gates Jaclard for the demoralizing effect his departure had upon
Blanquist preparations for an insurrection in August 1870.[51] In
the aftermath of the Commune, the Blanquists in exile in London cast their support to Marx in the hope of displacing Bakunin
and his anarchist faction.[52]

Despite the rivalry of the International in the last years of the
Second Empire, the Blanquist conspiracy began to assume the
proportions of a better disciplined and more elaborate organization with specific revolutionary objectives.[53] Beginning in 1867,
and with increasing seriousness of purpose until 1870, Blanquist
militants created a secret network of paramilitary cells, each of
ten members and each unaware of the personnel in other groupings and of the size of the larger membership. These units mus-
tered regularly for nocturnal training exercises, sessions at
which, one former militant claims, they were often inspected by
Blanqui, who loitered nearby in disguise.[54] Inspector Lagrange,
the police official responsible for the surveillance of subversives
at Paris during the Second Empire, claims that this secret society
possessed a combined membership of nearly three thousand by
1870. Historians sympathetic to the Blanquists generally accept
this estimate.[55] But the reliability of the figure is questionable,
since Lagrange, who offered it in testimony before the military
court of inquiry which was investigating the origins of the Commune, had good reason to exaggerate. The Blanquists themselves vaunt the fact that they escaped police detection by avoid-
ing written records and by passing all orders verbally.[56]

Even if the figure is approximately accurate, it reveals little
about the effectiveness of the organization, which acted overtly
only twice during the Second Empire. As evidence of their potential strength, the Blanquists usually cite the first of these

mobilizations, the funeral parade for Victor Noir on January 12, 1870, in which a sizable Blanquist contingent (estimates range between seven hundred and two thousand) marched behind the cortege.[57] But the capacity of this organization to act was tested only once, some six months later (August 14, 1870) in an abortive raid on the arsenal of the fire station at La Villette in eastern Paris. The inability of Blanquist leaders to muster more than a tiny contingent for this insurrection (estimates vary between sixty and one hundred), or to carry the plan of action beyond the first stage before fleeing in disarray, suggests that the Blanquist secret society, if it did exist in anything more than skeletal outline, was undisciplined and unreliable.[58] If the Blanquists succeeded in fooling the police about the character of their organization, they also succeeded in fooling themselves about what that organization could do. Most of those counted as Blanquists were not conspirators, but sympathizers, whose loyalties to the Blanquist underground were tenuous and whose willingness to be mobilized depended upon the occasion.

Fear of subversion led the imperial police to overestimate the danger posed by the Blanquists as a secret society. In an early effort to uncover their plot, the police rounded up some forty-one Blanquist students and workers caucusing at a popular drinking hall in the Latin Quarter on November 11, 1866. The incident, subsequently known as the Café Renaissance Affair, is often cited as an early example of Blanquist revolutionary militancy.[59] In fact, it was an extraordinary gathering of Blanqui's disciples, assembled to admonish the Blanquist delegation to the congress of the First International at Geneva for defying Blanqui's order to refrain from participation. Far from preparing for an insurrection, the Blanquists were still in the process of exploring their relations with other groups opposing the imperial regime. Blanqui's order was unusual, the plenary assembly of Blanquist conspirators unprecedented. The police were disappointed to find no evidence of plots against the empire. The Blanquists were equally disheartened, since, despite their best intentions, they had by that date hardly begun to expand their secret organization.[60]

The Blanquist penchant for intrigue further contributed to this exaggerated image of their conspiratorial role. From the earliest days of their association (1864-65), Blanquist students had adopted code names in their correspondence and had prescribed rites of initiation as part of the training of newcomers to their fold.[61] These were the innocuous activities of a tiny circle of enthusiasts, for whom insurrectionary schemes were still largely fantasies. But as the years passed, the harsh realities of confronting the police, together with the fear of betrayal by police spies masquerading as political radicals, turned such intrigue into a grim vendetta.

This sense of revolutionary activity as a deadly game is best exemplified in the activities of Raoul Rigault (1846-1871), a Blanquist youth who constructed his own counterespionage system against the imperial political police.[62] Rigault's personality provides a portrait of bohemian brilliance. Despite keen abilities and high grades, he was expelled from the lycée at Versailles in 1866 for insubordination. For several years thereafter, he frequented the cafés of the Latin Quarter, where he became known as an amusing and flamboyant spokesman for radical causes. It is reported that he always carried a copy of Hébert's *Père Duchesne,* which he had committed to memory and from which he quoted freely at the slightest prompting. He gained access to the Blanquists' group by visiting some of them in prison and soon became one of the stalwarts of their cause. Between 1867 and 1870, he was convicted twelve times for his words and deeds attacking church and state. After his prosecution for the first of these—his role in the Café Renaissance Affair—Rigault became bitter toward the police and especially their informers who had infiltrated Blanquist ranks. He decided to study the workings of the political police. For a time he donned judicial garb as a means of gaining entry to the sessions of the Sixth Chamber of Correctional Police, which dealt with political crimes. There he scrutinized the police agents who testified, recording as much physiognomic and biographical data as he could manage. He then checked their names on the electoral lists for the wards surrounding the Prefecture of Police in order to trace their addresses. In the late afternoons, he sometimes waited opposite the prefecture, on the Rue de Jérusalem, to identify police agents as they exited and to follow them to their favorite haunts. Within a few years, he had constructed an intelligence file on the police more impressive than that which they possessed on the Blanquists.

Rigault was able to verify his data during the Siege of Paris in the autumn of 1870, when he was appointed a special police commissioner and thereby gained access to the political police files of the Second Empire. His secretary, Gaston Da Costa,

attests to the remarkable accuracy of Rigault's detective work
when measured against these files.[63] "Rigault has a vocation,"
Blanqui once muttered astutely. "He was born to be Prefect of
Police."[64] By the spring of 1871 he was the prefect, and he began
to take revenge. As the "grand inquisitor" of the Blanquist entourage, Rigault eventually became its most controversial figure. His friends pitied him as a comic figure; his enemies feared
him as a satanic one.[65] Either way, he lived the doctrine preached
by the Blanquists with a fervor so ruthless it bordered on caricature. In the play of spy and counterspy, he made manifest the
stark contrast of culture and counterculture which informed the
conceptions of many Blanquist conspirators.

Rigault saw the world in Manichaean terms; but not all Blanqui's followers were so doctrinaire or so dedicated. Beyond the
conspiratorial nucleus of the late 1860s there was a fair and
growing number of sympathizers. Among them were the few
surviving comrades of Blanqui's earlier campaigns: François
Cleray, Louis Watteau, and Louis Lacambre, all of whom offered
him asylum during the Second Empire; Arthur Ranc, who wrote
sympathetically about him; and Benjamin Flotte, who during the
Commune tried unsuccessfully to ransom him back from the
Versailles government.[66] Nor did all the students who idolized
Blanqui join his organization. Among those who preferred to
admire him from afar were Charles Longuet, editor of *La rive
gauche*, the best-known student newspaper of the era, and Paul
Lafargue, a medical student and occasional correspondent for
the Blanquist press.[67] Also in this circle of "Blanquists of the
second degree" were Jules Vallès, the novelist, and Pierre Denis,
a journalist, as well as Ferdinand Taule, a future scientist, and
Georges Clemenceau.[68]

There was, moreover, some movement out of the ranks of the
Blanquist conspiracy even during the Second Empire. Eugène
Protot and his fellow delegates to the Geneva congress of the
International would have been formally expelled at a mock trial
at the Café Renaissance in 1866, had not the police interrupted
the hearing.[69] Jaclard's defection to the International in 1869 left
a legacy of broken ties and bad feelings.[70] The more common
pattern, however, was for militants to exit less obtrusively, usually to enter the ranks of the radical republicans, who shared the
Blanquists' commitment to Jacobin values and yet enjoyed a
larger measure of political respectability. Alphonse Humbert,
Germain Casse, François Viette, Léonce Levraud, and Emile

Villeneuve, all Blanquist conspirators of the Second Empire, became legislators and municipal councillors in the Third Republic.[71] Such defections were ongoing, although the fall of the Commune in 1871 and the amnesty of the Communards in 1880 provide major dividing lines demarcating the dissolution and reformation of Blanquist organizations.

Few Blanquist militants, even among those who were expelled, severed their ties with the inner circle without retaining some sympathy for Blanqui and some sense of a Blanquist identity. Protot, for example, while shunned by some of his former Blanquist companions, defended others as a trial counsel during the Second Empire and worked in close harmony with several Blanquist leaders during the Commune.[72] As these veterans of the Blanquist youth movement of the Second Empire passed into the ranks of the radicals of the Third Republic, they began to see Blanqui differently—not as a conspirator bent upon overthrowing the regime, but as a statesman of the revolutionary tradition which was slowly realizing its objectives by fashioning more democratic institutions for the young republic.

The outer circle of Blanquist sympathizers widened continuously through the first two decades of the Third Republic, its boundaries corresponding roughly to the widening orbit of influence of the legend of Blanqui. Seeing Blanqui as an emblem of an advancing tide of political democracy, some Blanquist militants were prepared by 1880 to propose a fundamental reconstruction of the movement as a geographically broad-based party employing more diversified tactics. In effect, they raised the question of whether conspirators and sympathizers might not merge into a single political formation. But concerns about what such a formation might be and what objectives it should seek bothered most of the veterans of earlier campaigns, who sensed that a larger party would mean more superficial commitments and an end to the fraternal feeling of the inner circle. The debate divided and demoralized Blanquist leaders during the 1880s and prepared the way for the schism of the movement in 1890. Throughout the 1870s and 1880s, however, the original structure of an inner and an outer circle bequeathed by the youth movement of the 1860s remained intact.

The inner circle continued to be what it had been from the outset: a comradeship of dedicated revolutionaries, bound by rites of initiation, a code of secrecy, and a commitment to the conception of a revolution as a coup d'etat. Despite the death of some leaders during the Commune and the deportation of others to penal colonies overseas during the 1870s, the inner circle, periodically renewed and reconstituted, remained a fairly stable sect of forty to a hundred active members. Several of the most prominent Blanquist leaders during the Third Republic, such as Edouard Vaillant, Edouard Marguerittes, and Gabriel Ranvier, joined the group only in the aftermath of the Commune, while Ernest Roche, a champion of the early traditions of the Blanquists, became associated with them in the 1880s. But a tiny nucleus participated in all the campaigns of this thirty-year span and gave the movement a certain continuity of leadership. Among the veterans of the Blanquist youth movement of the 1860s who survived to direct Blanquist activities in the 1880s were Alfred Breuillé, Emmanuel Chauvière, Charles Da Costa, Gaston Da Costa, Emile Eudes, Emile Gois, Albert Goullé, Ernest Granger, Henri Place, and Octave Martinet.

Despite continuities of leadership, organizational structure, and ideological viewpoint, the Blanquists from the end of the Second Empire ceased to play a serious role as conspirators hoping to inspire a popular insurrection. Each new political formation—the Revolutionary Commune of the 1870s, the Central Revolutionary Committee of the 1880s, and the Socialist Revolutionary Central Committee of the 1890s—was of less importance than its predecessor as a subversive organization. The Blanquists clung to the image of conspiracy, but the image was increasingly remote from their activities.[73] The inner circle of the Blanquist movement remained as ever committed to revolution. But that commitment in the aftermath of the Commune meant propagating their viewpoint rather than changing their world. That viewpoint, epitomized in the legend of Blanqui, was during the early years of the Third Republic merging with the broader perspectives of the entire Jacobin ideological inheritance. From the time of the Commune, the Blanquists passed from their role as activists in a revolutionary movement to another as ideologists of the cult of the revolutionary tradition. The new role gave them a new prominence. During the Second Empire, they had been but one among many revolutionary factions. In the Third Republic, they became spokesmen for a revolutionary heritage renewed and amalgamated in the myth of the Commune. Thenceforth their ritual remembrance of insurrections past displaced their plans for future insurrections.

Historians in their curiosity about the conspiratorial role of the Blanquists have sometimes overlooked their more obvious public role as ideologists. First as journalists for the revolutionary press, but also as liturgists for ritual demonstrations, the Blanquists were continuously given to demonstrative statement and theatrical display. This public role, which dates from the earliest days of the youth movement, parallels and eventually supersedes the conspiratorial one. The continuity of the Blanquist movement lies not only in its personnel and its organizational structure, but also in its rituals. These, too, would undergo a certain development during this era; for the Blanquists' political notions of the 1880s had their sources in the Blanquist atheist ideas of the 1860s.

CHAPTER III

Atheist Foundations of Blanquist Thought

Neither political conspiracy nor loyalty to Blanqui was enough to sustain the Blanquist movement. What unity the Blanquists possessed through vicarious identification with the revolutionary past was reinforced by more present-minded intellectual convictions. For the Blanquists were confirmed atheists, and their atheist attitudes provided the primary source of their revolutionary zeal. In their self-image as conspirators they were acting out a philosophical position. Just as the revolutionary movement led by Blanqui was a clandestine one which he believed would break upon the world with catastrophic fury, so atheism for his followers was a kind of hermetic knowledge about to be overtly revealed. It is interesting that Giordano Bruno, the most important apostle of hermetic thought during the Renaissance, figured prominently in the Blanquist pantheon of martyrs for the Free Thought movement. Thus secrecy for Blanquist youth was initially a means of self-understanding as much as it was an actual preparation for insurrection.

If the Blanquists' secret role as political conspirators contributed little to the revolutionary movement during the Second Empire, their highly visible involvement in the Free Thought movement influenced it more substantially. The Free Thought movement (La Libre Pensée) was the principal agency for the dissemination of radical atheism during the Second Empire.[1] It won favor among students of the Latin Quarter in the early 1860s as part of a broader renaissance of interest in the religious question. As in matters more obviously political (his defense of the temporal power of the papacy, for example), Louis Napoleon's deference to high ecclesiastical officials in the shaping of educational policy was bound to promote a new wave of anticlericalism. Well-known intellectuals at the University of Paris made the issue a topic of public controversy. The historians Jules Michelet and Edgar Quinet contrasted the historical evolution of the Church's doctrines with its claims to dogmatic consistency, claims which in the modern world, they contended, impeded the historical fulfillment of the values of liberty and justice announced in the French Revolution.

Equally important was the new interest in religious anthropology. Auguste Comte's work inspired a lively curiosity about comparative mythology. A spate of books on Christian origins appeared, the most impressive of which was Ernest Renan's *Vie de Jésus*, which treated Christ sympathetically but as a mythological figure. Such literary celebrities as Charles Sainte-Beuve and Victor Hugo contributed to the discussion by defending the right of proponents of the lay viewpoint to be heard. Most of these intellectuals were advocates of natural religion; by placing revealed religion in historical perspective, they hoped to free religious understanding from the strictures of dogma, mystery, and superstition. For them, religious understanding was not a matter of divine grace but rather of humanist wisdom about the world. The teachings of these progressives had a clearly professorial air. The Free Thinkers, generally younger and not as well-known, were familiar with their claims for rational religion, but rejected them in favor of a thorough-going empiricism in which the religious question was dismissed altogether. The German materialists Feuerbach and Büchner, not the French agnostics Quinet and Renan, were their heroes.

Considered narrowly, the Free Thought movement was not a Blanquist organization. Yet Blanquist students played an instrumental role in its founding, lent the movement its militant tone, and by 1870 effectively directed its fortunes.[2] If some of its sponsors (Louis Asseline, Auguste Coudereau, and André Lefèvre) prudently kept the discussion of atheism on an academic plane, Blanquist intellectuals endeavored to make clear its integral relationship to radical politics. The Free Thought movement first gained attention through the publicity surrounding the International Student Congress at Liège (October 29-November 1, 1865) and in the controversy which stemmed from it at the University of Paris in the following months.

In its inception and planning, the congress was not especially intended either for atheists or for youth. Rather, it was convoked to air the religious questions which were arousing so much intellectual interest, and distinguished spokesmen for a variety of traditional, progressive, and agnostic viewpoints were invited to attend. When most of these authorities declined their invitations, the congress acquired a more youthful composition,

and one decidedly more hostile to religion than had originally
been intended. The French delegation, composed largely of Blanquist students, soon dominated the proceedings and set them
upon a contentious course. The tone was set at the opening
session when the French delegation draped the tricolor in a black
shroud and paraded it around the hall as a symbolic gesture of
mourning for the death of academic freedom in France. A series
of Blanquist orators, notably Germain Casse and Albert Regnard, then delivered animated presentations of their atheist
creed, pointing out whenever possible its political and social implications. In a historical sketch of the Free Thought movement
written some years later, Regnard cited the Liège congress as
the first public manifesto of the neo-Hébertist viewpoint. The
conveners disbanded the congress early, but not before its atheist participants had laid plans for a society entitled Act As You
Think (*Agis comme tu penses*) to coordinate future efforts of the
Free Thought movement on an international plane.[3]

If the sponsors of the Liège congress were disturbed by its
outcome, governmental officials in France felt doubly humiliated.
Louis Napoleon's advisors were concerned that the radical rhetoric of the French students at the congress might be interpreted
by foreign observers as evidence of his weakening support at
home. Ecclesiastical officials, already disturbed by the tenor of
the religious controversy, were irate that French university students should have used an international forum to flaunt their
atheist doctrine and demanded that the government take action
against them. Thus the controversy over the congress soon became the "affair of the schools." Yielding to public pressure, the
Academic Council of the Universities of France banned the participants from the University of Paris forever and from other
universities for at least one year. Rey, Regnard, Lafargue, Bi-
gourdan, and Jaclard, interns and medical students, as well as
Casse and Losson from the law school, were expelled forthwith.
These students had been easily identified as participants. But
university authorities decided to discipline other students simply
for showing open sympathy for the Liège participants. Judging
these measures heavy-handed and capricious, the students staged
a strike, marked by sit-ins, street demonstrations, boycotts, and
the disruption of classes. The Blanquists watched these activities
closely, abetted the agitation, and even staged a public banquet
and demonstration on January 21, 1866, on the Rue des Amandiers in eastern Paris in the hope of rousing workers' support.

The turmoil in the Latin Quarter lasted for much of the winter, but the orders of expulsion were not rescinded.[4]

Academic officials wanted to treat the incident as the rebellion of irresponsible students. Yet it was hard for them to disclaim the seriousness of intellectual purpose of some of the leading participants. Exemplary in this respect was Dr. Albert Regnard (b. 1836), the most articulate spokesman for free thought at the Liège congress and a key target of the Academic Council in the "affair of the schools."[5] Regnard had for some time been a Blanquist sympathizer; the affair propelled him toward a more complete identification with the cause. An intern at the hospital La Charité in Paris, he had already established his reputation as a brilliant medical student for his pioneering studies in neurological research. In 1864 he had won the Esquirol prize, offered by the Society for Psychological Medicine for the year's best study on mental health. Even before the affair, he had roused the ire of the dean of the School of Medicine, Ambroise Tardieu, by successfully opposing the latter's efforts to meddle in the activities of the student medical society. Regnard's interests were as wide as his independence of mind. He was thoroughly familiar with recent studies in materialist philosophy and had translated the classic work by Ludwig Büchner, *Kraft und Stoff* [Energy and Matter] (1857), into the French in 1865. His speech at Liège thus represented his first opportunity to state publicly the implications for educational policy of a subject upon which he had carefully reflected. Expelled from the hospitals of Paris for his role in the affair, he completed his professional requirements at Strasbourg and continued with his medical research uninterrupted. But he was embittered by the experience and thenceforth participated in the activities of the Free Thought movement with a new sense of urgency. He drew closer to the Blanquists and became, next to Tridon (whose work he greatly admired), the leading theoretician among them.

The Liège congress was the kind of intellectual festival which appealed to the Blanquists' sense of apocalyptic moment. Yet during the remaining years of the Second Empire, they played a less glamorous but more sustaining role in the Free Thought movement as journalists. Between 1865 and 1870, they contributed energetically to a series of ephemeral newspapers dedicated to the task of popularizing atheist thought. The first of these, *Candide* (May 3-27, 1865), was exclusively a Blanquist enterprise. Drawing upon the discussions of the prison visits with Blanqui and publishing some of his essays, Tridon and his staff tried to present the atheist viewpoint in a playful, mocking fashion, interlacing satires of contemporary issues with more polemical exposures of historical ones. Their barbs were insufficiently subtle to stave off the imperial censors, and *Candide* was suppressed after only eight issues.

More academic but no less militant in tone was its successor, *La libre pensée* (October 21, 1866-February 24, 1867). Edited by Regnard and a staff of colleagues from outside the Blanquist circle, the paper took on Catholic spokesmen, Louis Veuillot and Monsignor Félix Dupanloup, in a hostile debate, which ended in the prosecution of Regnard (and his managing editor Eudes) for "insults to religion and public morality." Blanquist journalists were only marginally involved in *La pensée nouvelle* (May 19, 1867-May 2, 1869), which devoted itself exclusively to a philosophical discussion of atheism and which scrupulously avoided comment upon contemporary issues which might have invited censorship. In a closing letter to subscribers (May 14, 1869), however, its editors conceded that it was time to relate the problem of atheism more directly to present-day political issues.

A new militancy on the part of the Free Thought movement was made possible by the more liberal rights of press and assembly granted in an imperial law of June 1868, and it was in these circumstances that the Blanquists again came to the fore in its propaganda campaigns. The major organs of the Free Thought movement at Paris in the last years of the empire, *Le démocrite* (January 11-February 20, 1868 and December 3-17, 1868) and *La libre pensée* (January 24-July 30, 1870), were edited entirely by Blanquist staffs. The former, a vitriolic news sheet directed by Rigault and Henri Place, was twice suppressed despite the liberalized press law. Therein Rigault published an attack on the idea of tolerance, which won him considerable notoriety (most of it unfavorable). Rigault's viewpoint was particularly disheartening to liberal Republicans, who prided themselves upon the success of their hard-won struggle to extend individual liberties under the empire. Such a concession Rigault only ridiculed as a sign of weakness, citing Calvin's burning of Servetus and Robespierre's guillotining of the Hébertists to show where tolerance led.[6] Vaunting these and more blasphemous attitudes, Rigault became a popular orator at public rallies (permitted for the first time in 1868), where he scandalized some listeners and titillated others with his attacks on marriage and family and his outspoken advocacy of free love.[7]

If Tridon and Regnard were its principal theorists and Rigault its most outlandish spokesman, the Free Thought movement was more modestly sustained during the last years of the empire by Henri Place (1847-1902).[8] Descended from a republican family from Moulins, Place, too, came to Paris as a student in the mid-1860s only to abandon his classes in order to devote himself to radical journalism. He supported himself by becoming a printer. By 1868 he was a member of the Blanquist circle. Writing under the pseudonym Henri Verlet, he contributed articles to a number of student newspapers before assuming the editorship of *La libre pensée* in January 1870, a post acquired through his participation on an ad hoc committee to select delegates for the Naples Anti-Council (December 8-10, 1869), the Free Thinkers' response to Vatican I. The committee continued to caucus in the hope of founding lay schools at Paris under the auspices of the Free Thought movement. The newspaper was founded to publicize both initiatives, and Place turned to his Blanquist companions for an editorial staff. Place possessed the ability to simplify and condense the more erudite studies by Tridon and Regnard, to relate radical atheism to recent work in philosophy, and to place the development of the Free Thought movement in historical perspective. He also tried to coordinate the activities of the Free Thought movement across France. Thus he sought to work in close association with Denis Brack, editor of *L'excommunié* at Lyons, and with Charles Le Balleur-Villiers, an articulate spokesman for atheism at Montpellier.

The optimism with which Place set upon his tasks seemed confirmed by the initial success of these projects. Albert Regnard's participation as Parisian delegate to the Naples Anti-Council proved as provocative as his orations at the Liège congress four years before. Place and Casse had also been selected to represent Paris, but were unable to attend because of insufficient funds. They aided Regnard by drafting a program calling for freedom of inquiry, freedom of conscience, and human responsibility for moral decisions as counterpoints to the dogmas emanating from Rome. The Naples Anti-Council, convened by the Italian politician Giuseppe Ricciardi, was designed to answer the religious claims of the Vatican Council with those of the new creed of secular progress. Anticlerical in inspiration, the council's proceedings turned out to be more militantly atheist than its organizers had anticipated. Regnard's aggressive defense of atheism frightened Ricciardi into suspending the proceedings.[9]

Although its events followed the same pattern as those at Liège, Naples was more than an echo of the earlier congress. With support from across Europe, the Free Thought movement appeared to the Blanquists to be gathering momentum and even a certain respectability. Regnard returned home triumphantly to lecture to a crowd of more than six thousand Free Thinkers at Lyons (January 12, 1870).[10] Contributions to the lay school fund began to accumulate during 1870, and at least one school would have opened in the fall but for the advent of the Franco-Prussian War.[11]

Atheism, of course, had its revolutionary implications, and the Blanquists consistently drew them in expounding their creed. In its simplest and most accessible expression, the propaganda of the Free Thought movement was designed to ridicule every aspect of religious practice. Anecdotes of clerical folly provided a leitmotif for weightier subjects treated in other columns. Saint Simeon Stylites, the famed fifth-century pillar sitter, of course received lots of copy. The lives of the saints were reviewed in disbelief, and monasticism was dismissed as so much useless self-indulgence.[12] One Blanquist reporter, Alfred Breuillé, began a series of articles on Parisian churches but stopped with two, one on Notre-Dame cathedral and the other on Sainte-Chapelle. Having described two dimly-lit church interiors in derisive terms, he concluded that there was little more to say.[13]

Much of the satire was designed to underscore the menace of church influence in public education under the Second Empire. Not only was the religious viewpoint useless, the Blanquists contended, it was downright pernicious in its teachings of obedience and passive resignation. The Blanquists attacked revealed religion as the principal weapon with which imperial authorities insured the political obedience of the masses and thereby perpetuated the status quo.[14] The most prolific author of this genre of satire was the Baron Antoine de Ponnat, an inveterate apostle of Free Thought, who published several volumes of anecdotes about the seamier side of church history.[15] Amid the satire, however, some of the younger Blanquist authors had something more serious to say, and they even became theologians of sorts in order to criticize religion more effectively. Tridon, Regnard, and

Rigault flaunted their knowledge of Scripture and enjoyed turning biblical passages to make atheist points.

The serious side of the Blanquists' discussion of atheism was its denial of the idea of Providence, that is, of a power transcending the phenomenal world and ordaining historical change. God, the Blanquists argued, was an illusion which man had created to allay his fears, and religion was man's excuse to escape into a world of fantasy. In creating an imaginary world, the believer neglected the world of sense experience, which set the actual limits of human need and human understanding. For the Blanquists, religious faith and scientific knowledge could not be reconciled. Whereas religion prompted man to create a fictitious world, atheism forced him to come to terms with the real world in which he was required to live.[16] Human problems, Tridon contended, had to be considered in light of human "suffering"— in light of the passion which issues from man's immersion in the texture of material phenomena. Thus the Blanquists emphasized that their concern with "suffering humanity" was a matter of realism, not romanticism. Indeed, the Blanquists scorned not only religious ideas but the romantic imagination generally as a harmful distraction.[17] For them, there was nothing fanciful about human aspiration. "Freedom is a matter of blood and bone," Tridon commented sternly.[18]

In this sense, atheism for the Blanquists was an exhortation to courage. The atheist denial of the idea of Providence heightened the sense of human responsibility, the capacity to live, as the Blanquists expressed it, "without God or master." The courage of atheism was the courage to affirm life in all its manifestations: realism in unmasking illusions, skepticism in considering abstractions, and a hard pessimism in accepting life as an ordeal. The Christian doctrine of Providence taught resignation to suffering in sentimental hope of spiritual immortality. The atheist doctrine of "suffering humanity" taught action as a form of witness to the tragic value of human creativity. If there was no God, then man was called upon to be godlike. Atheism implied a willingness to act upon one's convictions, and it was with this in mind that the Blanquists were determined to make their attitudes known.[19] They conceived of themselves as demythologizers in conscious revolt against the Romantic imagination with which so many progressive intellectuals tried to salvage their religious notions. Religious myths, they declared, were an affront to common sense, diseases of the mind which prevented men from facing facts.[20]

Facing facts, of course, meant understanding matter. Revelations of a supernatural world would, the Blanquists believed, eventually yield place to scientific knowledge of the material world. In this respect, they readily acknowledged their debt to Auguste Comte for laying the intellectual foundations upon which atheism could flourish in the present age. Regnard praised Comte for his historical vision of human progress from the religious imagination of primitive man to the positive consciousness of modern man, who would henceforth live without recourse to abstract speculation. Nevertheless, some Blanquists were distressed with the positivist cult of Comte's last years, with its rites and rituals for the initiated. Some accused him of having repudiated his earlier views out of personal vanity, others of having succumbed to premature senility. For Comte's preoccupation with the symbolic objectification of positivist ideas appeared to the Blanquists to be in contradiction with the iconoclasm of his prime. Under the circumstances, it was difficult to make of Comte an emblem for the atheist cause. The Blanquists sympathized with those of Comte's disciples who felt compelled to abandon him. One of these, Célestin de Blignières, was a regular contributor to Place's *La libre pensée*.[21]

Yet the Blanquists were not simply iconoclasts. They, too, had a coherent world-view, even if they believed it was founded on a perception of reality unencumbered by mythic disguise. The Blanquists were determined to banish the idea of Providence; but they were also willing to endow matter with providential powers. Repeatedly, Blanquist authors returned to the theme of the dignity of matter: the dignity of matter was derived from its eternity—its vastness across space and its unending metamorphosis in time. Man could understand matter; he could fashion it to serve his ends. But he could neither create it nor deny its power. For the Blanquists, matter was not only the source of knowledge; it was as well the matrix of life and energy. In the workings of the material world, man discovered the sources of his own creativity.[22] The Blanquists borrowed many of these ideas from Ludwig Büchner, who extolled a materialist cosmology. Regnard was so taken with the originality of Büchner's work that he translated it into the French.[23] Place wrote a series of articles outlining Büchner's theory and explaining its importance in the struggle to overcome the Romantic imagination.[24] "Hugo or Büchner, the poet or the savant," he mused confidently, "which one will leave the deeper mark upon history?"[25]

In its deepest sense, the Blanquists' denial of Providence was a denial of the possibility of nonbeing. In the viewpoint of the Christian apologist Blaise Pascal, for example, the prospect of annihilation was the measure of human greatness. For the Blanquists, in contrast, the grandeur of matter lay in its capacity to inspire wonder at an organic, eternally renewing cosmos in which man is but an infinitesimal part. For this reason, Blanquist atheism was marked by a sense of immortality in its belief in the immutability of the natural processes underpinning the visible cycles of growth and decay. Man discovered in the rhythmic workings of the material cosmos his ceaseless obligation to fashion a human world which conforms to its patterns. The concept is reminiscent of the Platonic idea of the Demiurge, the divine power that molds a preexisting universe.[26] Such a conception conjured up images of man as a skilled craftsman, and it suggests why the Blanquist typology of the ideal worker was expressed in this sense.

In the formulation of these atheist ideas, the Blanquists claimed no special originality. But Tridon's effort to trace them to their sources became the basis of a painstaking inquiry into religious origins in general. This historical study, *Du Molochisme juif*, was his last and most important monograph, on which he worked for most of the 1860s but which remained unpublished until 1884, some thirteen years after his death. In it he argued that atheism was but a modern version of an ancient doctrine. It grew out of the polytheism of Greco-Roman civilization, a benign religion of natural processes whose logical issue was modern materialist philosophy. Christianity, in contrast, was derived from the monotheism of Semitic culture, a pernicious religion of revelation whose worship of a nonexisting spirit rendered impossible any understanding of the ordered, material world. Such conceptions led Tridon to formulate his vision of the cultural history of the West as a titanic struggle between the Aryan (atheist) and the Semitic (Judeo-Christian) mentalities—a history demarcated by a golden age (that of the Greco-Roman world), an age of decadence (that of the Christian Middle Ages), and the present age (announced, yet not realized, in the French Revolution), which offered the prospect of a return to the ancient Aryan wisdom.

Tridon contended that there was nothing inevitable about this alternating rhythm of opposing viewpoints. Christianity had prevailed in Europe quite by accident because of the capacity of the early Church fathers to ritualize their religious beliefs. To them he conceded a certain begrudging admiration. History was not fated, but capricious, and Christianity would never have endured in Europe but for the will of these religious leaders to succeed. All of this, he argued, was a tragic turn of events, for it established the institutional forms with which the Church imposed a millennium of intellectual darkness with all the attendant forms of political and social oppression.[27] In this way, Tridon translated the atheist conception of the endless metamorphosis of the same cosmic reality into a historical vision of man repeatedly discovering and forgetting the same eternal truth. His paradigm of opposing mentalities projected not a vision of progress but one of eternal return. The conflict between Aryan and Semitic ideas did not offer the possibility of dialectical resolution. Whether presented as a conflict between faith and reason, spiritualism and materialism, revelation and empiricism, or chaos and order, the struggle through history of these opposing modes of thought had been ceaselessly repeated yet never transformed.[28]

Tridon's model of the history of the West explains why the Blanquists viewed the French Revolution as a redemptive event: it was of singular importance because it marked the rebirth of atheistic consciousness. The task of the revolutionaries had not been to create a new reality, but rather to resurrect a primordial harmony. As a primarily philosophical revolution, it represented the culmination of the patient and painful struggle of Free Thinkers to overcome the oppression of religious obscurantism which dated from the Middle Ages.[29] The illustrious lineage of martyrs for Free Thought from Bruno and Vanini to Diderot and d'Holbach had played its part in this movement of liberation.[30] Yet the revolution was especially significant because it was the work of simple, anonymous people, the honest tradesmen and skilled artisans of the Parisian faubourgs. For the first time in history, the Blanquists claimed, the idea of emancipation had become a popular cause. The "people" were the true heroes of the revolution, a fact obscured by early nineteenth-century historiography, which focused upon the legal world of clever oligarchies and pompous politicians. Even Michelet's idealization of the people was for the Blanquists too abstract to convey the sense of elemental passion out of which the little people of Paris rose in revolt against the burden of eighteen hundred years of material privation. It was the atheist foundation of this popular revolution, forgotten since its tragic suppression, which Blanquist intellectuals were determined to reveal. Again, it was Tridon who presented the essential argument, in this instance in his essay *Les Hébertistes*, first published in 1864 and to this day his best-known work.[31]

Les Hébertistes was Tridon's attempt to draw the political implications of radical atheism. Literally, it was a history of the faction of that name which dominated the politics of the Revolutionary Commune of Paris during the Terror of 1793, idealized the virtue of the sans culottes, and sparred with the Committee of Public Safety for a larger share of power in revolutionary politics. Figuratively, the essay offered some basic propositions which Tridon clearly believed applied to any revolutionary situation. The first of these suggested a typology of revolutionary leadership which reflected Tridon's need to analyze the problem of inner conviction in revolutionary commitment. As in his distinction between the atheist and the religious mentalities, the lines between radicals and reactionaries were sharply drawn. While Tridon clearly relegated the moderate leaders of the revolutionary assemblies to the latter camp, he was far more interested in drawing distinctions among the radical revolutionaries themselves.[32] The capacity to lead in a revolutionary situation for Tridon depended upon the depth of the leader's belief in the virtue of the popular revolution. In matters of religion, faith had been a liability; in matters of society, it was a decided asset. The faithless leaders were the evil ones, and also the best-known.

Such was the case of Robespierre, the ideal type of authoritarian leader. Robespierre was a believer of sorts, but not in the people. Tridon portrayed him as cold and austere, too removed from the people to sense their needs or empathize with their plight. Unable to trust the popular will, Robespierre instituted the cult of the Supreme Being as a ruse to enforce civil obedience. In this act, he revealed his hidden reactionary tendencies. His deism was but an updated version of Christian monotheism. That is why, Tridon argued, he opposed the de-Christianization program of the Hébertists.[33]

More treacherous still were the Girondins, characterized by Tridon as selfish individualists who possessed neither religious nor social ideals. The Girondins flaunted their radical views, but they were like actors wearing masks on the historical stage. What distinguished them from genuine revolutionaries was their lack of passion. Despite their high-sounding rhetoric, their motives were petty. As the skeptics of the revolutionary camp, they molded their politics to their opportunities and their propaganda to their ambitions. Above all else, the Girondins were cunning. Tridon's point (and it became a favorite one with the Blanquists) was that those who masqueraded as revolutionaries were more dangerous than those who openly presented themselves as reactionaries. Tridon chose Charlotte Corday, Marat's assassin, as the personification of the Girondin: outwardly beautiful and loving, inwardly deceitful and vengeful. Tridon's image of the Girondin became for the Blanquists the ideal type of the faithless revolutionary.[34] It was an image born of their fear that men wearing masks might surface in their own midst, as had happened in the Café Renaissance Affair. The idea related well to the larger theme of the interplay between secrecy and revelation which pervaded Tridon's writings on the religious question and, for that matter, which informed the Blanquists' approach to politics generally.[35]

The mark of revolutionary virtue for Tridon was the capacity to lead and yet to be of the people. Of all the parties that aspired to direct the revolution, he contended, the Hébertists alone understood the relationship. The Hébertists were intellectuals, yet they were willing to share the suffering of the people. Like the people, their manner was rough and unrefined. On the rostra and in their newspapers, they spoke and wrote in a robust, popular idiom rather than in the elegant style of the more illustrious tribunes of the revolution. Outsiders considered their newspaper, *Le Père Duchesne*, vulgar, but it spoke for the people while accepting its responsibility to educate them.[36] Most important, the Hébertists were atheists, and their activities were a necessary consequence of their atheist convictions. In the lay schools they founded and the hospital services they extended, in their tender concern for the poor, the aged, and the infirm, they sought continually to demonstrate that moral aspiration is rooted in material need.[37] The Hébertists showed the people the relationship between understanding and power. In this way, they announced the birth of ideology. What they offered was not simply a new body of knowledge, but also a new way of action. Monotheism taught self-abnegation. Atheism taught self-affirmation.[38]

Among the Hébertists, Tridon singled out three personalities who played complementary roles in carrying out the work of the radical revolution. There was of course Jacques Hébert himself, the journalist who maintained that delicate balance between leadership and participation through his ability to convey to the people the meaning of the egalitarian ideal. Tridon also extolled Anacharsis Cloots, the foreign-born orator who proclaimed that the wider destiny of the revolution was to promote a new ideal of fraternity among the nations of the world. But his deepest praise was for Pierre Chaumette, the prosecutor of the Commune, who was revered for the moral authority he exercised in revolutionary Paris. Each played a different revolutionary role: Hébert, teacher; Cloots, prophet; Chaumette, lawgiver. Each exemplified a different revolutionary virtue: Hébert, magnanimous leadership; Cloots, inspiration; Chaumette, justice.

Tridon endowed these Hébertist heroes with superhuman powers which personified the ideals of the entire revolutionary community. He also described three ideal personalities of the Revolutionary Commune of a lesser order: Antoine Momoro, the ardent journalist; Charles Ronsin, the "warrior" who organized the revolutionary army; and Jean-Paul Marat, the journalist who personified revolutionary fury. Herein were the makings of a hierarchy within the typology. Presumably, Tridon avoided further elaboration for fear of making this hierarchy too explicit; the focus was supposed to be upon differentiation among equals.[39] In this process of elaboration, however, he created a revolutionary mythology, his contempt for religious mythology notwithstanding. To describe this popular revolution of anonymous participants in terms of a trinity of ideal types could only be justified on mythological grounds. To underscore the point, he noted the correspondence between these ideal personalities of the revolution and those of the early stages of the atheist movement: Hébert with Giordano Bruno; Cloots with Lucillo Vanini, and Chaumette with Servetus.[40]

To his typology of revolutionary personalities, Tridon added a typology of revolutionary events. For he believed that there was a logic to the revolutionary struggle. The philosophical revolution of the Hébertists was not simply a historical experience to build upon, but a timeless consciousness waiting to be reawakened. The return to revolutionary precedent, therefore, was also a return to archaic time, where change was measured in terms of recurrent cycles of consciousness recalled out of a primordial golden age. The Hébertist experience of 1793 expressed the archetype of the rise and fall of revolutionary consciousness, demarcated by the revolutionary days of August 1792, when the

Hébertists ascended to power in the Revolutionary Commune of Paris, and the "last days" of March 1794, when the Hébertist leaders were executed.[41] Thus Tridon formulated an early version of the doctrine of permanent revolution.

Revolutionary days for Tridon were popular festivals of rebirth. They signified a metamorphosis of illusion and reality in the sudden manifestation of the hidden consciousness of the people. The potential power of the "damned of history" (the atheist pariahs who worked secretly for the intellectual liberation of mankind), which had seemed illusionary to their enemies, was revealed as real. The actual power of the reactionary forces who enjoyed privilege and position was at the same time revealed as an illusion.[42] Tridon placed great emphasis, therefore, upon the corresponding fall of Louis XVI; and his execution day, January 21, 1793, assumed an important place in the Blanquists' revolutionary calendar.[43]

The "last days" were those of martyrdom. They marked the fall of atheist revolutionaries from power, usually through betrayal by faithless revolutionaries. In the case of the French Revolution, Tridon argued, the vision of the good society which the Hébertists had tried to implement in the Revolutionary Commune of Paris could not overcome the machinations of Robespierre, who isolated the Committee of Public Safety from the people, or those of the Girondins, who roused the suspicions of provincial France against the popular revolution at Paris. Still, Tridon maintained, 1793 was to be remembered as a holy year in the annals of the atheist crusade, and its last days offered precedents to be remembered.[44] Tridon's doctrine of last days suggested that revolutionary action was of value not only for its efficacy, but also as a form of witness to the immortality of the revolutionary movement. He emphasized that the Hébertist leaders, like their Free-Thinking predecessors, Bruno, Vanini, and Servetus, knew how to die well.[45] The courage to accept death for the revolutionary cause reaffirmed the tragic value of action. Its memory was important, for therein revolutionary energy was preserved for the future. Tridon's tableau of the last words of the Hébertists as they stood before the guillotine is in this respect poignant: "If some of them despaired, it was for the future, not for themselves. 'What crushes me,' cried Hébert, 'is the knowledge that the Republic will perish.' 'No,' explained Ronsin, 'it is immortal.'"[46]

It was with this in mind that Blanquist youth hoped to take up the tasks of the Hébertists, as the Hébertists had taken up those of the atheist martyrs before them. In a way, the nineteenth century represented for the Blanquists a concentrated replica of the history of the West to the time of the revolution.[47] During this period, they claimed, France had passed into the Dark Ages of religious and political oppression once more. In an obvious parallel between the conditions in the Second Empire and those in imperial Rome, Tridon blamed Caesarism for creating an atmosphere in which Christianity could flourish.[48] The Blanquists believed, therefore, that their present task was to rehabilitate Blanqui and other nineteenth-century martyrs for human liberation—counterparts of the Free Thinkers who had prepared the way for the French Revolution. By the late 1860s, they were analyzing contemporary political events as if they were about to witness a repetition of the revolution of 1793.[49]

The Blanquists' need to relive as well as remember the past explains their special fascination with Chaumette, the prosecutor of the Revolutionary Commune of 1793. Their interest was based on Chaumette's insight into the role of ritual repetition in the making of a philosophical revolution. In his love of popular festivals, Chaumette gave the atheist revolution its visible symbolism. It was he who planned the Festival of Reason in Notre-Dame cathedral on November 10, 1793, thereby casting the form in which revolutionary Paris would thenceforth honor and re-enact the atheist achievement. Such ceremonial rituals, the Blanquists believed, were not only symbolic acts but essential means of enacting their philosophical convictions and conveying them to a wider audience. Just as man fashions a preexisting material world, they contended, so he fashions preexisting ideas. These cannot be created out of nothingness; rather, they must be re-awakened and reaffirmed. In ritual repetition one is reminded of the hope of resurrection. Thus Chaumette, as he faced the judges who were about to condemn him, asked not for his life but for its remembrance.[50]

It is hardly surprising that the Blanquists should have developed rituals of their own. Perceiving the significance of rites of passage as a means of affirming atheist as well as religious belief, they soon made sponsorship of civil burial ceremonies one of the most characteristic aspects of their participation in the Free Thought movement. The Civil Burial movement began in the mid-1860s as a mutual aid society, organized by Blanquist students to assist working-class families with the financial and emotional problems of this difficult rite of passage. Their intent was to spare the poor the expense of lavish funerals which the religious traditions of nineteenth-century society required and to lend support to atheist workers who might be tempted in their grief to fall back upon religious prepossessions which they had struggled to overcome. The Blanquists stressed the decorum of these simple ceremonies, which offered readings, brief eulogies, and the casting of forget-me-nots, in contrast with the extravagance of the corresponding religious rites.[51]

It is important to note that the Civil Burial movement was the principal access route of Blanquist youth to the working class of Paris during the 1860s. The first contacts appear to have been made by Blanquist medical students, who provided free medical care for needy families. These were followed by social hours hosted by the Blanquist wine dealer, Edmond Levraud, where fine wines prepared the way for discussion of this more sobering subject. Such soirees were sponsored frequently and were well attended by Levraud's Blanquist friends. On these occasions, workers were exhorted to join the Civil Burial Society and to draw up wills prescribing lay funerals for themselves. They were encouraged to attend the funerals of members of the society, even when they had not known them personally. Blanquist students seem to have been faithful to this ritual witness, and the workers, sometimes bemused that these rites could be of such importance, usually straggled along.[52] Charles Da Costa, reminiscing about his Blanquist youth, claimed that the Civil Burial movement promoted a deep rapport between students and workers. Acquaintances made at the ceremonies, and afterward in the cafés adjoining the cemeteries, often served as the beginnings of more enduring friendships—solidified by later fraternization in the cafés of the Latin Quarter. The ease and intimacy of these associations, Da Costa contended, broke down class distinctions and thereby evoked for the young Blanquists idealized images of the comradeship in the revolutionary community of Paris in 1793.[53] The accuracy of these fond recollections is confirmed by the reports of imperial police investigators, who, baffled by the importance attached by the Blanquists to the Burial Society, investigated it as a facade for some more menacing political conspiracy. Thus when the police descended upon the Café Renais-

sance in November 1866 to arrest the Blanquist clan assembled
on charges of political conspiracy, they directed most of their
interrogation to the nature and function of the Civil Burial
movement.[54]

Most civil burials were occasions of anonymous witness by
anonymous comrades in atheism, although the death of a Blanquist loved one sometimes added a note of special pathos. When
Blanquist militant Gustave Genton was denied permission to
leave his prison cell to attend the funeral of his infant son on
April 30, 1867, more than four hundred sympathizers followed
the cortege to the cemetery in silent support.[55] The burial of
Albert Regnard's young wife (January 25, 1869), who had died of
an illness contracted during her husband's imprisonment, served
as the setting for one of his most eloquent eulogies—a tribute to
death, the reality before which all illusions vanish.[56]

In time, however, the Blanquists' involvement in the Civil
Burial movement extended to rites with more obvious political
overtones. In the late 1860s, they were drawn into anniversary
ceremonies commemorating the death of Alphonse Baudin.
Baudin, a medical doctor and a committed republican, fell on the
barricades in the faubourg St. Antoine on December 2, 1851,
while resisting the coup d'etat of Louis Napoleon. The conditions
of his heroic death, long forgotten, were first widely publicized
in 1866 in a book by Eugène Tenot.[57] As a man of science and a
man of action, Baudin fired the imaginations of the republican
youth of the 1860s, who venerated him for his courageous opposition to Louis Napoleon against overwhelming odds. As one
among a number of republican groups promoting the cult of
Baudin, the Blanquists, beginning in 1867, made pilgrimages to
his grave at the Montmartre cemetery on the anniversary of his
death in the hope that remembrance of his role in the last days
of the Second Republic might hasten the coming of the revolutionary days in which the Third would be born. The memorial
ceremony assumed the proportions of a festival of the republican opposition on December 2, 1868, when more than a thousand pilgrims assembled to honor Baudin. On this occasion a
newcomer to the Blanquist circle, Théophile Ferré (1846-1871),
delivered his first public speech against the empire. Recruited at
the event was Emmanuel Chauvière (1850-1910), who was arrested with other Blanquist students in a skirmish with police
following the ceremony. The momentum generated by these

2. The cult of Baudin: Ernest Pichio's depiction of Baudin on the barricades resisting the coup d'etat of Louis Napoleon, December 2, 1851. Phot. Bibl. Nat.

demonstrations was channeled into a fund-raising campaign to build a monument to Baudin, in which thirty-three newspapers across France participated.[58]

The drama attending the rites of remembrance for Baudin was reawakened for the Blanquists at the funeral of Victor Noir on January 12, 1870. Noir, a reporter for Henri Rochefort's *La Marseillaise*, was killed by Louis Napoleon's half-brother, Pierre, for having written disparagingly of the imperial family. More important in death than he had ever been in life, Noir was given a funeral which became a major event for the republican opposition. Rochefort urged his republican comrades to turn out en masse for a day of republican mourning. The Blanquists pointed out the relationship between this observance and those for Baudin. One reporter for *La libre pensée*, A. Brun, claimed that Noir, as he had set out to visit Pierre Bonaparte, had cavalierly remarked that should he die, he wished to be remembered in a manner befitting Baudin.[59] So it was. An enormous crowd of sympathizers assembled at the mortuary in Neuilly on the western outskirts of Paris for the march (estimates of the size of the crowd range from one to two hundred thousand), their fervor undampened by cold and steady rain. This was the first of only two occasions during the empire that the Blanquists publicly presented themselves as a paramilitary force, marching in ranks one thousand strong. The Blanquists, together with a band led by Gustave Flourens, urged the parade organizers, Rochefort and Charles Delescluze, to lead the procession across Paris, past the Imperial Palace, through the working-class districts, to the cemetery Père-Lachaise on the eastern edge of the city. Warding off this demand, Rochefort diverted the cortege to the cemetery at Neuilly rather than brave a confrontation with the imperial police.[60] Angered all the same over the political character of the funeral, the police began to round up well-known participants during the following month on charges of conspiracy, while at his trial for the homicide of Noir, Pierre Bonaparte was exonerated by the High Court.[61]

Reflecting upon the significance of the event several years later, Blanquist militants asserted that the funeral of Victor Noir

3. The funeral of Victor Noir, January 12, 1870, became a precedent for the political funerals of the Third Republic. Phot. Bibl. Nat.

might easily have been an occasion for the overthrow of the empire.[62] But from the outset the demonstration exhibited more of the hallmarks of a festival than of an insurrection, which reflects something of the ambiguity of the Blanquists' position as revolutionaries. Rites of passage and commemoration were for them important means of educating the people to civic responsibility. The tendentious use of festivals, particularly those of anniversary remembrance, followed logically from both the historical and philosophical aspects of their vision of revolution. The value of remembering the revolutionary heroes and events of the past, they believed, was derived from the reaffirmation of truths affirmed by these revolutionaries in their own day. These truths, the Blanquists explained, are objective and eternal, and men must return to them repeatedly for inspiration. To remember the past is therefore to prepare for the future. But whether that future promised transformation as well as reaffirmation remained problematic, for their conception of revolution had been thoroughly internalized. Much depended upon a decisive testing of their ideology, one which would force a division of political leaders along the lines proposed by Tridon in his history of the revolution. If the Blanquists could emerge from such a struggle victorious, they would remember their rituals as a spur to radical reconstruction; but if defeated, ritual activity could as easily become a substitute for it. This was precisely the testing provided by the Paris Commune of 1871.

CHAPTER IV

The Commune as an Atheist Drama

The Paris Commune of 1871 has been interpreted in many ways by historians, yet never quite as the Blanquists perceived it: as the renewal of the "philosophical revolution" announced yet unfulfilled in the Hébertist experience of 1793. Hence when the events of March to May 1871 transpired, the Blanquists had long since cast the images of what the Commune was supposed to be. The term "commune" figured prominently in the Blanquist vocabulary during the late 1860s and especially during the Siege of Paris by Prussian troops in the fall of 1870.[1] The translation of the religious question into a political one had been prepared in the last years of the Second Empire by the widening orbit of the Free Thought movement, and especially by its new-found militancy. With the advent of the Franco-Prussian War (August 1870), the activities of the Free Thought movement were momentarily suspended.

The conflict nonetheless remained for the Blanquists an atheist drama. It is no surprise, therefore, to learn that the staff of La patrie en danger, the Blanquist newspaper which monitored the war effort, was essentially the same as that of La libre pensée, which had popularized the atheist crusade.[2] The philosophical doctrine of opposing mentalities (religious and atheist) developed by Tridon and popularized by his Blanquist comrades translated easily into a political doctrine of opposing nations (legal and real) as the Blanquists began to decipher the meaning of the war. Whether phrased as a conflict between the Prussian king and the French people, the provisional government and the "revolutionary commune," or the provinces and Paris, their essential conception of the struggle was that of quarreling communities of like-minded peoples for whom there could be no meeting of minds.[3]

The Blanquists believed, therefore, that the coming of war was something for which to be grateful, for it helped to clarify the terms of the struggle, everpresent but often obscured. They loved martial imagery and underscored its importance in reinforcing their conception of atheism as a militant cause. An armed insurrection, they explained, was the appropriate issue of a philosophical revolution, as it made tangible the sense of participation in a movement of intellectual liberation.[4] It is in this context that Blanqui's *Instructions pour une prise d'armes*, written in 1868 and circulated among his followers at the end of the empire, must be appreciated. Not only was it a manual on the tactics of insurrection, it was an affirmation of his faith in the moral energy which could be generated by a people under arms. It was the enthusiasm of the citizen-soldier, Blanqui argued, which gave him the advantage over the conscript, who was motivated only by fear. A popular army, if properly organized and disciplined, could wear away the resolve of a professional one.[5]

In the columns of *La patrie en danger*, Blanqui and his followers spread this message and delineated its revolutionary implications. War policy, they claimed, equalized conditions within a nation, as it required rich and poor to share limited resources and to accept participation in a common struggle. A new sense of community would emerge from such comradeship. The needs of war also dictated a strong central government, one which could deal effectively with domestic problems through long-range planning and which could design bold strategies for military preparedness. Daily, the Blanquists exhorted the Government of National Defense to adopt a more aggressive and comprehensive war policy and offered specific suggestions on rationing, manpower conscription, and even military strategy for its implementation. Beneath their commentary was the assumption that actively sharing in the use of power provided the only authentic means of creating a just society. It was through shared ordeal that a "commune" became truly "revolutionary."[6]

The Blanquists argued that an active, visible enemy steels a people's resolve and catalyzes the moral energy needed to carry on the struggle; hence they praised their avowed enemies. As Raoul Rigault, the staunchest proponent of this viewpoint, explained, at least one knew what one's declared opponents stood for.[7] Far more dangerous than the visible enemy without was the invisible enemy within. Cited in this category were those republicans in positions of political authority whose lack of revolutionary conviction sapped the will of the people to fight for liberation. From the first days of the Franco-Prussian War, the Blanquists had accused the Bonapartists of complicity in Bis-

marck's design to render France subservient to Prussia.[8] Within
a month of the fall of the Napoleonic regime (September 4,
1870), they were prepared to consign most of the republican
leaders of the provisional government to this category as well.

The French Revolution provided them with more than a distant model by which to measure the government's performance.
The most insistent theme of Blanquist journalism during the
Siege (September 1870-January 1871) was the parallel between
the weaknesses of the present Government of National Defense
and the Girondin Ministry of 1792-93, the inadequacy of whose
efforts on both the war and the home fronts compromised the
military struggle and threatened the revolution. The failure of
both the Girondins and their neo-Girondin successors, they
claimed, was rooted in lack of faith that the war could be won.[9]
For success was dependent upon daring to take advantage of
opportunities in which the will to power might provide the mar-
gin of victory. Repeatedly, the Blanquists insisted that revolutionary courage alone could prevail over superior military might.
However inauspicious the prospects, success in battle was ever a
possibility. Willpower, not technology, was the essential ingredient. Blanquist journalists referred to the battles of Valmy and
Jemappes as examples of victories by the revolutionaries of 1792
against nearly impossible odds.[10]

In pursuing this line of argument, the Blanquists found it
useful to return to ideological sources. Willpower, they believed,
could only be derived from the moral courage inspired by atheism. Therefore, as the military situation of the French armies
deteriorated in October, Blanquist journalists reminded their
readers of the atheist origins of the revolution then in progress.
Henri Place argued that revolutions had been most successful in
those historical eras in which atheist influence had been prevalent. By mid-November, both he and Regnard openly expressed
their disappointment that the old religious idols had not fallen
with Bonaparte as anticipated, and they soon turned their attention once more to the projects of the Free Thought movement.[11]
Place hoped that Free Thinkers would be able to establish committees in each of the arrondissements of Paris, although only a
few appear to have been formed before the siege was lifted in
January 1871.[12]

Nonetheless, activities that had been sponsored by the Free
Thought movement were much in evidence. Civil burials, particularly those directly related to the war effort, were given

considerable publicity. Gustave Tridon described the civil burial ceremony for Messrs. Lapie and Baudot (October 27, 1870), workers killed in an accidental explosion at a Parisian munitions factory, as a "funeral worthy of Mirabeau." Purportedly it was one of the most solemn festivals of the siege, attended by thirty thousand mourners bearing the banners of their clubs, committees of vigilance, and national guard battalions. Blanqui, among others, delivered a eulogy.[13] A similar ceremony was held in late November for the "sharpshooters [*tirailleurs*] of Belleville" who had died in the Battle of Maisons-Alfort.[14] The committee to establish lay schools, dormant since July, was reactivated. Lay schools were in fact established during the siege in a few Parisian arrondissements (third, fourth, and eleventh), despite some hostility from the Municipal Council.[15]

The Blanquists' desire to expose the enemy within involved more than a critique of governmental inertia. It included charges of treason as well. Blanquist journalists hinted at the tacit alliance of the neo-Girondins, the libertarian elite of the new republic, and the Orleanists, the libertarian elite of the old empire. They pointed to the continuity of self-serving interests in the supposed transition from the old regime to the new. The neo-Girondins of the Government of National Defense, they contended, were false friends preparing to betray the republic by suing for peace. As war heightened the prospect of revolution, they claimed, so peace would insure the preservation of the status quo. Charges of defeatism, muted in the Blanquist press during the early months of the siege, were stated more vociferously by November, when the government began to arrest members of the staff of *La patrie en danger* who had been involved in protest demonstrations.[16]

The attack on governmental lethargy was, in turn, linked with the graver issue of internal subversion, presented by Raoul Rigault in a dramatic exposé of the police spies of the Second Empire. Rigault, shortly after the proclamation of the republic on September 4, 1870, had spent two months as a special police investigator (*commissaire spécial*) combing the files at the Prefecture of Police for evidence of spies who had infiltrated the revolutionary movement during the 1860s.[17] In early November, he resigned his post and began to publish his most sensational findings in *La patrie en danger*. Each day, he described the interests and activities of a different police official or informer. His most telling accusations were against Blanquist comrades or those closely associated with them; notably Joseph Largillière, wood worker, veteran of the 1848 revolution and Blanquist militant of the 1860s, and Jean-Baptiste Roux, law student and Blanquist comrade of the Latin Quarter, both of whom were exposed as informants in the Café Renaissance Affair. Also censured were Greffe, a carpenter active in the Civil Burial movement, and Joseph Ruault, a stone cutter, both cited as secret agents of the imperial police receiving regular stipends for spying on Blanquist and other republican groups.[18] Such evidence lent credence to the Blanquists' proposition that defeat was more likely to result from inside corruption than from outside power. For the Blanquists, the enemy within bore not only the hallmarks of ineptitude but also the stigma of malicious intent.

For this reason, the "revolutionary days" of the Franco-Prussian War became for the Blanquists ritual confrontations with their ideological adversaries. There were four such uprisings in the fall and winter of 1870-71: August 14, the storming of the fire station arsenal at La Villette by about one hundred armed Blanquists; September 4, the invasion of the assembly hall of the Legislative Body by a crowd (in which the Blanquists figured prominently) as a prelude to the proclamation of the Third Republic; October 31, a demonstration of National Guard units at City Hall, at which Blanqui briefly menaced the leaders of the Government of National Defense for their military ineptitude; and January 22, an insurrection of National Guard battalions led by Blanquist militiaman Théodore Sapia to protest the negotiations for an armistice with Prussia.

Although none of these uprising succeeded in achieving Blanquist objectives, the Blanquists believed them to be valuable for their lessons about the nature of the struggle. Indeed, each successive revolutionary day seemed to them to clarify further the military tasks of the atheist crusade. August 14 and September 4, they believed, had made the Parisian people aware of the secret complicity of the French emperor and the Prussian king, while October 31 and January 22 had made them conscious of the more treacherous intrigues within the republican movement to prostrate France before Prussia. Later, they would argue that the Commune, created to draw physical lines between two spiritual nations, was the logical consequence of this struggle and revealed what had actually been at issue throughout the siege.[19]

The Blanquists' conception of the ritual relationship between these revolutionary days and past revolutionary events was underscored by the manner in which they recounted them. Blanqui, for example, offered tediously detailed narratives of the events of August 14 and October 31 without interpretation, as if their meaning were transparent in their simple presentation.[20] Gaston Da Costa's discussion of the insurrections of the siege likewise emphasized description rather than analysis, as did the memoirs of Emmanuel Chauvière and of Ernest Granger.[21] Their perception was that these demonstrations reenacted a point of view whose meaning had already been established in an earlier historical experience and was therefore self-evident. The revolutionary days of the siege were primarily celebrations of ideological confrontation in which presence was as important as efficacy. In this sense, they were but more vigorous and visible expressions of the kind of political vigilance which the Blanquists demanded nightly in the popular rallies of the clubs of Paris.

In such a setting the Blanquists played their most conspicuous role during the autumn of 1870. The Club Blanqui, a peripatetic gathering which ambled on successive evenings from the cafés of Belleville to those of the Rue d'Arras, gained a reputation as the most popular forum for the airing of radical ideas.[22] Blanquists presided over other clubs as well: Gabriel Brideau over the Club du Maine; Edmond Mégy over the Club des Batignolles, and Théophile Ferré over the Club de Montmartre.[23] The Blanquists were not newcomers to the political clubs of Paris. They had practiced oratory of this sort since 1868, when the imperial government had legalized such assemblies. Nor were the themes discussed fresh or original: atheism; social justice; oppressive social mores; restrictions on intellectual freedom; historical precedents for revolutionary action—these subjects had been their common parlance for some time, though they were now put forward with a new urgency.[24] But such issues were couched in a language too abstract to be of much interest to a governing body, even one responsive to the notion of popular vigilance. Concrete proposals affecting domestic or war policy, when they were offered by the Blanquists, were narrowly conceived in terms of the experience, real and imagined, of the Revolutionary Commune of 1793.

With such a compelling emphasis upon public witness to their convictions, the Blanquists clearly gave second place to plans for secret insurgency. Gustave de Molinari, who patiently transcribed the proceedings of a number of the revolutionary clubs during the siege, is convinced that the Blanquists were just as happy that their uprisings did not succeed, because they did not conform adequately to their idealized conception of any of the popular insurrections of the French Revolution.[25] Hence the tableau of three thousand Blanquist militants waiting in the wings for the proper moment to execute a coup d'etat, conjured up by the Imperial police official Lagrange for the official parliamentary inquiry in the Commune's aftermath, does not correspond to the manner in which the Blanquists conceived of their role once the republic had been declared on September 4.[26] Rather, they believed that their task was to dramatize the conflict for others and thereby to unmask the enemy within.

Exposing false revolutionaries also reaffirmed for the Blanquists the central significance of comradeship in the making of a revolution. Community meant not only the achievement of a future ideal, but also participation in the present ordeal. Community was discovered through the shared experience of struggle in which comradeship was revealed as the primary source of power. The Blanquist vision of a revolutionary commune was based on this proposition. As a conception of community the Blanquists judged it superior to that instituted by the provisional Government of National Defense because of its spontaneity (as opposed to the provisional government's legalism); its organic unity (as opposed to the government's aloofness from the governed); and its capacity to act forcefully (as opposed to the government's policy to speak equivocally).[27] The contrast was based upon Tridon's theory of opposing nations. But the Blanquists' claim for the superiority of a revolutionary commune in directing the war effort was founded upon a complementary theory of Paris as the hearth (*foyer*) of revolution. The idea was that revolutionary energy radiates from the revolutionary community at its dynamic center. The task of extending the revolution, therefore, was a matter of reenacting the primal solidarity of the revolutionary experience on a wider plane. The leadership which Paris might provide for this movement of national liberation, the Blanquists believed, need not stop at the city's gates or even at the French frontiers, but could energize the struggle of oppressed people everywhere.[28] Hence the Blanquists' praise for Anacharsis Cloots—who in 1793 had proposed that the French Revolution become a world revolution—was reiterated in their praise for his modern counterparts, the Italian Giuseppe Garibaldi and the Frenchman Gustave Flourens, who had journeyed to distant lands to further the cause of national liberation.[29]

Reduced to its basic paradigm, the theory of Paris as the hearth of the revolution offered the image of a widening circle of revolutionary energy. It provided a resolution of sorts to the ceaseless conflict which the logic of the theory of opposing nations seemed to imply. The expanding wave of revolutionary energy overcame and suppressed its reactionary opposition. The latter force was neither annihilated nor transformed, but was driven underground and, with constant vigilance, rendered harmless.[30] The theory of the hearth was not without ambiguity. In its images of widening access to the revolutionary community, it universalized the Parisian experience. On the other hand, it implied that the level of energy a revolutionary movement could generate was inversely proportional to its distance from Paris.

Indeed, this geographical aspect of the theory became for the Blanquists more nuanced still. Their desire to make more precise the source of revolutionary energy prompted them to distinguish between the regions of the Parisian cityscape. The eastern faubourgs were designated as the hearth of Parisian revolutionary ardor and, within this region, the Père-Lachaise quarter as the hearth of the faubourgs.[31] All these refinements reiterated the Blanquists' obsession with the sources of their own revolutionary energy in the Hébertist experience of 1793. In later years, they would use a variation upon the theory of the hearth to lend importance to their claims for the inspiring power of their own comradeship on the eve of the Commune. Newcomers would be absorbed into the Blanquist group during the Third Republic, but the veterans of the campaigns of the 1860s would never be completely comfortable with those outside the original confraternity.[32] If revolutionary action did not succeed in transforming the larger society, it nonetheless offered the revolutionary community as a source of consolation. That sentiment, too, harked back to 1794, when the revolutionary movement inspired by the Hébertists had been forced to go underground.

The conflict between particular comradeship and universal aspiration implicit in the theory of the hearth became explicit in the revolutionary days of the siege. Just as these four uprisings punctuated a shift in the Blanquists' perception of the enemy from a force without to a force within, so their perception of their own role changed from one of leadership of the revolution to one of guardianship of the revolutionary ideal. In seeking to extend their revolutionary comradeship, they lost the organizational cohesion they appeared to have been building in the last years of the empire. The uprising of August 14, the storming of the arsenal at La Villette, is the only example of an insurrection autonomously inspired and led by Blanqui's student followers of the 1860s. The assault on La Villette was attempted in the belief that popular insurrection against the crumbling Second Empire was imminent. La Villette was chosen both for its stores of weapons and ammunition and for its proximity to Belleville, the Parisian quarter most sympathetic to the revolutionary cause.[33]

The Blanquists' expectations that their raid would galvanize mass popular support were not entirely naive. Popular agitation had smouldered in eastern Paris since the imperial police had first begun to round up suspected participants in the funeral parade for Victor Noir some eight months before. These arrests, launched in February 1870, led to the incarceration of Rochefort, the flight of Flourens and Tridon abroad, and the erection of barricades in Belleville. Demonstrations of protest in that quarter continued from February through May. Exasperated with the incessant agitation, the police undertook a systematic round-up of political radicals in the late spring and placed sixty-two of them on trial for conspiracy in a much publicized series of proceedings at Blois in July. Many of those accused fled abroad. Most of those who remained were acquitted.[34] Blanquist observers were as much struck by the ineptitude of this action as they were by its repressive character. In a manifesto published on the eve of the trial, Rigault and Gois (both of whom had been indicted) mocked the imperial authorities for the theatrical quality of the whole affair.[35] The Blanquists admitted that they had been conspiring against the empire for some time. But their actual revolutionary organization bore no resemblance to the contrived one that Bonapartist officials had fabricated. The government of the Second Empire, it seemed to the Blanquists, was ill-equipped to deal with subversion in the best of times. With the advent of war, they were convinced, the regime had lost its bearings and could be easily toppled.

The uprising of August 14 involved considerable planning. Ernest Granger contributed his entire inheritance to purchase guns for his comrades. Emile Gois forged the daggers they would carry into action. The assault upon an arsenal, the Blanquists believed, would provide the first step in the arming of the Parisian population for a larger insurrection. As a target, their first choice had been the fortress at Vincennes, where Granger and Eudes, slipping past its sentinels unobserved, had for several weeks been making preliminary inspections. The decision to shift the offensive to the fire station at La Villette was made only a few days before the assault because that edifice was situated near the "hearth" of revolutionary Paris and because the Blanquists anticipated that the firemen might be sympathetic to their cause. Neither calculation worked to the Blanquists' advantage. Far from fraternizing with the Blanquists, the firemen resolutely resisted their entry. In the ensuing exchange of volleys, one arsenal guard was killed and one was wounded. The populace of Belleville shunned the entire event.[36] Granger recalls an eerie feeling of isolation as he and his companions ran to safety through the empty streets adjoining the fire station.[37]

More disappointing still was the turnout of militants. Although the Blanquists boasted of a disciplined following of at least a thousand, they were able to mobilize no more than a hundred on this occasion. If they possessed a network for communicating orders, it failed to function on that day.[38] The storming of La Villette was a fiasco. Easily resisted and rapidly dispersed, the Blanquists fled in panic. Blanqui later blamed the failure of the uprising on a tactical error in timing, Granger on the choice of target, Eudes on the defection of some comrades to the International during the preceding months. Its real significance, however, was that it disabused the Blanquists of whatever illusions they may have harbored about their capacity to incite a popular insurrection. Without admitting it, they were prepared to accept a more modest role. If they sometimes acted with éclat, their participation in the revolutionary days of the siege had none of the operational planning which had preceded the attack at La Villette.[39]

From that time on, the Blanquists were content to be absorbed into the larger revolutionary horde. This was apparent in the uprising of September 4. On that day, the Blanquists abandoned their paramilitary organization to mingle with the revolutionary crowd. Individuals were highly visible. Ernest Granger, for example, led the crowd into the Bourbon Palace where the Legislative Body was deliberating and ascended the podium to interrupt the proceedings. Gaston Da Costa claims that September 4 was largely a Blanquist affair. But though individual Blanquists were prominent in the drama of casting out the deputies of the old regime, control of the new was quickly seized by others. In no sense did the Blanquists direct the events of the uprising. No Blanquist was named to the provisional Government of National

Defense. The most significant event of the day for the Blanquists was the freeing of their comrades Brideau and Eudes from the Cherche-Midi prison, where they were awaiting execution for their part in the storming of La Villette. Thus images of comradeship figure more obviously than do those of victory in most Blanquist accounts of the day.[40] Whereas comradeship had been seen as a force for reconstructing community on August 14, by September 4 it was viewed as a community of consolation in the midst of uncertain revolutionary turmoil.

Discarding their own organization as a political base of operation, the Blanquists during the siege sought individually to infiltrate the National Guard; and there their role was considerable. A striking number of Blanquist militants were chosen for positions of leadership in the battalions of the National Guard during the autumn of 1870. Of seventy-eight new battalions mobilized in Paris during the siege, no less than sixteen were commanded by Blanquists. Many other Blanquists served as officers on the staffs of these military units.[41] As well-known public orators of the late 1860s, they had gained recognition and thus acclaim in the open forums where Guard officers were elected. At the same time, Blanquist military leaders appear to have had remarkably little contact with one another. Emile Eudes, who commanded the 138th Battalion, for example, claims that during the entire course of the siege he never saw his comrade Emile Duval, who led the 157th.[42] Nor do the Blanquists appear to have had much influence upon the ad hoc committees which emerged to coordinate the activities of revolutionary Paris. On both the Central Committee of the Twenty Arrondissements, formed at the outset of the siege, and the Central Committee of the National Guard, created at the beginning of the Commune, the Blanquists had only token representation.[43]

The demonstration of October 31 reveals the extent to which the Blanquists, considered as revolutionary activists, had been scattered. When Blanqui proceeded on that day to City Hall (where the provisional government was meeting) at the head of his battalion (the 169th), he made no effort to contact other Blanquist battalion commanders. Some units headed by Blanquists did converge on City Hall, but they had devised no prior strategy. Nor did Blanqui, once he had arrived there, include any of his followers on his list of candidates for a Committee of Public Safety (proposed to supplant the Government of National Defense). Moreover, he quickly discarded the list when leaders of the provisional government offered assurances that they were determined to carry on the war effort.[44]

Likewise, the demonstration of January 22 was remembered for its vignettes of personal Blanquist comradeship rather than for its insurrectionary effectiveness. On that date, several National Guard units gathered at City Hall to protest the cessation of hostilities with Prussia on terms which amounted to surrender. Within the crowd were numerous Blanquist Guardsmen, notably Théodore Sapia, a professional soldier who had cast his lot with the Blanquists and upon whom they counted for military leadership. Sapia had presided over the session of the Central Committee of the Twenty Arrondissements, which had planned the demonstration, but this was not a Blanquist initiative. Blanqui purportedly waited in a café near the square where the demonstration was held—but as a witness, not an organizer.[45] January 22 would be reverenced by the Blanquists as the last day of the siege, a day on which unsuspecting National Guardsmen, in a final display of vigilance for the "fatherland in danger," were fired upon by Breton militiamen (*gardes mobiles*) loyal to the provisional government in a cruel act of betrayal. In subsequent commentaries about the day, Blanquist writers have little to say of its historical significance but take special care to recreate a tableau of the massacre itself, especially the scene of Sapia dying in the arms of his comrades.[46]

Having lost their cohesion as a paramilitary organization during the siege, the Blanquists lost their capacity to shape the organization of the revolutionary movement in its aftermath. The fabled Blanquist network of secret societies, to the degree that it had ever existed, dissolved to be replaced by the revolutionary committees of the International and of the National Guard. The unity of the Blanquists during the siege was rather in the viewpoint they had expressed as journalists and club orators. In the process, they publicly cast themselves as ideologists rather than activists. As Regnard protested when several of his comrades were arrested for having participated in the demonstration of October 31, the Blanquists were not a political faction but a group of republicans who shared a common vision of the revolutionary ideal. Their power, he claimed, was in the moral authority of their public pronouncements.[47] In effect, the Blanquists, unable to lead the revolutionary movement, decided instead to act as monitors of its ideological orthodoxy.

This orientation explains the nature of their role in the Paris Commune of March to May 1871. The Commune served them as a stage on which the gathering drama of ideological confrontation, rehearsed during the siege, would be played to its denouement. During the Commune, the Blanquists were determined that their historic revolutionary ideal should live again. The succession of events was for them a revelation of the logic of Tridon's archetypal model of revolution—from the "revolutionary day" of March 18, on which the Commune was proclaimed, to the "last days" of Bloody Week (May 22-28), when it was destroyed.[48] Indeed, with the fall of the Commune relentlessly approaching, the Blanquists were determined that their last acts should precipitate a violent clash of the ideological forces at play. The rituals with which they had celebrated the violent events of the revolutionary tradition during the Second Empire and the siege yielded in the final episode of the Commune to ritual violence in the desecration of churches, the destruction of public monuments, and the execution of political hostages.

Of all of the agencies of the Commune, therefore, the political police was the one over which the Blanquists chose to assert their control. Through that organization they were able to carry out their atheist crusade most effectively. On March 29, Rigault and Ferré were named Civil Delegates for General Safety. Rigault served as chief delegate at the Prefecture of Police from that date until April 24, when he was forced to resign by moderates of the Communal Assembly who could no longer tolerate his behavior. Ferré acceded to the post on May 13 to face awesome decisions concerning the fate of the Commune's hostages in the last days of fighting. The Prefecture of Police thus became the primary instrument of the Blanquists' attack on internal subversion, providing in turn a staging ground from which to influence the judicial system as well. On April 26, Rigault was named public prosecutor (*procureur*) of the Commune (the post held in 1793 by his idol Chaumette). The high and middle echelons of both the police and the prosecutor's office were staffed with Blanquists. Drawing together a network of agencies through their personal and institutional ties, they made internal security a special sphere in which they exercised nearly exclusive control.[49]

This focus of the Blanquist effort during the Commune has never received adequate attention from historians. Maurice Dommanget, for example, stresses the variety of their roles. His study of the Blanquists during the Commune catalogues the activities of individuals, of dissidents as well as loyalists, of sympathizers as well as disciples. His inference is that, despite their apparent dispersion, Blanquist militants held a significant number of leadership posts in the Commune. Hence the group played a decisive role in shaping the policies of that regime.[50] But Dommanget's claim for a comprehensive role for the Blanquist party during the Commune dissolves under scrutiny; for its leaders made no special effort to act in concert to shape either the military or the political policies of that government. The standard histories of the Commune identify between eight and eleven members of the Communal Assembly as Blanquists.[51] But they did not constitute a separate voting bloc within that body. On matters of policy, the distinction between Blanquists and Jacobins tended to disappear. The crucial split within the assembly was between those favoring a strong central authority (Blanquists and Jacobins together) and those preferring a larger measure of local autonomy (Proudhonists and federalists).[52] Moreover, some of those identified as Blanquists by historians (Vaillant, Cournet, Chardon, and Ranvier, for example) had in fact had little association with earlier Blanquist formations, or else they officially aligned themselves with the party only in the ensuing exile. The presence of individual Blanquists in the Communal Assembly has relatively little importance as a category of distinctly Blanquist leadership.[53]

Nor did the Blanquist party enjoy special status in the Commune's army, despite the significant number of leadership positions in the National Guard battalions carried over from the siege by Blanquists. A few held major military commands. Both Duval and Eudes were named to the Military Commission and personally led the first offensive of the war, on April 3. But Duval was captured and executed on that ill-fated mission and Eudes relegated to a less important post. Subsequently named commander of a legion of active reserves, Eudes staffed his headquarters with Blanquist confederates (Emile Gois, Albert Goullé, A. Poirier, Léopold and Octave Caria), but these men did not act as a consolidated interest group within the army. Eudes did have his own special services company, Les Enfants Perdus, an elite unit with a distinctive costume. Elements of this company were

4. Les Enfants Perdus: a militiaman of the elite guard of General Eudes during the Commune. Phot. Bibl. Nat.

used by Blanquist officers in the last days of fighting to execute hostages; but it was, in terms of the military campaigns of the Commune, an insignificant body. The chance for Blanquist military leadership had been lost at the outset. In his memoirs, Eudes laments that his preliminary efforts to construct a revolutionary army of battalions led by Blanquist commanders (Duval, Chauvière, Ferré, and himself) had been dashed by the speed of events in the early days of the Communal uprising and subsequently by the Central Committee of the National Guard.[54]

If sympathizers exaggerate the Blanquists' role, critics focus too narrowly upon the diabolical influence of a few leaders, notably Raoul Rigault and Théophile Ferré. These were the "spoiled children [*les galopins*] of the revolution," in the words of Maxime du Camp, the Commune's most hostile critic.[55] Du Camp claims that most of the atrocities committed by the Commune were the responsibility of these "sinister" figures. He portrays Rigault

5. Raoul Rigault as prefect of police during the Commune. Phot. Bibl. Nat.

and Ferré as juvenile, inept, and gratuitously cruel. Their evil
deeds he attributes to ill-formed character, to adolescent behavior run amok.[56] Rigault and Ferré did provide their critics with
rich opportunities for pursuing this line of argument. Anecdotes
about their behavior, often macabre, abound, and hostile historians have exploited them to the fullest. There was, for example,
Rigault's decision concerning the status of the Prefecture of Police. He had vowed to abolish it in some of his more flourishing
speeches at the end of the empire. This pledge he honored upon
assuming office by changing the name of his organization to the
Ex-Prefecture of Police without changing any of its functions.
Rigault could thus amuse his critics even if he did frighten them.
In judging his role as Delegate for General Safety, moreover,
they find him to have been a small-minded dictator, self-indul-

gent, arrogant, and most of all capricious.[57] Thousands of suspects were arbitrarily incarcerated during his reign, in clumsy imitation of what he believed had transpired in the Revolutionary Commune of 1793.[58] Even his friends portray him as lazy and conceited, a man who reveled in the perquisites of office without being willing to face the responsibilities. In a letter to Eudes written in the early days of the exile, Edmond Levraud, who had been a bureau chief at the Prefecture, privately confided his dismay that Rigault had largely abandoned the essential tasks of his office after the first few days. Levraud claims that Rigault continued to pass his afternoons in the cafés of the Left Bank, as had long been his custom, and left the bulk of the work to his subordinates.[59]

A similar case has been made about Théophile Ferré, whose critics are quick to point out the physical and formative factors which left him bitter and vindictive. It is said that he was conspicuously ugly. A clerk by profession, he hailed from humbler origins than did most of his comrades. Like Rigault, he was initiated into the Blanquist entourage through prison contacts in the late Second Empire. He entered radical politics with éclat in December 1868, when he delivered a tirade at the anniversary ceremony for Alphonse Baudin at the Montmartre cemetery. To be sure that he would be noticed, he climbed atop a burial monument to shout a series of revolutionary slogans. Such a pose was not unusual. A diminutive man, he was obliged to stand on tiptoe when delivering an oration. His enemies claimed that he shrieked rather than spoke. Ferré's style may have been a bit frenetic. But the ardor with which he hurled invectives against the emperor and his empire made him a popular speaker in the clubs of Belleville and Montmartre in 1869 and 1870. Arrested and prosecuted in the trial at Blois, in the summer of 1870, he defended himself with bravado and was acquitted. At the outset of the siege, he enrolled in the 152nd National Guard infantry battalion from Montmartre. Active in the vigilance committees of that quarter, he was elected to the Communal Assembly on March 26 by a substantial majority; and he was named by that body to serve with Rigault as Civil Delegates for General Safety. During the Commune, Ferré drew close to Rigault, whom he served as assistant prosecutor (*substitut*) and whom he succeeded as chief delegate at the prefecture. In that post he signed the death warrants for some of the Commune's hostages in the last days of fighting.[60]

Blanquist sympathizers agree with the critics that Rigault and Ferré were fanatics. But they contend that the intense passion with which they pursued their ideological convictions was a necessary ingredient in the making of a revolution. The problem was not their excess, but the lack of such enthusiasm among the majority of Communards. In seeking to rehabilitate Rigault's much maligned image, Gaston Da Costa, his secretary and constant companion, points out the contradiction in his personality between a skeptical mind and a fanatical heart. Acknowledging Rigault's faults and even his misdeeds, Da Costa retains a certain awe before Rigault's unmatched daring.[61] Of Ferré, Da Costa speaks no less generously. He dwells fondly upon Ferré's unconquerable energy and his faith in his cause—"the faith which makes heroes"—which he sustained throughout his ordeal of trial, imprisonment, and execution in the aftermath of the Commune.[62]

But neither the critics nor the sympathizers pay sufficient attention to the direct connection between Rigault's and Ferré's acts and their intellectual convictions. If they were both ruthless (as their critics charge) and passionate (as their apologists claim), they were also fully conscious of what they were doing and had no moral compunctions about it. The suspects they marked for arrest show a clear pattern of stereotyping: priests, policemen, and, the most nefarious of all, friends revealed as police informers. Their deeds corresponded directly to their ideological vision of the world. It is easy to single them out as ideologues acting out of fervent conviction. But just as the critics have failed to appreciate their motives, so too they have overestimated their personal power. Their Blanquist subordinates at the Prefecture of Police, if less obviously fanatical, shared their values and willingly pursued the same objectives. It was the faithful camp followers of earlier Blanquist groupings, and the clever and ambitious men who now rallied around them at the prefecture, who carried out their policies thoroughly and with unquestioning devotion. Not only Rigault and Ferré, but also their comrades, the Blanquists and student friends of the Latin Quarter, conducted the search for political subversives in the name of a noble ideology which would transform the world. The significance of the Blanquists in the Commune, therefore, is at once lesser and greater than ordinarily characterized: lesser in that it was focused upon the province of internal security, greater in that the involvement of the Blanquists in the work of the police agencies of the Commune was deeper, more thoroughgoing, and more carefully calculated than their critics ever imagined. The degree to which the Blanquists infiltrated and assumed control of the upper and middle echelons of the police organization, the prison administration, and certain agencies of the judicial system suggests a painstaking seriousness of purpose. It was the cumulative effect of so many militants working to make a revolution in which the enemy to be overcome was perceived as an internal force, identified by its ideology, which accounts for the arrests, imprisonments, and executions carried out in the name of the Commune.[63]

The Blanquists who served in Rigault's cabinet at the prefecture typify the faithful lieutenants who, out of personal devotion or ideological conviction, carried out their tasks, often unpleasant ones, without moral scruples. The personal loyalty of Gaston Da Costa (1850-1909) to Rigault is a case in point. As Rigault's intercessor, confidant, and secretary, he was unkindly referred to by some Communards as Rigault's dog. During the Commune, he was Rigault's chief of cabinet at the prefecture. Critics of the Commune sometimes cite Da Costa as an example of the regime's juvenile leadership. When he assumed his official duties he was but twenty. Even in his personal development, he had followed in Rigault's footsteps: he had an aptitude for mathematics, passed his baccalaureate in science at age sixteen, and aspired to enter the Ecole Polytechnique. His early involvement in the Blanquist circle deflected him from his studies toward radical journalism and political activism. He interpreted as a ritual coming of age his first trial and imprisonment for participating in a Blanquist political demonstration in 1866.[64] When Rigault was named a special police investigator during the siege, he called upon Da Costa to serve as his personal secretary. Thus Da Costa was involved in Rigault's research on the police informers of the Second Empire. When Rigault was named delegate to the Prefecture of Police during the Commune, Da Costa was momentarily reluctant to join him; Rigault had him "arrested" by some of his friends and dragged to his new post. (All of this was so much banter.) Da Costa took up his duties as chief of cabinet with enthusiasm and, one might say, a certain nonchalance. Those interrogated by him were never quite sure whether the affable youth understood the full significance of the activities in which he was involved. In addition to his duties of questioning and incarcerating political suspects, he took special charge of the ongoing search for the secret police informers of the Second Empire, which remained one of Rigault's primary interests. In his history of the Commune, Da Costa gives a sense of his outlook upon his duties when he describes his role during the last days of the Commune in transporting hostages from Mazas prison in the center of the city (about to be invaded by troops from Versailles) to the prison La Grande Roquette on its eastern reaches. That he was delivering them for almost certain execution presented him with no moral dilemma. He feared that the mob might seize and assassinate his charges en route, but the mission itself did not especially bother him. His political ideology enabled him to treat this responsibility in routine fashion. To convey hostages identified as "traitors" was a test of courage, not of moral choice.[65]

If Da Costa agreed to serve out of loyalty to Rigault, Dr. Albert Regnard, appointed secretary general of the Prefecture of Police, accepted his post for ideological reasons. One historian conjectures that Regnard, known as an intellectual, a researcher in medicine, a talented journalist, and a friend of Tridon, accepted the position as a consolation after having lost the election for a seat in the Communal Assembly. In fact, the secretary generalship gave him an ideal opportunity to turn theory into practice. As a leading theoretician of the Free Thought movement, he saw this responsibility as a logical means of pursuing his ideological crusade. His campaign for atheism had failed to undermine revealed religion as rapidly as he had hoped it would. With the founding of the Commune, he believed that the time had arrived to attack the clergy directly and so to accelerate the process. The task of ferreting out his ideological enemies under wartime conditions pulled together his wide-ranging intellectual interests. Regnard's other major activity during the Commune was his role in the reorganization of the national theater so that it could inculcate the new civic virtue. It was his attempt to give a more positive expression to the motive which likewise drew him to the prefecture.[66]

In the descending hierarchy of the political police, the list of Blanquist militants lengthens. Some had been friends or acquaintances of Rigault in the Latin Quarter. The key figure in their placement was Alfred Breuillé (1847-1929), one of the most unassuming members of the Blanquist entourage. An unsuccessful candidate for the Ecole Polytechnique, he turned to radical politics under the empire. From 1866, he participated in the demonstrations and shared the prisons of his Blanquist companions. During the Commune, Rigault named him a special commissioner and chief of personnel at the prefecture. In addition to appointing and supervising a variety of special agents, Breuillé assumed responsibility for much of the day-to-day administration of the internal security operation. Whereas Rigault cut an image of the flamboyant eccentric, Breuillé played the complementary role of the steady bureaucrat at the prefecture. Unlike Da Costa, however, Breuillé declined Rigault's invitation to follow him to the prosecutor's office in mid-May.[67]

The Blanquists at the prefecture controlled not only the measures for arrest but also those for incarceration. As chief of the First Division, Edmond Levraud (1837-1880), the wine dealer and stalwart of Blanquist causes since the first comradeship of the mid-1860s, was given overall supervision of the prisons. Levraud provides another example of the capable subordinate who carried out his duties scrupulously.[68] Assisting him were a number of Blanquists and sympathizers, each responsible for a different prison. Many of the prison guards were carryovers from the imperial administration, some of whom later claimed that they retained their posts to blunt the capricious effects of revolutionary justice. But the Blanquists knew that if they exercised exclusive control of the right to detain or release those arrested, they could accomplish their objectives without worrying overmuch about the loyalty of their rank-and-file personnel.[69]

In the police organization itself, however, the appointment of Blanquist personnel extended well beyond the central administration at the prefecture. Rigault and his staff named friends and followers as police commissioners in many of the arrondissements of Paris. There were Blanquist special agents in the train terminals and Blanquists leading the municipal police. Others were appointed for special services. There was a group of inspectors specifically assigned to track down priests suspected of espionage and to inventory and requisition the effects of the city's churches. There was another group assigned to the police archives of the Second Empire to pursue the investigation of police informers begun by Rigault during the siege.[70] The few officials appointed to positions of authority who had not been part of the Blanquist confraternity were selected for their docility. Frédéric Cournet replaced Rigault as delegate at the prefecture with the latter's knowledge that Cournet could be counted

upon to do his bidding.[71] A more poignant example is that of
Philippe-Auguste Cattelain, chosen as chief of security in Rigault's cabinet. An engraver by profession, Cattelain was a simple
and exceedingly naive man with no previous interest in politics.
In his memoirs, he recounts how bewildered he was when called
upon to serve in this high post. Even in retrospect, he seems to
have had little insight into Rigault's character or purposes.[72]

The limits of the Blanquists' infiltration of the police force
were set only by the time and personnel available. Many non-
Blanquist minor functionaries retained their posts because there
was no one to replace them. This problem was an enduring
source of worry to the Blanquists, some of whom pondered its
consequences for many years thereafter. During the exile,
Breuillé carried on an interesting correspondence with Eudes
about members of the prefectoral administration whom they
suspected had been agents of the Versailles government.[73] Thus,
even after the war was lost, some Blanquists found solace in the
continuity of their pursuit of the enemy within.

Blanquist influence extended to the judicial system as well,
although in this sphere it assumed a different cast. The relationship between the police and the judiciary during the Commune
reflected the tensions of a Blanquist feud of long standing.
Eugène Protot (1839-1921), named Delegate for Justice, set
distinct limits upon Rigault's ability to conduct his war on subversion. Protot, persona non grata to Blanqui, was the young
lawyer who had spoken at the First Workingmen's International
in Geneva (1866) in defiance of Blanqui's orders to abstain.[74]
Protot had severed formal ties with the group, but he maintained friendships with many Blanquist students and by 1870
appears to have drawn close to the faction of dissidents (led by
Jaclard) which had drifted toward the International. Protot greatly enhanced his professional reputation among political radicals
by his successful defense of Blanquist militant Edmond Mégy at
his trial at Blois in August 1870. Mégy was accused of having
shot and killed a policeman sent to arrest him for participation in
an alleged conspiracy. Protot saved his client from a sentence of
execution by building his defense upon the legal technicality that
the policeman had arrived before sunrise, the legal hour for
delivering a summons.[75] Protot's courage in taking the case, despite official intimidation, and his clever handling of it won him a
reputation as the lawyer of radicals. In the winter of 1870-71, he
successfully defended Pierre Vésinier and Paolo Tibaldi against

charges of treason for having participated in the demonstration of October 31.[76] On March 26, he was elected to the Communal Assembly by a large majority. Appointed Delegate for Justice, Protot surrounded himself with friends from his student days, most of whom had some Blanquist association. Among the Blanquists in his cabinet were Léon Sornet, a railroad employee and a veteran of Blanquist groups of the Second Empire, and Charles Da Costa, law student, journalist, and brother of Gaston.

Protot was ideologically close to the Blanquists, but his formation as a lawyer had instilled in him a respect for libertarian principles which made it difficult for him to accept the more tyrannical measures invoked by Rigault's Committee for General Safety. He and his assistants waged an ongoing battle with Rigault's entourage over arbitrary arrests and detainments. It was Protot, moreover, who drafted the Law on Hostages in order to prevent the Communal Assembly from carrying out the summary executions demanded by Rigault. In seeking to contain the excesses of the Committee for General Safety, Protot played a narrower, more conventional role than he might have otherwise; and he never had an opportunity to implement his youthful dream of a more democratic judicial system responsive to the needs of the poor.[77] At the same time, Protot was basically supportive of Rigault's campaign against internal subversion and, partly out of ideological sympathy, partly out of naïveté, was drawn into it as the ordeal of the Commune wore on.

The war against the Catholic clergy, identified as the nucleus of the enemy within, was a primary mission of Rigault's staff from the outset.[78] The first priest was arrested on March 31, 1871, only a few days after Rigault was installed in office. Rigault's capacity to carry out his anticlerical campaign was greatly enhanced on April 2, when the Communal Assembly nationalized the effects of ecclesiastical houses held in mortmain and authorized an official inquiry to inventory them. Attempts by the clergy, real or imagined, to resist the enforcement of this decree provided Rigault with a pretext for arresting priests whom he wished to detain for ideological or political reasons.

Rigault and his cabinet took immediate measures to put the decree into effect. Among the first arrested for violations of its enforcement was Monsignor Georges Darboy, archbishop of Paris. Arrested on April 3 on charges of conspiring to violate the decree and on vague references to complicity with Versailles, he was transported to the prefecture to be interrogated personally by Rigault. It was a triumphal moment of historical truth for the delegate, who reminded his charge that their meeting signified a symbolic reversal of the roles their ideological kin had been playing for eighteen hundred years. Darboy was imprisoned and his vicar general, the Abbé Legarde, with him, for no better reason than that the latter had voluntarily accompanied the archbishop to the prefecture. Darboy's detention as an enemy of the Commune was all the more unfortunate in that he had no personal loyalties either to Versailles or to the Vatican. A liberal prelate, he was quite independent of Rome and had opposed the proclamation of the doctrine of papal infallibility.[79] His arrest, moreover, concurred with the defeat of the Commune's first offensive, in the aftermath of which Generals Duval and Flourens had been executed. When this news was announced at the meeting of the Communal Assembly, Rigault called for the immediate execution of the archbishop in retaliation. The demand was set aside, but the roundup of priests was accelerated in April, as military operations foundered in a quagmire of indecision and disputed leadership.

Darboy's arrest was followed by that of the Abbé Gaspard Deguerry, curé of La Madeleine and former confessor of the empress, for having tried to flee through his garden when a police agent came to inventory the effects of his rectory. The arrest and incarceration of the pastors of the other major churches of Paris followed the same pattern. More than two hundred priests were arrested during the first three weeks of April under the provisions of this decree. Special police agents learned that the aggressive pursuit of clerics was an easy access route to official favor, and certain investigators, such as Georges Pilotell and Benjamin Le Moussu, became notorious for the zeal with which they tracked them down.[80]

The campaign against the clergy as a subversive force represented more than compensation for military victories the Communards could not win at the front. It drew deeply upon the atheist mythology of the clergy popularized by the Free Thought movement during the Second Empire. The very existence of clerical houses, silent enclaves of an alien ideology in the midst of revolutionary Paris, aroused Blanquist suspicions that they were staging areas for paramilitary conspiracies of the sort that the Blanquists themselves had plotted under the empire. The Blanquists were prepared to believe that the monasteries and convents of Paris held caches of arms and ammunition, as well as treasure chests of the fabled wealth of the Church. The first inspections of ecclesiastical houses, carried out by Rigault's police agents under the provisions of the decree nationalizing movable church property, were actually intended to discover such contraband, believed to be hidden away in secret chambers and subcellars. The fact that the investigators turned up nothing in the first week of searching did not restrain the Jacobin press from reporting the seizure of sizable stores of weapons, nor a credulous populace from believing such stories. Indeed, these press reports helped Blanquist police officials to believe in their own legends of the clergy and so to intensify their investigations.[81]

In the course of a search for a secret cellar at the convent on the Rue Picpus in mid-April, police agents unearthed some bones

6. The interrogation of Archbishop Darboy at the Ex-Prefecture of Police, April 3, 1871, was an example of the Blanquists' vendetta against the clergy. Phot. Bibl. Nat.

and skeletons. Official interest in the investigation shifted sud-
denly from fantasies of military conspiracies to morbid curiosity
about the mysteries of life in religious houses. Jacobin journalists gave free rein to visions of clerical sadism as they opened
their imaginations to the circumstances under which these suspected victims of priestly torture must have died. Such specula-
tions were a kind of inversion of the Blanquist conception of
"last days," in which images of the secret and humiliating death
of the victims of Catholicism represented the antithesis of their
images of the public and noble death of the martyrs of atheism.
Popular interest was considerable. On successive evenings in
late April and early May, crowds of as many as twelve thousand
curious onlookers gathered in front of the convent.

The masses were not the only ones intrigued. Rigault assigned
National Guard contingents to make systematic excavations of
this and other religious houses in Paris in the expectation of
uncovering cadavers and instruments of torture. Protot made
on-site inspections with an official physician whose scientific
expertise, he hoped, would enable him to verify suspicions about

7. Skeletons at Saint-Laurent: a sketch from a Communard newspaper dramatiz-
ing rumors of clerical sadism and perversion. Phot. Bibl. Nat.

the seamy side of the religious life. Official autopsies revealed that the bones were those of people long deceased, most of them aged, but this information was withheld from the public. Instead, fabulous stories of cruelty and perversion held revolutionary Paris mesmerized while the last military defenses of the Commune were crumbling. As late as May 18, Protot still found time to visit a convent to view the remains excavated there—as if verifying the crimes of the enemy within could somehow redeem the impending fall of the Commune.[82]

The Blanquists' crusade against their anonymous ideological enemies must be juxtaposed to their vendetta against specific police informers of the Second Empire, a cause to which they attached equal significance. Rigault, of course, had done considerable preliminary work during the siege on informers masquerading as radicals and had published many of his findings in the Blanquist press. As delegate to the prefecture during the Commune, he decided to stalk his prey. He created a special "section of political archives" at the prefecture under the direction of Antony Jeunesse and Emile Giffault, Blanquist companions of his student days. Gaston Da Costa, who had shared in Rigault's initial investigation, was assigned to aid them.

In the remnants of the police files which imperial police official Lagrange had failed to destroy, Giffault found documentary evidence corroborating Rigault's accusations against Largillière, Ruault, and Greffe. He tracked down Largillière and Ruault in National Guard battalions, the former serving with a company guarding the Ministry of Finance, the latter on the front at Asnières, defending a barricade. Accused of being secret agents, they were confined by Rigault "under the greatest secrecy possible," as he put it, in keeping with his sense of the ideological appropriateness of such seclusion. Greffe, an organizer of the Civil Burial movement during the 1860s, had the misfortune to be spotted by a police agent while marching in a lay funeral parade for a fallen National Guardsman. Although the crimes of these men—acts of betrayal out of the past—possessed an ideological immediacy for Rigault, they bore no relation to the present strategies of the government at Versailles to infiltrate the agencies of the Commune, which were not seriously impeded by Rigault's counterespionage operation. Rigault also pursued and arrested "traitors" of the revolutionary days of the siege: Gustave Chaudey, adjunct mayor of Paris, accused of having ordered the massacre of demonstrators on January 22; and Henri-Joseph

Chevriaux, commander of the *garde mobile* at City Hall which had freed members of the Government of National Defense from Blanqui and other radical National Guard commanders on October 31, 1870.[83]

If the need to apprehend the enemy within lent unified meaning to the Blanquists' conception of the struggle, so did their search for a savior from outside. It was in this way that Auguste Blanqui, invested by his followers with nearly miraculous powers, acquired mythological status for the Commune as the incarnation of revolutionary will. Blanqui had been arrested on the eve of the Commune (March 17, 1871) at the home of his friend Dr. Louis Lacambre in the Lot, where he had retreated in disgust over the defeatist sentiment pervading the Bordeaux Assembly. From the outset of hostilities, the Blanquists gave their concerted attention to the task of retrieving him. They believed that Blanqui was the missing element in the Commune's leadership, a figure who could play the role that had been Hébert's in 1793. Ernest Granger, considered by his companions the most resourceful agent for such a delicate mission, was dispatched to fetch Blanqui. Granger arrived at Lacambre's home only to learn that Blanqui had been transported to the nearby jail at Figeac. Without money to bribe the guards for Blanqui's release, Granger hastened back to Paris, where the needed funds were authorized by the Committee for General Safety. By the time he returned to the Lot, Blanqui had been removed to a distant isle in the Bay of Morlaix, and Granger was obliged to journey back to Paris with nothing to show for his adventure.[84]

Yet the efforts to retrieve Blanqui continued, so essential did his followers see him as a unifying figurehead for the Commune. In early April, Rigault and his Blanquist companions at the prefecture devised a strategy for negotiations with Adolphe Thiers, head of the provisional government at Versailles, to trade the archbishop of Paris for Blanqui. As a symbolic manifestation of the ideological conflict which the Blanquists believed was at issue, the exchange seemed an exquisite idea. The plan was to persuade Archbishop Darboy to draft a letter condemning the summary executions of Communard soldiers captured in the offensive of April 3. The Blanquists hoped this would prepare the way for direct negotiations about an exchange of hostages. The strategy unfolded in two initiatives. On the morning of April 8, Gaston Da Costa visited the archbishop at Mazas prison to deliver the request. Darboy was happy to cooperate. His letter was sent immediately by a clerical courier to Versailles.

Thiers showed no interest in the gesture, but Rigault continued his efforts undaunted. Benjamin Flotte, Blanqui's companion in the revolutionary campaigns of 1848, followed up Da Costa's overture with a more concerted effort. Between April 9 and 24, he visited Darboy in his cell frequently. At Flotte's urging, the archbishop wrote a second letter to Thiers on April 12, this time speaking more frankly about the possibility of an exchange. Flotte also asked the American ambassador Elihu Washburne and the papal nuncio Monsignor Flavio Chigi to intercede by making clear to Thiers the real danger faced by the archbishop if the exchange were not concluded. When there was no reply from Thiers by April 24, Rigault became impatient. His comrades tried to persuade him not to count too heavily upon the trade, but the repatriation of Blanqui had become an obsession for him. Finally he sent Flotte to Versailles to treat with Thiers directly. "We can't leave Blanqui to the Versailles government," Rigault ranted theatrically as Flotte was about to depart. "Offer him all the hostages if necessary."[85] At his audience with Thiers on May 12, Flotte dutifully offered to trade all the Commune's hostages for Blanqui. But Thiers was unmoved, and the negotiations came to a definitive close.[86]

As the sense of urgency about the Commune's precarious situation mounted, these two Blanquist concerns, the search for subversives within and the return of Blanqui from without, were conjoined in the application of the Law on Hostages, which had been enacted on April 5. The law provided that certain political prisoners, condemned by a special tribunal as traitors, would be designated hostages, liable to immediate execution, as security against the execution of Communard prisoners of war by the Versailles government. The measure was pressed upon the Communal Assembly in the demoralizing days of early April, when the defeat of the Commune's first offensive and the summary execution of Generals Duval and Flourens raised fears about the disposition of captured Communard soldiers. To some extent, it was a tactic designed to lessen the hysteria of Blanquists and other extremists in the Communal Assembly who demanded the immediate execution of Darboy and other priests recently arrested.

A second decree, enacted on April 22, prescribed the procedures by which grand juries would be selected from National

Guard candidates. It also assigned to the prosecutor of the Commune broad powers to arrest potential hostages and to convene
the juries.[87] Rigault's move from the Prefecture of Police to the
prosecutor's office on April 26, therefore, gave him the opportunity to put this judicial innovation into practice. Only one
group of prisoners was ever brought to trial under the provisions of the decree, a contingent of fourteen municipal policemen alleged to have fired on the insurrectionary crowd on March
18. They were brought to trial on May 19. The men were non-
entities, and no evidence was presented that they had fired on
the demonstrators or that such an act could, in any event, be
construed as treasonous. Rigault berated them all the same with
his Manichaean conception of political allegiance. "Let's be frank,"
he cajoled one group of the accused.

We do not force anyone to share our viewpoint. Were you to deny that
you are Bonapartists, we would perhaps not have the power to force
you to admit that. What we do want is that you express a viewpoint. We
Republicans, if we were not in our place but in yours, would say to you:
"You are the strongest, strike us down"; but that would not prevent us
from hating you and despising you.[88]

Twelve of the fourteen were formally declared hostages by the
jury. At the conclusion of the proceedings, a crucifix which had
hung unnoticed above the tribunal caught the prosecutor's attention and was ordered removed before the court convened the
following day, when several priests were slated for prosecution.
Spared that formality by the entry of troops of Versailles into
Paris, nearly a hundred de facto hostages were nonetheless sent
to their execution in the desperation of the last days of fighting.[89]

These "last days" of the Commune—Bloody Week (May 22-
28) in the annals of the revolutionary tradition—provided the
unifying image through which the struggle would be remembered by the Blanquists during the Third Republic. If the Commune had not been the fulfillment of their vision of 1793, it had
been at least a repetition of its heroic striving and its tragic
defeat. As such, they believed, it would reinforce the call to
revolutionary courage for future generations as an example of
the resilience of the atheist cause.[90] But although the memory of
these last days by surviving Blanquist militants blurred into a
coherent whole of high moral purpose dauntlessly sustained in
the face of certain defeat, the reality of their participation in the

events of Bloody Week presents a mixed picture of confusion and vengeance.

There was, of course, a certain grandeur in the defense mounted by the Parisians. The tenacity with which they manned the barricades, the determination with which they resisted the relentless advance of the overwhelmingly superior forces of Versailles, seemed to obliterate the indecision, the inertia, and the empty posturing of their leaders over the preceding two months. The Commune found its nobility when all was lost. Yet the epic quality of its struggle to stay destruction was marred by the atrocities to which many Communards gave themselves during the last days of fighting. The incidents were many and varied, and Blanquist militants figured at least marginally in nearly all of them. Some of the executions were carefully planned, as Blanquist authorities took their vengeance upon specific enemies. Others were more haphazard episodes, characterized by official acquiescence to popular demands for the blood of real or imagined enemies. Most poignant were the formal executions of the hostages, who died for their identification with the Blanquists' stereotypes of ideological adversaries.[91]

In seeking to apologize for the atrocities of the last days, Communard writers as well as some sympathetic historians draw a portrait of vigilante justice in a city in disarray.[92] The Communal Assembly held its last, inconclusive session on May 22, as the Versailles troops advanced rapidly toward the center of the city. The remnant of the Committee of Public Safety, which moved its headquarters to the town hall (*mairie*) of the eleventh arrondissement in eastern Paris, had limited communications and exercised uncertain control. Central political authority had for all practical purposes disappeared. The streets were in the hands of frenzied mobs, determined to ferret out and punish those subversives in their midst whom they believed had betrayed them. In such circumstances, these commentators contend, the Commune's leaders could but mitigate the worst excesses of the mob. Gaston Da Costa, for example, praises the leaders of the last days as courageous men caught up in impossible circumstances. He condones the executions they ordered as unavoidable measures, requirements of the last, desperate acts of the war. If the crowd engaged in willful violence, he continues, it did so as a reaction to the arbitrary massacres of captured Communards by the invading Versailles soldiers. Ultimately, Da Costa claims, the

Versailles government was responsible for the atrocities committed by both sides. Its policies could only have elicited an atavistic response from the Parisian crowd, driven to despair by what it had suffered for a lost cause.[93]

But Da Costa's focus on the anarchy of the Parisian crowd and the cruelty of the Versailles army does not exonerate the Blanquists (or, for that matter, other Jacobin leaders with strong ideological commitments) of personal and collective responsibility for their acts. Others may have actually performed the acts of violence and harassed those in positions of responsibility to sanction them, but Blanquist ideologists had carefully and calculatingly prepared the situation. In publicly libeling the clergy, they had lent authority to rumors of clerical treachery and credence to the sensational stories of clerical sadism. In designating hostages, they had formally identified the ideological victims. In sum, they had primed the masses for ideological warfare. The last battles of the Blanquists were against the symbols of the enemy rather than the enemy itself.

In these battles they proclaimed the value of ritual iconoclasm. As a preface to their campaign of arson during Bloody Week, the Blanquists played a crucial role in the demolition of the Vendôme column, the famed monument to Napoleonic glory. For two months, workmen chipped away at crucial points of its superstructure so it would come tumbling down in a resounding clutter at an appointed hour. Protot and his companions held *agape* luncheons daily in a restaurant across the way, from which they could witness the project's progression. The actual toppling of the column on May 16 was carried out as a triumphant festival, even though everyone knew that the days of the Commune were numbered.[94] The chapel of Louis XVI, the chapel of General Bréa (commander of the repression of "June days" in 1848), and Thiers's townhouse had been razed during the previous week with only slightly less ceremony.[95] The destruction of the townhouses and palaces of central Paris followed. As the Versailles troops approached the Seine, General Eudes ordered the firing of a number of public buildings, among them the Tuileries Palace, the Palace of the Legion of Honor, and the City Hall. Ferré ordered the burning of the Palace of Justice.[96] In all, more than two hundred houses, ten palaces, and two theaters went up in flames.[97] Da Costa and other Blanquists justify these acts as legitimate measures of defense to cover the retreat of the last remnants of the Commune's forces.[98] But many of the buildings

8. The toppling of the Vendôme column, May 16, 1871, an example of ritual iconoclasm by the Communards. Phot. Bibl. Nat.

destroyed had no military value. For some Blanquists, it is clear, the collapse of the Commune required a fiery retribution. Despite the adverse publicity he received in later years for his part in the arson, Eudes had no regrets. "The people instinctively admire such acts," he confided to Edouard Vaillant in a letter of 1874.[99]

As Versailles soldiers penetrated the defenses of the central districts of Paris on May 22, the fate of the hostages became an immediate issue. The previous evening, at the prefecture, Rigault, Ferré, and about fifteen of their associates held their last conference, at which they decided to transfer the hostages from Mazas prison to that of La Grande Roquette, situated not far from the mairie of the eleventh arrondissement from which the remaining officials of the Commune would send their last directives.[100] There, in the so-called hearth of revolutionary Paris, within the Commune's last defense perimeter, a number of Blanquist militants were brought together to pursue to its conclusion the logic of the war against subversion they had begun. Blanquists were involved in all the major incidents of execution of hostages and political prisoners during Bloody Week.[101]

Rigault, who had orchestrated the war on ideological subversives, had time for but one act of vengeance before he himself was struck down. Sensing that his days were numbered, he decided to give himself to his remaining obsessions. These had come to focus upon Gustave Chaudey, who personified his fears and hatreds of Girondin treachery. Chaudey, the Blanquists believed, was responsible for the massacre of National Guardsmen in the last days of the siege. By the final days of the Commune, the echoes of that affair reverberated loudly in Rigault's mind. During the reign of the Commune, Sapia's widow had visited Rigault periodically and had pressed him for Chaudey's execution. But the charges against the former municipal official had never been substantiated, and moderate Communards were alarmed when Rigault had him arrested. Chaudey appeared to many Communards a committed republican, a man of courage and integrity who had accepted heavy responsibilities during the siege and given clear evidence of loyalty to the Commune. But for Rigault, the case was closed. He was determined to supervise the execution personally. On the morning of May 23, in the uniform of a colonel of the National Guard, he paid a visit to Sainte-Pélagie prison, ordered Chaudey removed from his cell to the yard, and personally commanded the firing squad that killed him. Chaudey's only satisfaction was to have accepted his fate bravely. Rigault then had some policemen, selected from the rolls of hostages detained there, dispatched for good measure.[102] But this was almost a distraction for him. The execution of Chaudey had given him the sense that his task was completed.

With Chaudey died Rigault's sense of purpose. He did not return to the prefecture that evening, and the next day he wandered aimlessly among the barricades of the Latin Quarter, which were about to fall to Versailles. Maxime Vuillaume, Jacobin journalist and astute chronicler of the Commune, recounts his last encounter with Rigault at a café on the Place de la Sorbonne about noon that day. Rigault, more pensive than usual, laconically described the execution, as if that act had provided the key to the riddle he had been trying to unlock all his life.[103] From there he departed for the barricades at the Pantheon. Still resplendent in dress uniform, he fell an easy target to Versailles soldiers advancing through the Rue Gay-Lussac about three hours later.[104]

Théophile Ferré had no qualms about continuing Rigault's work. He had his own vendetta against Georges Veysset, an admitted spy for Versailles, whom he put to death on the Pont Neuf on May 24 during the preparations to evacuate the prefecture.[105] In the following days, he willingly signed the death warrants for hostages. The executions themselves, however, were carried out by faithful Blanquist henchmen, officers of lesser rank such as Emile Gois, Gustave Genton, and Emile Fortin— pleased to gain some small victory in a struggle which they feared they would otherwise lose completely.

Prompted by mob fury, sanctioned by Ferré's pen, and carried out by Blanquist zeal, the executions of the fifty-eight hostages detained at La Grande Roquette were parceled into three groups between May 24 and 26. The massacre was triggered by the lynching of Charles de Beaufort, an officer attached to the headquarters staff of the delegate for war. Beaufort was denounced by soldiers of the 66th Battalion who, for personal spite rather than substantive causes, blamed him for heavy losses they had suffered in a recent battle on the front lines. Spotted by these Guardsmen on the morning of May 24 near the mairie of the eleventh arrondissement, Beaufort was hauled before Ferré by the Guardsmen, spurred by a furious mob. Ferré, intimidated by the mob, hastily convened a court-martial with his Blanquist confederates Gois, Genton, and Fortin as judges. Although they had no evidence against him, these judges tried to appease the

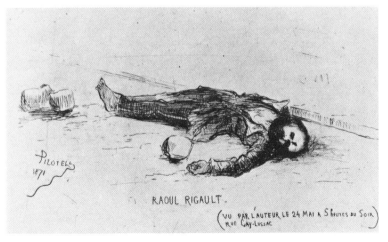

9. The death of Raoul Rigault, May 24, 1871. Sketch by Georges Pilotell. Phot. Bibl. Nat.

10. Théophile Ferré as prefect of police signs the execution warrant for the hostages, May 24, 1871. Phot. Bibl. Nat.

crowd by ordering Beaufort stripped of his rank and sent to the barricades as a common soldier. But releasing him to the incensed crowd waiting outside was tantamount to condemning him to death, and he was immediately devoured by them.[106]

The lynching, far from appeasing the crowd, whetted its appetite for blood. A second delegation, emerging anonymously from the crowd, visited Ferré that afternoon to demand death for the hostages. Without hesitation, Ferré signed an order for the execution of six of them, leaving the choice of actual victims to the discretion of his subordinates, Fortin and Genton, whom he sent to La Grande Roquette to carry out his order. They, in turn, foisted the decision upon Jean-Baptiste Francois, governor of the prison, who sensed that the most prestigious hostages would have to be the first to die. François chose Louis-Bertrand Bonjean, a former president of the Supreme Court of Appeal, and five priests. When pressed by Fortin to include Archbishop Darboy on the list, Francois demurred and demanded a written order from Ferré. The delegate was glad to oblige. "And especially the archbishop," he scrawled on the bottom of his original execution order when it was returned by Fortin. The six hostages died in the prison courtyard before a firing squad supervised by Blanquist militants. Benjamin Sicard, an officer on the staff of the prefecture, commanded the squad; Fortin and Genton acted as witnesses.[107]

The execution of these hostages primed the most vengeful Blanquists to dispense with even the formality of Ferré's approval. On the morning of May 26, Antoine Clavier, Alexandre Girault, and François Liberton, Blanquist police agents assigned to the twelfth arrondissement, with unidentified comrades, called at La Grande Roquette and at gunpoint forced François to surrender Jean-Baptiste Jecker, a banker reputed to have acquired a vast fortune through financial swindles in Mexico. In a brief interrogation near the prison, his accusers reproached Jecker for his wealth but nonetheless tried to extort some of it

11. The execution of Archbishop Darboy and five other hostages of the Commune at the prison La Grande Roquette, May 24, 1871. Phot. Bibl. Nat.

from him. When that failed, they marched him to a ditch in a neighboring park and put a bullet through his head.[108]

That afternoon, Emile Gois, General Eudes's aide-de-camp, accompanied by his personal execution squad and volunteers from Eudes's elite guards, Les Enfants Perdus, went to the prison to demand the remaining hostages. When François timidly asked for release orders, Gois and his men brandished their weapons. The cells were emptied forthwith. The contingent of thirty-six policemen, ten clergymen, and four accused police spies was subjected to the further ordeal of a march through the streets of Belleville, jeered and jostled by the furious crowd. Herded into an alley off the Rue Haxo, on a hill above the Père-Lachaise cemetery, the hostages were halted. It may have been the narrowing circle of territory belonging to the Communards which prompted Gois to choose this spot. But it was also ideologically fitting that these forlorn hostages should have been brought back to the hearth of the Père-Lachaise quarter, the Blanquists' most sacred ground. Gois asked Eudes for orders concerning the disposition of the hostages, but the Blanquist general refused to assume that responsibility, as he had refused to authorize their transfer from the prison a few hours before. A few remaining members of the Communal Assembly who were present pleaded for the lives of the hostages. But the time for such a decision had passed. Gois's execution squad could not be restrained. The hostages were mowed down indiscriminately in irregular volleys. Three hundred fifteen more de facto hostages, incarcerated in other Parisian prisons, were spared the same fate by the arrival of Versailles troops.[109]

The last battle of the civil war continued through the following night (May 27-28) amid the tombstones of the Père-Lachaise cemetery. In the morning, when the bodies of the massacred hostages were discovered by Versailles troops, 147 National Guardsmen, chosen at random in the quarter, were marched to a wall on the southeast corner of the cemetery and executed in retaliation. Amid the 25,000 executions which it is estimated the Versailles army carried out in its vast and terrifying reprisals, the massacre of the National Guardsmen at "the wall," the final event to issue from the ideological conflict, became for the Left in later years the most sacred legend of the last days of the Commune.[110]

From the atheist crusade against religious superstition to the political crusade against the enemy within, the Blanquist war

12. Ernest Pichio's sketch of the massacre of the *fédérés* at the wall of the Père-Lachaise cemetery, May 27-28, 1871. It promoted the legend of the "last days" of the Commune. Phot. Bibl. Nat.

against subversion had in the end been reduced to the shooting of hapless priests and policemen who had by chance fallen into their net. Their execution, as visible symbols of the enemies of the Blanquists' youth, was a pathetic diminishing of the "philosophical revolution" to which they had originally dedicated themselves. In the face of defeat, these militants succumbed to the emotional need for an apocalyptic last judgment which would immortalize their brief reign.

Despite the later efforts of the Blanquists to associate the courage of their dead with the heroism displayed by the Hébertists in the face of the guillotine, most Blanquists in fact chose exile rather than martyrdom. Among the best-known militants, Rigault alone decided to fall with the Commune in its last days. Gaston Da Costa, Genton, and Ferré were among the few cap-

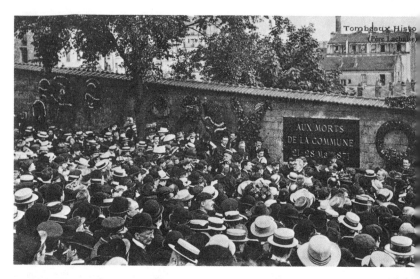

13. The wall of the *fédérés* as a sacred space for the Left in the late nineteenth century. Phot. Bibl. Nat.

tured leaders of the Commune actually condemned to die by the special courts-martial convened to try their cases.[111]

For his role in the execution of the hostages, Ferré expressed no regrets at his trial. To the judges who sentenced him, he uttered one parting cry of defiance: "Fortune is capricious. To posterity I confide the care of my memory and of my vengeance."[112] His comrades cherished the memory of this moment and of Ferré's courage during the deathwatch. Gaston Da Costa tells how the jailers tried to break Ferré's resolve by placing his crazed brother in his cell on the eve of execution. But Ferré accepted the ordeal stoically, and went to the stake on the plain of Satory calmly smoking a cigar.[113] Genton died with similar courage a few months later.[114] The young Da Costa's jailers claim that he lost his nerve during his incarceration under sentence of death.[115] That may explain his obsession with the concept of courage betrayed by his book on the Commune. His sentence was commuted and he was deported, with Henri Place and some lesser-known Blanquist militants, to New Caledonia. There they carried on a haphazard correspondence with their more fortunate comrades, lamenting the absence of Blanqui's comradeship under trying prison conditions.[116] Blanqui himself was held incommunicado at the prison at Clairvaux until 1879.

But the majority of the Blanquists regrouped in London to ponder how the revolutionary phoenix could rise from its ashes once more.[117]

The Blanquists' role in the Commune was less coherent than the myth of that experience which they were to bequeath to the world. In clinging to the notion of the moral unity of the Commune, they were unable to reconcile the differences between what the Commune was and what they believed it ought to have been. Their post-Commune reflections, therefore, coincided more closely with their pre-Commune hopes than with the actual events of March to May 1871. From this point, the delicate balance they had tried to maintain between creativity and repetition in their conception of revolution was for all practical purposes tipped in favor of the latter. With the advent of the Third Republic, the events of the Commune, together with Blanquist hopes for its return, were fast receding into the past, as new problems emerged and a new socialist ideology was offered to deal with them. At a time when the Left had become more willing to believe in the Blanquists as the bearers of the revolutionary tradition, the Blanquists themselves were finding it more difficult to make practical sense of their conception of the revolutionary struggle. This became evident in the encounter of the Blanquist exiles with Marx and the Marxists, the apostles of the new socialism, during the 1870s.

14. The execution of Théophile Ferré on the plain of Satory. Phot. Bibl. Nat.

CHAPTER V

Exile and Disarray: The Marxist Alternative

The Paris Commune provided the testing ground for the Blanquist myth of the revolutionary tradition; the decade of exile in England which followed furnished a setting for its attrition. The story of the Blanquists in exile during the 1870s is one of the disintegration of their conception of revolution. With a loss of vision came a loss of purpose. By the time they were permitted to return in the amnesty of 1880, they sensed that they were faced with a choice between old Hébertist traditions and new socialist directions. Proud of their role in the Commune, they loudly proclaimed their loyalty to the old way; but the sense of the myth, derived from the radical atheist crusade of the 1860s, was for the most part forgotten, and with it the guiding insight into the meaning of revolutionary action it had offered. The widening appeal of the new socialism, closely associated with Marxist thought, was a force in left-wing politics with which they were obliged to reckon, and with which they anxiously and unsuccessfully tried to reconcile their Hébertist convictions.

To some extent, the loss of purpose was rooted in the disorienting experience of exile. Denied any communication with Blanqui, saddened by the incarceration or execution of a number of their most energetic comrades, those Blanquists who escaped the sweep through Paris by the Versailles troops during Bloody Week faced life in a foreign land with some dismay. The majority reassembled in London, where they formed a mutual aid society to assist Communard refugees.[1] Besides this group they founded another with a more obvious political orientation, the Revolutionary Commune (La Commune Révolutionnaire). To this society a number of important Communards rallied, among them Edouard Vaillant, Frédéric Cournet, and Gabriel Ranvier, thereby lending prestige to the Blanquist claim to speak for the revolutionary movement in exile.[2] But this group was soon plagued with factionalism and embarrassed by the widely publicized charges that, as the Commune's end had drawn near, the Blanquists had given themselves not only to arson and unjustified executions, but to thievery as well.

The extent of their looting was revealed in the Caria Affair in London in August 1872. In a newspaper edited by Blanquist dissident Pierre Vésinier, Octave Caria, one of Eudes's former staff officers, accused the general and his subordinates Emile Gois and Albert Goullé of having absconded with medals, jewels, and even the linens which had adorned the Palace of the Legion of Honor. The members of the Revolutionary Commune refused to give the charges a hearing, but they were obviously chagrined a few months later when the linens were identified in a London pawn shop.[3] Caria's accusations nonetheless drove General Eudes (the acknowledged leader of the group in exile) to seek the obscurity of a teaching post at a private academy in Edinburgh—a course of action urged by his friend Alfred Breuillé, who argued that in such a setting he could establish a reputation as a "perfect gentleman" and so weather the tide of criticism. Eudes subsequently taught French at the naval academy at Portsmouth. He good-naturedly appreciated the irony of a situation in which he, one of France's most notorious revolutionaries, was preparing the children of the English aristocracy to defend a monarchy.[4]

The exile also revealed the disenchantment of Blanquist intellectuals with the political course of the Commune. The excesses of Blanquist activism had driven Gustave Tridon from the fold even before the fall of the Commune. Disheartened by policies he believed made a travesty of his vision of the Hébertist Commune of 1793, Tridon broke with his Blanquist comrades in the Communal Assembly by refusing to vote for the creation of a Committee of Public Safety. He abstained from the activities of Bloody Week and spent his last agonizing struggle with terminal illness alone in Brussels, where he succumbed on August 29, 1871.[5] His defection was followed by that of his chief apostle, Albert Regnard, who, while residing in London, remained aloof from the Blanquist society. Regnard continued to praise the Hébertists in his writings; as an author, the exile was one of his most productive periods. He remained deeply devoted to the memory of Tridon. With Louis Watteau, he was responsible for the publication of Tridon's manuscripts in the 1880s and hence for the renewed interest in Tridon's thought.[6] But he was openly critical of Blanqui for being insufficiently appreciative of the efficacy of intellectual endeavor in forwarding the revolutionary cause.[7] If Regnard remained true to the sources of Blanquist ideology, he did so only by divorcing himself totally from his former comrades.

With the deportation of Henri Place, the alienation of Regnard, and the death of Tridon, the Blanquists in exile lost the principal theoreticians of the youth movement from which their group had sprung. More disorienting still was their encounter with Karl Marx, from which so much had initially been expected. Three days after the fall of the Commune, Marx had delivered a public address in behalf of the Workingmen's International entitled "The Civil War in France," in which he denounced the government of Adolphe Thiers for its illegal arrogation of political sovereignty, its cunning provocation of the civil war, and its unstated complicity in Bismarck's grand design for Europe.[8] The praise he lavished upon the Communards, together with the cordiality with which he received them as refugees in London, led the Blanquists to believe they could benefit from an association with this renowned theoretician of the new socialism.[9] Marx's statement likewise prompted the Blanquists to consider the merits of the International in a new light. During the Second Empire, they had repeatedly attacked the French section of the International as a timid, compromising group, fearful of facing the realities of political power.[10] Marx's reaffirmation of the importance of political action in his discussion of the Commune gave the Blanquists new hope that the International could serve their ends. They were wooed as well by Marx's apology for the Commune's incendiarism and execution of hostages as necessary defensive measures for a nation at war. The work of the Commune, the Blanquists reasoned, could be continued, indeed, extended onto a European plane; and, despite the defeat of the Commune, they were flattered to believe in the role Marx ascribed to them.[11]

The alliance of Blanquists and Marxists in London in the 1870s was destined to be short-lived. It foundered quickly in controversies over tactics within the General Council of the International—to which a number of Blanquist exiles (Vaillant, Cournet, Ranvier, and Edouard Marguerittes) were elected almost immediately upon their arrival in London.[12] These quarrels reflected an underlying incompatibility of viewpoints which the Blanquists, in the flush of much-needed revolutionary solidarity, failed to consider until their break with the International was an accomplished fact. Yet the differences were implicit from the outset in Marx's address, if it is considered as anything more than a document on political strategy. Whereas the Blanquists believed the Commune to be a recreation of the revolutionary community of 1793, Marx extolled the events of 1871 as a totally new experience based upon new realities. Whereas the Blanquists conceived of themselves as a vanguard of professional revolutionaries reenacting a tradition dating from the Hébertists, Marx spoke of the Commune as a proletarian revolution which prefigured a wider social transformation. The Blanquists had long insisted upon the need for the professional revolutionary to identify vicariously with the life situations of the common man; Marx's interpretation of the Commune in effect obviated a role for an elite of professional revolutionaries whatever its sympathies.[13]

To have accepted this interpretation of the Commune would have obliged the Blanquists to alter their conception of the revolutionary tradition beyond recognition. For Marx characterized the civil war in France as the political manifestation of class struggle, the issue of the economic changes wrought by the coming of industrial capitalism. In the actions taken by the Thiers government against Paris before and during hostilities, the direct relationship between state power and class interest was exposed with dramatic clarity. For the Blanquists, social conflict was real, but it was better expressed in terms of the contrasting ideas of community represented by the conflict. The rising of the people was inspired by a nationalist ideal, with atheism as its unspoken source. The immediate task, the Blanquists believed, was the eradication of an alien philosophy in both its political and religious manifestations, not the uprooting of class society or the withering away of the state.

Marx declared the Commune to be "emphatically international" in its orientation toward the social question. But the Blanquists, while sympathetic toward oppressed people everywhere, envisioned their revolution as an autonomous uprising, turning on a nativist conception of community. For Marx, the coming of the classless society announced by the Commune remained an event in the offing. For the Blanquists, the Commune represented the ideal society already formed in microcosm. Its advent had been made possible not by promoting class distinctions, but by overcoming them in the alliance of workers and intellectuals, the alliance which had fostered all the urban insurrections of the nineteenth century. On the issue of the Commune at least, Blanquist nationalism, which envisioned the shared commitment of a like-minded community striving for liberation, was fundamentally at odds with Marxist socialism, which argued that social antagonisms deeper than moral intentions were preparing the way for the new social order. While Blanquists and Marxists might share common concerns, ultimately there could be no converging of their perspectives on the good society.[14]

These differences became evident soon enough in the General Council of the Workingmen's International. The Blanquists had taken seriously Marx's assertion that the Commune was an expression of the International's wider commitment to political revolution, and they counted on Marx to support their plans to use the organization to foment political subversion in France. For tactical reasons, Marx tolerated the Blanquist position. It provided him with additional leverage in his quarrel with the anarchist faction, based in Geneva under Bakunin and James Guillaume, which for several years had threatened to depoliticize the entire organization. Blanquist support at the London conference of 1871 enabled Marx to win passage of a resolution committing the International to concerted political action, a measure which prompted the anarchists to quit the organization.[15] But the impetuous presence of the Blanquists made Marx wary. Having weathered the anarchist challenge, he had no interest in seeing the Blanquists turn the International to serve their own ends, especially as their call for immediate action in France ran counter to his French strategy. Although the Commune had rekindled much of his former faith in insurrectionary action, its defeat convinced him that future revolutionary movements in France would have to await patiently the maturing of economic processes. At the Hague conference a year thereafter (1872), he successfully conspired to transfer the General Council to New York City, where, far removed from the concerns of the European labor movement, it had little chance of survival.[16]

The Blanquists, bitter about having been outmaneuvered by Marx, publicly took exception to his plans for the International. In a pamphlet entitled *Internationale et révolution*, published in the wake of the Hague conference (September 15, 1872), the Blanquist members of the General Council expressed their deep regret that Marx had denied the International the opportunity to become a "powerful lever of revolution." They offered as well the admonition that there really was no alternative to the concerted use of political force, a "dictatorship of the proletariat," as a means of dealing with the social question. Resigning from the International, the Blanquist contingent denounced the organization for its abstract conception of internationalism and reaffirmed its commitment to the French revolutionary tradition.[17] What they had wanted, the Blanquists now realized, was less world revolution than the recognition that theirs had been the primal revolutionary experience for the world. Thus they retreated into their own circle, the Revolutionary Commune, a society of some forty-four refugees, where, enduring the mockery of their erstwhile Marxist comrades, they pondered once more the meaning of the Hébertist vision as they awaited the day when they could reenter France.[18]

Out of this process of self-evaluation came two pamphlets, the publication of which punctuated the remaining years of the Blanquists' exile. In 1874 they published a manifesto, *Aux Communeux*, in which they rededicated themselves to the ideals in behalf of which the campaigns of March to May 1871 had been waged: atheism, communism, and revolution.[19] These were the same ideals that the original Blanquist group had advanced in the first issue of *Candide* in 1864. Though the Commune of 1871 had displaced that of 1793 as the touchstone of revolutionary experience for the Blanquists, they likewise expressed their deepening sense of the interrelationship of past revolutionary precedents. The Commune in their collective memory took on the character of an epiphany in which images of revolutions past and future congealed. In passionate terms, the Blanquists called upon the Communards to guard the memory of the atrocities committed by the Versailles troops during the Commune's last days: the executions at Satory, the burial of the wounded with the dead, the savage repression of the population of Paris, and the transportation of Communards to New Caledonia. Forthrightly the Blanquists reiterated their acceptance of responsibility for the incendiarism and execution of hostages during Bloody Week. They noted that a regime can be destroyed only when its monuments and symbols, as well as its institutions, are attacked. But in defending iconoclasm, they admitted the significance of icon itself, just as their plea for the remembrance of the Commune was implicitly a call for its ritual commemoration. The document *Aux Communeux* thus reveals the Blanquists' growing consciousness of the role of myth and symbol in ideological commitment, a consciousness they had been unable to appreciate fully before the testing of their conceptions in the ordeal of the civil war.

A second pamphlet, *Les syndicaux et leur congrès*, written in 1876, expressed the Blanquists' concern that the growth of the trade union movement in France, coupled with the banishment of French revolutionary leaders, might deflect the working class from revolution as a political cause.[20] The French Section of the International, which the Blanquists held accountable for this dangerous trend, now took on the trappings of the enemy within to be consigned to the infamous company of Girondin groups which had previously betrayed the revolutionary cause. The cast of characters had changed for the Blanquists in exile, but the paradigm of conflict remained intact. Drawing a distinction between Communards (*Communeux*) and syndicalists (*syndicaux*), the Blanquists denounced trade unionism as a capitulation to the requirements and procedures of the "legal world," a world which they refused to believe had widened with the coming of the Third Republic. Instead, they expressed their scorn for the "parliamentary republic" and judged it unworthy of the revolutionary tradition with which republicanism had always been associated. Characteristically, they noted that the error of these labor leaders lay not simply in their moderate, reformist policies, but "in their temperament and character." Like their Girondin predecessors, the syndicalists' reformism was a masquerade for their acceptance of the status quo.

These attempts to define a theory of revolution only earned Marx's private scorn and Engels' public ridicule for the Blanquists. In an article of 1874, specifically written to discredit the Blanquists and appearing subsequently in a widely circulated preface to the *Civil War in France*, Engels dismissed them as anachronisms, trapped by their determination to relive a past which had lost its relevance for present problems.[21] Their insistence upon atheism, he argued, was passé, and their commitment to the Commune as a sacred event forced them to live in morbid self-deception. Their myth of the Commune as the new Jerusalem of the revolutionary cause displayed only ignorance of the workings of the long-range processes of history. Hence their account of the atrocities committed by the Versailles government was a futile effort to inspire a new insurrection, for spontaneous willfulness was no match for historical necessity in a country as yet unprepared to renew the struggle. Engels further insinuated that the relation of the Blanquists to Blanqui was more vicarious than real and pointed out how few of the present entourage had ever been in personal contact with the master. If the "so-called Blanquists" claimed to act in accordance with Blanqui's esprit, Engels concluded, they nonetheless failed to appreciate the nondoctrinaire, creative character of his revolutionary activism.

Despite this drawing of the lines between Blanquists and Marxists both politically and ideologically in the mid-1870s, Marxist terminology abounded in the Blanquist documents of exile. Phrases borrowed from the Marxist lexicon peppered texts which otherwise reaffirmed the original Blanquist vision. These neologisms Engels correctly ascribed to Edouard Vaillant, a newcomer to the Blanquist ranks, whose sympathy for the new socialism he noted with condescending amusement. In a letter written to his friend Friedrich Sorge in November 1872, Engels commented upon Vaillant's repeated use of Marxist phrases as if they were inventions of his own.[22] Though Vailliant may have neglected to acknowledge the Marxist sources of his ideas, he did grasp Marx's fundamental insights to a degree which escaped most professed French Marxists; and he sought to blend them with Blanquist concepts in a new ideological synthesis which might better serve the revolutionary cause in France.[23] From the vantage point of the Blanquist veterans of the campaigns of the 1860s, however, Vaillant's theories, far from providing a new synthesis, created only confusion. In this sense, his intrusion into the Blanquist circle was the most disorienting experience of all.

The confusion Vaillant promoted was derived not only from his fascination with the new socialism, but also from his commitment to a new politics. During the years of exile, he encouraged his comrades to consider a broader array of political tactics in preparation for their return to France. In a pamphlet drafted on the morrow of the amnesty of the Communards, *Le suffrage universel et les élections municipales* (1880), he pointed out the advantages they could gain by moving out of Paris into the middle-sized cities of France for a concerted effort of propaganda, including participation in electoral campaigns.[24] This proposal was greeted with a certain skepticism during the exile by some of Vaillant's comrades. Emile Eudes, for example, questioned whether such a reorientation was compatible with the Paris-based fraternal unity which had been such an essential part of their earlier revolutionary endeavor.[25] Blanqui himself, in his brief dealings with Vaillant on the staff of *Ni Dieu, ni maître* in 1880, found the latter's pronouncements pompous and ordered his editorial secretary, Breuillé, to scrutinize the articles carefully before publishing them.[26] Moreover, Blanqui believed Vaillant's decision to base himself in Vierzon rather than Paris after the amnesty was an unorthodox and unnecessary departure from the Blanquists' traditional conviction that Paris could be the only genuine center of revolutionary action. Vaillant was especially solicitous of Blanqui and did what he could to patch up the disagreement between them.[27] Yet the question of the relationship of Vaillant's new methods and the Blanquists' hallowed traditions remained unresolved at Blanqui's death in 1881.

It should be noted that Vaillant (1840-1915) came to Blanquism by a circuitous route and with a somewhat different intellectual formation from that of his newfound comrades.[28] Although he studied at the Sorbonne and other schools at Paris in the early 1860s, receiving doctorates in science and medicine, he participated only marginally in the political causes in which Blanquist youth tested their ideological conceptions. In 1866 he departed for Germany, not to return except for brief visits before the advent of the Franco-Prussian War. At a succession of universities there (Heidelberg, Tübingen, and Vienna), he delved into German social philosophy and was especially influenced by the materialist Ludwig Feuerbach. He thus became an atheist by intellectual conviction, but his atheism was never the inspiring spur to revolutionary combat that it was for his Blanquist contemporaries in France.

Despite periodic sojourns in France, Vaillant was only superficially acquainted with the Blanquists during the Second Empire, and during the siege and the Commune he steered a course largely independent of them. In contrast with the Blanquists, he was a leading organizer of the French Section of the International and of the Central Committee of the Twenty Arrondissements during the siege, and he played a major political role in the Commune as a member of the Executive Commission and as Delegate for Public Instruction. Only in the aftermath of the Commune did he formally affiliate with a Blanquist organization. In the 1890s, when the schism of the Blanquist movement was an accomplished fact and the hatred of the old guard for Marxism was open, Vaillant's absence from the Blanquist struggle against the empire would be held against him. But during the 1870s and the early 1880s, he was easily accepted by members of the Blanquist party, indeed, he was appreciated by them. Vaillant brought to the group his distinguished record of service to the Commune, the prestige of his professional accomplishments, and his able journalistic talent. He clearly played a major role in their experimentation with new forms of publicity in the 1880s; and he was the first Blanquist to hold public office, initially as a municipal councillor at Paris and subsequently as a member of the Chamber of Deputies. In his move toward the new socialism, he lent the Blanquist cause the prestige of that identification at a time when the mystique of the revolutionary tradition was beginning to wane.[29]

At the same time, it is important not to exaggerate Vaillant's role as a social theorist, or his influence on his Blanquist comrades in this respect. He was destined to become a major personality in the Socialist party; yet it is worth noting that he never produced a book-length study concerning either socialist theory or practice. Nor did his countless newspaper articles on contemporary politics add up to a synthesis of the Blanquist and Marxist viewpoints considered on a theoretical plane. Drawn during the Commune to the Blanquists for their energy, he was attracted in exile to Marx for his depth of thought. The documents of exile reflect Vaillant's first attempt to reconcile his respect for the French revolutionary tradition with his Marxist sympathies. After the amnesty, his attention turned increasingly to practical considerations, interests which became compelling from the time he entered public office in 1884. While his socialism became more explicit, his politics became less doctrinaire. His primary allegiance, as it developed out of his political practice, was to an eclectic socialism, closer in approach to that advocated by the revisionist Marxist Eduard Bernstein than to that advocated by Marx himself. For all his useful endeavor in behalf of the socialist cause, Vaillant never achieved a unified theoretical viewpoint. He may have acquainted his Blanquist comrades with some Marxist phrases and concepts, but he failed to provide them with a comprehensive grasp of Marxist theory; and he only alienated some by his growing indifference to the Hébertist values which most Blanquists were increasingly prompted to reverence.[30]

The Blanquists had not only to contend with Marx, or with Vaillant's interpretation of him. They had to come to terms as well with the Marxist movement in France, which emerged during their absence in the renaissance of social theorizing which took place in left-wing circles in the early years of the Third Republic. Socialism, the watchword of the intellectual avantgarde, rapidly gained broad currency. By the 1880s, many leftwing politicians sensed that "socialist" was an attractive label for electoral campaigning, as it seemed to place them upon the advancing tide of social change.[31] The introduction of Marxism into France in the early decades of the Third Republic must be understood in this context. If socialism conveyed the mystique of new beginnings, Marxism cloaked it with the mantle of scientific respectability.

French Marxism, identified closely with the Workers party (Parti Ouvrier) of Jules Guesde (1845-1922), bore the imprint of the special needs of the Left in the early Third Republic. Guesdism was initially a youth movement which emerged out of the student gatherings at the Café Soufflet in the Latin Quarter in the mid-1870s. Guesde, who dominated the party, was, like Blanqui, an intense, slightly bizarre figure.[32] Ungainly in bearing and emaciated in appearance, he conveyed an air of physical weakness; yet he was by nature an orator of great power and by experience an organizer of considerable skill. While the typical Blanquist militant had migrated from the provinces to Paris in his prime, Guesde had journeyed in the other direction. A Parisian by birth and education, he wrote for a number of republican newspapers in the Midi during the last years of the empire. He played a secret role in the organizational activities of the International in that region, as well as a public one in rallying the citizens of Montpellier to the new republic following the revolution of September 4 at Paris. Guesde could easily have won political office in Montpellier, but he preferred to turn his mordant pen against the faults of the provisional government. During the spring of 1871, he cast his wholehearted support to the Paris Commune, albeit from afar. For his articles criticizing the Versailles government he was convicted and sentenced to five years' imprisonment. But he had already escaped to Geneva, where he mixed with the Proudhonist refugees of the Commune and even played a part in the Bakuninist opposition to Marx's efforts to dominate the International.

Guesde's opinions in the last years of the empire were those of the typical radical republican: democratic, anticlerical, and reformist. His work among the exiles at Geneva during the early 1870s acquainted him with anarchist teachings without winning his lasting allegiance to them. Guesde had the zeal of a revolutionary and the sentiments of a democrat. What he lacked was a doctrine. This he discovered upon his return to Paris in 1876, where he wrote for the radical press and mixed with the radical student milieu. In this setting, he became interested in the economic sources of political power and was rather dramatically converted to collectivism. The new socialism gave system to the sentiments which had always inspired him. With his student friends he read, discussed, and absorbed many of Marx's essential ideas. But his reading of Marx was colored by his somewhat rigid personality, and his presentation of collectivist doctrine bore a scholastic tone.[33]

Having acquired a creed, Guesde was prepared to use his considerable talents to build a socialist movement in the country at large. His student friends were easily persuaded to join him in the venture. They, too, wished to move beyond Jacobinism as a revolutionary ideology and the Commune as a revolutionary experience. Although every Blanquist was a veteran of the Commune, few of Guesde's comrades had been more than vicariously involved, and most viewed it as an experience to which there needed to be no further appeal. These young men were in search of a theory which might deal more authoritatively with social problems than did the Hébertist doctrine with which the Blanquists honored the revolutionary tradition. In the activities of the Blanquists they noted an idealization of revolutionary movements which they believed to be self-defeating. There was an element of the theatrical in the activities of the Blanquists, a degree of passion in their manifestoes, which they found distasteful. The Guesdists wanted a more objective approach to the social question, one which drew its insights not from the revolutionary experience of the past but from the new science of society. What appealed to Guesdist youth in Marx's writings was his theory of history as a vast unfolding of socioeconomic processes which transcended the immediate concerns of political activists. Marxism seemed to offer a dispassionate, scientific understanding of the deeper logic of historical development which was inevitably leading capitalist society toward its destruction in a revolutionary crisis. Without abandoning a belief in the coming of revolution, the Guesdists had found a way to detach it from an exclusive commitment to street riot and coup d'etat. The intent of the Guesdists, therefore, was to demythologize the history of revolution—a field which for the Blanquists had become sacred ground.[34]

There was in all of this an ironical turn upon the youthful experience of the Blanquists. As students in the Latin Quarter in the 1860s, they had offered science as an alternative to religion as a means of understanding the material world in which human nature is formed. For the Guesdists, however, Marxism offered a science of history rather than of nature and thus dealt objectively with problems the Blanquists preferred to leave in the more subjective realm of chance, will, and precedent. For the Blanquists, it was the evocative power of concrete historical precedent which energized their activities in the present. The images of the Hébertists of 1793 and the Communards of 1871 acted powerfully upon the minds of men because they had been involved in actual events which revealed the meaning of human will and courage. To this cyclical view of history—that is, the eternal return to creative precedent—the Guesdists offered a linear alternative. Revolution was the culmination of a historical process which developed in accordance with laws which could be neither accelerated nor retarded by individuals, parties, or mass demonstrations. In the very realm where the Blanquists denied the idea of Providence, the Guesdists were prepared to introduce it once more.[35]

The new socialism of the French Marxists thus fostered a climate of fatalism, with far-reaching implications for the role of the militant committed to revolutionary change. For the Blanquists, the militant was a gadfly. It was his task to immerse himself in the popular milieu in order to sound public opinion in a thousand ways. The professional revolutionary did not inculcate values; rather, he ignited the latent will of the masses. The Guesdists, in contrast, preferred to stand above the crowd. The Guesdist militant conceived of his role as that of a teacher. The new-style revolutionary was not an activist in the tradition of Blanqui, but a purveyor of the new science of society which promised the liberation of the wage-earner in the dawn of a new historical era. Sub rosa plotting was therefore abandoned in favor of the open presentation of a doctrine whose logic was believed to be compelling.[36]

These conceptions of militancy were graphically contrasted in the images of the leaders with which each cause was identified. If Blanqui was known as a hidden figure who taught by personal example, Guesde was most readily recognized in his professorial role as public lecturer. More than one commentator has pointed to Guesde's "dialectical style," in which he developed his argument point by point, as if he were a logician deducing a theorem. If questioned, he would repeat the argument but was unwilling to be drawn into a more far-reaching dialogue.[37] The style won Guesde some of his most dedicated followers—men who were impressed with the learned character of what he had to say. But in Blanquist eyes, Guesde's priestly airs were not unlike those of Robespierre—removed, abstract, awkward, and austere. Thus the contrast between Guesde's intellectual elitism and Blanqui's instinctual populism epitomized contrasting styles of revolutionary practice to be tested in an era in which the nature of revolutionary action was open to question in a way it had not been before.

It was vexing to disagree with Marx about what a revolution was; it was infinitely more frustrating to dispute with his French followers about how to make one, especially as it was to serve as an inescapable issue of contention during the 1880s. Paradoxically, it was the Guesdists who to some extent made this dispute with the Blanquists possible through their zealous pursuit of amnesty for the Communards behind the banner, ironically enough, of Auguste Blanqui. The campaign at Bordeaux and elsewhere in 1879 to elect the imprisoned Blanqui to the Chamber of Deputies was designed to dramatize the issue of amnesty. It was by no means an exclusively Guesdist venture, but drew together a broad coalition of left-wing elements and depended heavily on the initiative of local leaders in such cities as Roanne, Lyons, and Bordeaux. The success of the Blanqui campaign at Bordeaux, for example, was due in large measure to the dynamic efforts of Ernest Roche (1850-1917), an engraver without previous political experience, who discovered his forensic talent in the course of the campaign. Roche, with a committee of local radical leaders, mobilized a coalition of radical, socialist, and revolutionary groups behind Blanqui's candidacy in opposition to the moderate republican incumbent. Blanqui's election in April 1879 was invalidated, as was his reelection in August. But the campaign helped win him a pardon and accelerated passage of the Communards' amnesty proposal in the Chamber of Deputies.[38] It was in publicizing and coordinating the campaign at the national level that the Guesdists played a crucial role. In effect, the Blanqui campaign was the first major political cause of the Guesdist party. The key figure in the Guesdist effort was Gabriel Deville, a journalist who worked tirelessly to give the local campaign at Bordeaux national attention and to promote Blanqui's candidacy in other cities so it could serve as a kind of national plebiscite for amnesty.[39]

If the Guesdists played a role in Blanqui's electoral victory at Bordeaux, in his liberation from prison, and in his public adula-

15. The aging Blanqui, circa 1880, depicted as the grand old man of the revolutionary tradition. Phot. Bibl. Nat.

tion everywhere, they contributed in an equally significant way to the taming of his legend in the popular imagination. For Blanqui was offered as the disembodied symbol of an event in which he had not actually participated. During the Commune, the Blanquists had mourned his absence as that of a savior whose active presence would have lent coherence and energy to the revolutionary struggle. Eight years later he was only the passive emblem for a campaign whose purpose was reconciliation rather

16. Jules Guesde, as apostle of the new socialism. Phot. Bibl. Nat.

than revolt. By seeking amnesty for the Communards, the Guesdists were implicitly arguing that the cause for which the Commune had done battle was no longer an issue, and that its militants presented no threat to the present regime. A stable republic, whatever its shortcomings, was a necessary staging ground for the socialist cause.

Such a view rendered the revolutionary tradition obsolete and Blanqui innocuous. It was a viewpoint to which the Blanquists in

exile remained unreconciled. For them, Blanqui continued to inspire awe.[40] For the Guesdists, he was simply an aging militant
who deserved respect. In describing his recollection of Blanqui
during the empire, Paul Lafargue, for example, sought to de-
bunk the stories of Blanqui as a sinister, conspiratorial figure.
Recalling his first meeting with Blanqui as a delegate to the
International Student Congress at Liège in 1865, he depicted a
gracious, warm personality who encouraged young revolutionaries to make their own way rather than to become disciples of
an older master.[41] But Lafargue's effort to recast the memory of
Blanqui in a benign image served also to desacralize it, and indeed to reduce it to somewhat sentimental proportions. Deville's
brochure *Blanqui libre*, which depicted Blanqui's life as a saga
nearing completion, had the same effect. Blanqui was eulogized
by the Guesdists for his suffering at the hands of oppression,
not for the specific conception of revolution he had championed.[42]
As the grand old man of the revolutionary tradition, he provided
a rallying point for the Left as it departed on a new quest for
what was as yet a vague, idealized conception of some future
socialist republic. As the emblem for a cause in which he was not
personally involved, Blanqui played a role analogous to that of
Baudin for republican youth a decade before or that of Boulanger
for the populist Left a decade after.

The Guesdists contributed substantially to the success of Blanqui's electoral campaign. But that campaign also accelerated the
Guesdist effort to popularize the new socialism. Guesde's speaking tour through the Midi in the summer of 1879, a tour devoted
in principle to a theoretical discussion of collectivism, took advantage of the aura of excitement surrounding the series of
elections in which Blanqui's name was placed in candidacy to
further the cause of amnesty. Guesde may have been pleased
with the outcome of the issue of amnesty, but he attached greater
importance to his more exclusive triumph at the Third Congress
of the Workers party, held at Marseilles in October of that year.[43]
The Marseilles congress was, in effect, the first major socialist
national convention. Attended by 130 delegates representing
forty-five cities, it marked the successful culmination of Guesde's
efforts to wrest control of the Workers party from its moderate
laborite founders. The congress approved collectivism as a goal,
established national and regional organizations, and instructed
Guesde to draw up a collectivist program in collaboration with
Marx for consideration at the next congress.[44]

For Guesde, it was more than a political victory. It was a testament to the growing appeal of a doctrine to which he himself had been but recently converted but whose truth he found so compelling that he was prepared to dedicate the rest of his life to its propagation. In later years he would reminisce about the gathering at Marseilles as "that immortal congress," the primal event of French socialism.[45] Thus the congress of Marseilles of 1879, not the Paris Commune of 1871, became the hallowed ground of the Marxist movement in France. With its emphasis upon the promulgation of the science of social change, the congress became the Guesdist movement's most characteristic institution. This explains why the Guesdists (and their historians) later attached such importance to party congresses in plotting the landmarks of the development of French socialism. Supposedly the purpose of these annual gatherings was to define theory. But because much of this effort was no more than the pro forma ratification of statements carefully prepared in advance, the party congresses functioned more obviously as festivals of the new socialism, underscoring the doctrinaire manner in which the Guesdists conceived of their task.[46]

From such an approach the Blanquists were quickly alienated. The Guesdist interest in the party congress as a forum for intellectual discourse contrasted sharply with their own preference for activism, or at least for its ritual remembrance. This point was made abundantly clear by Blanquist observers at the Marseilles congress. In a long letter to Blanqui in November 1879, Dr. Etienne Susini, a friend of long standing and a leading figure in the revolutionary movement at Marseilles, criticized the manner in which the congress had been conducted. Susini took exception to the vague formulas of the new socialism, and especially to the pontifical style in which Guesde and his colleagues presented them. As to the value of such congresses, he expressed his reservations: "Let us hope that the people, without expecting more of their congresses than they do of other long-winded assemblies, will proceed to remake the republic themselves, and without delay."[47] He praised the young engraver from Bordeaux, Ernest Roche, who had animated Blanqui's campaign in that city with his forensic talent, and who at Marseilles had fired the popular imagination at a postcongress rally with his bold political philosophy.[48]

Blanqui was in agreement. He appreciated the efforts of the apostles of the new socialism in enabling him to gain his freedom. But he clearly preferred those comrades who remained loyal to the ideas and values of the revolutionary tradition. Thus he politely turned down Lafargue's invitation to visit Marx in London to participate in the formulation of a program for the Workers party.[49] Instead he returned to Paris to rejoin his comrades of the 1860s, now straggling back from exile. Together they laid plans to edit a newspaper in the Hébertist manner, *Ni Dieu, ni maître,* and planned the nationwide speaking tour of 1880 which was Blanqui's last campaign.[50] Blanqui spurned Vaillant's proposal that militants establish themselves in provincial cities to widen the impact of revolutionary propaganda. Instead, he insisted that Ernest Roche, whose role at Bordeaux he especially admired, give up his activities there and join his group at Paris.[51] For the Blanquists, it was clear, Paris remained irrevocably the radiating center of revolutionary action.

CHAPTER VI

The Politics of Anniversary Remembrance

Shortly after Blanqui's release from prison in 1879, Ernest Roche wrote to him of the celebration in Bordeaux commemorating the anniversary of September 4, the proclamation of the republic. Roche described how the pageantry surrounding the event had grown each year, and how this year popular interest had focused on a liberty tree, adorned with a wreath inscribed to Blanqui. "Every year it is a place of pilgrimage for more than twenty thousand people," he explained. "They carry flowers and wreaths, they play music, they sing the 'Marseillaise,' and yesterday they cried 'long live Blanqui' at the top of their lungs! . . . It was wonderful. It is what we need at Bordeaux." Roche hoped the widening appeal of the legend of Blanqui which the amnesty campaign had revealed might become the basis for a new style of revolutionary politics. With a directness which Blanqui's veteran followers would never have dared, he criticized Blanqui for being insufficiently attuned to political experimentation. "Your error (happy error!)," he remarked, "seems to me to be similar to that of those philosophers of ancient times who, upon very little evidence, built a complete theory of nature, in which phenomena had to adjust to their preconceived notions, when they ought to have redesigned the theory."[1]

What Roche suggested was not as novel as he supposed. Unlike Vaillant, who pleaded the cause of new political directions before Blanqui at about the same time, Roche·called for the accentuation of an approach to politics in which Blanqui and his followers had always believed: the return to the ritual remembrance of the revolutionary tradition as the source of energy for fresh beginnings. The difference in Roche's proposal was the notion that the Blanquists could consciously use their revolutionary heritage as a political weapon. This possibility suggested itself in the outpouring of popular sympathy for Blanqui during and after his electoral campaigns of 1879—in the warm correspondence he received from old friends and new admirers, in the crowds lauding him during his speaking tour through France in the summer of 1880.[2] In his last days, Blanqui reigned unchallenged as the venerable elder statesman of the revolutionary tradition. The popularization of his legend inspired his followers to believe they could become spokesmen for the Left as the principal guardians of that heritage. Their primary interest thenceforth was in the question of how and how far the appeal of this legend could be extended. During the 1880s, the Blanquists formulated estimates of their political power not upon the size of their party, nor upon their participation in the congresses of the new socialist movement, but rather upon their capacity to popularize the cult of the revolutionary tradition as it related to Blanqui and through him to the memory of the Commune. This meant that during the 1880s they practiced not a politics of revolution, but a politics of anniversary remembrance.

The capacity to practice a politics of anniversary remembrance had been prepared by the experience of Blanquist youth in the Free Thought movement at the end of the Second Empire. One could argue that the Civil Burial movement, especially as it prepared the way for the funeral of Victor Noir and the commemoration of Alphonse Baudin, amounted to much the same thing with a less activist accent. With these traditions a certain continuity had been preserved, despite the disruptions of the civil war and the exile. Returning to Paris in 1880, the Blanquists found that a flourishing network of Free Thought groups had been established independently in their absence. Pleased with the interest, they were instinctively determined to take up the atheist causes which they had been forced to neglect for nearly a decade. It is significant to note that the first Blanquist newspaper published after the amnesty was a Free Thought venture, *La pensée libre*. Staffed by the same editor (Henri Place) and many of the same reporters as its predecessor, *La libre pensée*, this newspaper returned to the issues of civil burial and lay schools which had been put aside with the start of the Franco-Prussian War.[3]

Even during the exile, the rites of anniversary remembrance of the Free Thought movement had never been completely abandoned. The monument to Baudin, planned in the context of the republican agitation of the late 1860s, was erected at the Montmartre cemetery in 1872. Small groups continued to gather there on December 2 throughout the 1870s, and in 1880 one Free Thought newspaper still proudly offered its subscribers a photographic reproduction of Ernest Pichio's famous etching "The

Last Moments of Baudin."[4] For those in exile, the Brussels grave of Gustave Tridon occasionally became a place of pilgrimage.[5] In his first letter to Blanqui following the amnesty, Jules Vallès described his wanderings in those parts of the city where Tridon had suffered before his death.[6]

The amnesty campaign was quickened by demonstrations of anniversary remembrance at the burial plot at Père-Lachaise of Gustave Flourens, professor of natural history and soldier of fortune, who had fallen in battle for the Commune on April 3, 1871. Flourens, like Baudin twenty years before, had not been publicly mourned at his death. He had been buried in the midst of the civil war in a private ceremony attended only by his immediate family—his harried comrades having had no time to solemnize the occasion. But in 1876, and in greater numbers in each succeeding year, crowds gathered at his tomb on the anniversary of his death. By 1880 these pilgrimages were visibly adding momentum to the campaign for amnesty. In that year, a fund-raising drive for wreaths for his grave was publicized in the left-wing press, and a crowd of about fifteen hundred braved a driving rain to hear eulogies by former comrades now once more in the public eye, among them Emile Digeon, former leader of the Commune at Narbonne, and the recently liberated Blanqui.[7] From 1878, pilgrims to Père-Lachaise on these occasions marked out other holy places of the Commune as well, most notably the common grave which had served for the last militiamen (*fédérés*) of the Commune, who had fallen behind the tombstones or been executed near the wall in the final hours of fighting.[8]

Support for a politics of anniversary remembrance grew in many quarters during the campaign for amnesty; and the Blanquists returning from exile added to these ceremonies a new intensity and more than a touch of baroque extravagance. Consider, for example, the exhumation of the remains of Théophile Ferré at the cemetery at Levallois-Perret on July 26, 1881. Ferré had been buried without ceremony following his execution at Satory in 1871. Now, a decade later, his friends and relatives gathered to pay him tribute in the hope that this would rehabilitate his memory, so thoroughly had it been vilified in the intervening years by writers hostile to the Commune. The ceremony, however, was marked by practices altogether foreign to the simplicity of civil burial as observed by the Blanquists fifteen years before. The unearthed corpse was displayed so that onlookers could view the skull, portions of which had been shot away by the executioners. At the close of the eulogies, Marie Ferré, the sister of the deceased, invited friends to take pieces of hair still clinging to the victim's skull as souvenirs by which to remember him. The body was then wrapped in a red flag, itself a relic of the Commune, and reburied in the family tomb.[9]

Though the graphic, somewhat morbid aspects of this ceremony were never again equaled, they set a new style for Blanquist rites of remembrance in their capacity to elicit a deep emotional response to a personality of the Commune through an appeal to the senses. Blanquist burial rites of the 1880s assumed the trappings of the religious ceremonies which Blanquist youth of the 1860s had denounced in their plea for decorum in rites of passage. Blanqui's own funeral on January 5, 1881, is characteristic in this respect. The indomitable rebel succumbed to old age rather than to his political opponents. Felled by an attack of apoplexy following a rally sponsored by the staff of *La pensée libre* on the evening of December 27, 1880, he lay in a coma from which he never recovered before dying on New Year's day 1881. The widely publicized funeral ceremonies included a cortege estimated at two hundred thousand mourners, among them delegations from outlying departments and foreign lands. The procession marched in ranks, with banners of various revolutionary societies unfurled, to Père-Lachaise, where Blanqui was laid to rest not far from the trench where the last militiamen of the Commune had been executed. Eulogies were intoned for most of the afternoon.[10] Each year thereafter the Blanquists assembled on the anniversary of his death for the ritual walk across the Seine from the Place d'Italie, where he died, to his tomb at Père-Lachaise.[11] This was a pilgrimage in which every Blanquist militant felt morally bound to participate.

But the Blanquists were determined to honor the memory of their leader with some more lasting tribute. They initiated a campaign immediately after his death to erect a fitting monument at his graveside. In this project, they turned to the precedent of the campaign for a monument to Baudin. But to build one equal to Blanqui's memory, his followers believed, it would have to surpass all the others. They established an elaborate network of committees to oversee the fund-raising and commissioned the famous sculptor Jules Dalou to cast a life-size statue in bronze which would stand both as a memento of Blanqui and as a great work of art. Dalou took three years to com-

17. The burial of Blanqui, January 5, 1881—a political event. Phot. Bibl. Nat.

plete his work, then postponed the inauguration of the statue so he could place it on display at a salon. To help mark time, the Blanquists held an interim ceremony in January 1883 to inaugurate the pedestal which would eventually support the statue. Not until 1885 was the statue finally unveiled at Blanqui's grave.[12]

Years later, Alfred Breuillé fondly recalled the imposing funeral Blanqui's followers had given their mentor and recounted in detail the manner in which commemorative ceremonies were planned so as to heighten the awe surrounding his name.[13] But the attempt to apotheosize him in death as a public figure contrasted sharply with Blanqui's own search in life as a private citizen for anonymity. In effect, the Blanquists had buried not only the grand old man of the revolutionary tradition, but also the spirit of simplicity in which his lifelong reverence for death had been conceived.

The dedication of the monument to Blanqui was accompanied by other forms of tribute. In 1885, Ernest Granger, the executor

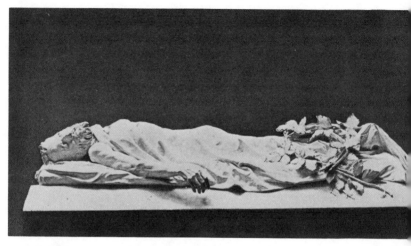

18. Jules Dalou's effigy of Blanqui, 1885.

of his papers, published an edition of Blanqui's writings on social
and economic questions under the title *Critique sociale*.[14] The work,
a collection of Blanqui's essays originally published as newspaper
articles, was intended to identify him with socialist theorizing, of
such interest to the Left in the 1880s. Equally important was the
simultaneous publication of Benjamin Flotte's book *Blanqui et les
otages en 1871*, which, in its descriptions of Flotte's abortive diplo-
macy to exchange a number of hostages for Blanqui, revisited
the theme of the critical role Blanqui might have played in sal-
vaging the faltering fortunes of the Commune.[15] In 1885 as well,
Gustave Geffroy began research for a biography of Blanqui
which he hoped would stand as the literary counterpart of Dalou's sculpture.[16] It was also in this year that the Municipal
Council of Paris was persuaded to rename a portion of the Boule-
vard d'Italie, Blanqui's last place of residence, in his honor.[17]
   The passion surrounding Blanqui's memory was also deepened
in the course of the decade because of the deaths of a number of
the most renowned personalities of the Commune: Theisz, 1881;
Trinquet, 1882; Vallès, 1885; Cournet, 1885; Amouroux, 1885;
Arnould, 1885; Pottier, 1887; Eudes, 1888, Gois, 1888; and Pyat,
1889—to name only the most prominent. Blanqui's, therefore,
was but the first of a series of grand funerals celebrating the
Commune. Each of these figures was memorialized annually in a
demonstration. Monuments were erected to the best known with

funds raised through public solicitation. As the decade pro-
gressed, not only the number but the scope of these observances
was extended. Elaborate rituals often attended the demonstrations, from the pageantry of the processions along well-marked
routes to the cemeteries, to the litanies of praise recited at graveside. Turnouts of two thousand were not unusual, and often the
numbers were more impressive still. It is estimated that more
than twenty thousand sympathizers attended the funeral of
Blanquist leader Emile Eudes, while sixty thousand gathered to
pay their last respects to Jules Vallès, the celebrated novelist and
newspaper editor.[18]

In all these ceremonies, the Blanquists participated vigorously,
frequently playing the guiding role, even in the tributes to Communards to whom they had not always been sympathetic. Eudes
and Emile Rouillon, for example, sat on a committee to raise
funds for a monument to Delescluze, despite the fact that Blanqui and Delescluze had hated one another.[19] For the Blanquists
believed that the ceremonial mobilization of the revolutionary
forces of Paris revealed and sustained the underlying strength of
their commitment to the revolutionary tradition, a commitment
often obscured by the outward sectarianism of left-wing parties
in Paris in the 1880s. Not only the men but the principal events
of the Commune therefore became part of the Blanquists' annual
memorial observance, and they soon reverenced a revolutionary
calendar as elaborate as the Christian one they so vigorously
scorned.

Nearly all the revolutionary groups joined the Blanquists to
commemorate Bloody Week on the last Sunday of May beside
the common grave at Père-Lachaise where the Commune's last
defenders were shot down. But some of the lesser events they
observed alone. In 1886, for example, a delegation went to La
Villette to celebrate the storming of the fire station there in
August 1870—an event, one might have supposed, they would
have preferred to forget. Their tribute to those who had fallen in
death and destruction was at least partially counterbalanced by
the festivals celebrating the Commune's founding on the Satur-
day evening closest to March 18. These were generally mirthful,
family affairs with wining and dining in banquet halls em-
blazoned with the banners of the subcommittees and satellite
groups of Paris.[20]

It is important to understand how dedication to the cult of the
revolutionary tradition reshaped the Blanquists' political prac-

19. Announcement of the campaign to erect a monument to the militiamen who fell at Père-Lachaise, 1883: the politics of anniversary remembrance. Phot. Bibl. Nat.

tice. For obvious reasons, the funeral and memorial demonstrations, sometimes the scenes of sporadic violence, raised specters in the minds of their opponents of insurrections past. The first annual pilgrimage to Blanqui's tomb (January 1882), for example, was marred by a clash with police, who tried to bar the demonstrators, eight hundred strong, from their chosen parade route.

Twenty-three were arrested on that occasion.[21] Denied the right
to commemorate the death of Théophile Ferré collectively, those
mourners who came to the cemetery at Levallois-Perret individually on November 26, 1881, were harassed and in some cases
arrested by police, who darted furtively about the graveyard to
prevent a crowd from congregating.[22] The funeral of Eugène
Pottier on November 8, 1887, was likewise dramatized by a violent quarrel between police and demonstrators.[23] At a ceremony
in honor of Bloody Week at Père-Lachaise on May 30, 1888,
Rouillon, a Blanquist militant, was fired upon by an anarchist
who was determined to turn the demonstration into an uproar.[24]
The funeral of Emile Eudes on August 8, 1888, was the scene of
an unruly standoff between demonstrators and police. Fearful
that random pistol shots might turn the crowd to panic, one
police official described the funeral with some hyperbole as
"the most substantial and terrifying demonstration since the
Commune."[25]

20. Violence at a demonstration commemorating Bloody Week, May 25, 1885.
Phot. Bibl. Nat.

Such a judgment reflected the traditional view of the Blanquists as inveterate conspirators bent upon inciting popular insurrection. Yet a coup d'etat in the image of the storming of La Villette was no longer even a remote hope in the Blanquist strategy. Rather, the politics of anniversary remembrance epitomized a style of political protest which rejected riot in favor of festival. Drawing upon the precedents of their youthful experience, they consciously emphasized the role of ritual activity as the most powerful means of manifesting the solidarity of the people of Paris in the revolutionary cause. In this they showed a surprising sensitivity to the techniques of the new mass politics, the possibilities of which were only beginning to be appreciated.

The Blanquists, for all their vicarious identification with the working class as the elect, had thitherto considered themselves quite self-consciously an elite. The politics of anniversary remembrance revealed the degree to which they had tacitly abandoned clandestine conspiracy for a public campaign to extend their popular contacts. Like other groups on the Left, the Blan-

21. The funeral of Emile Eudes, August 8, 1888. Phot. Bibl. Nat.

quists were increasingly aware of the power of public opinion and sought to appeal to it in new ways. If they did not share the Left's interest in the new socialism, they were instinctively drawn to the new politics, which widened the possibilities of revolutionary agitation. The revolutionary situation, they believed, would present itself as a broader and more elemental upheaval, one which could be directed but never catalyzed at will. By exploring the new possibilities of revolutionary action in the dawning age of mass politics, they hoped to renew contact with the traditions of popular vigilance and direct political action which had inspired their youth.

The politics of anniversary remembrance provided not only a basis for periodic demonstrations, but also the very structure of their more permanent organization. The Central Revolutionary Committee (Comité Révolutionnaire Central), the Blanquist headquarters during the 1880s, was the outgrowth of the ad hoc committee formed in 1881 to erect a monument to Blanqui.[26] The League for the Abolition of Permanent Armies, a satellite group whose activities carried Blanquist influence beyond Paris, was created in 1883 to pursue Blanqui's "last wish": the arming of the people.[27] But in a larger sense, the politics of anniversary remembrance, in its commitment to mass action, prepared the way for the democratization and diversification of the Blanquist organization. The Central Revolutionary Committee remained a tightly knit circle of about twenty veteran disciples of Blanqui. But Blanquist leaders made little effort to organize the subcommittees in Paris and its suburbs on the model of the parent organization or to impose a strict rule of discipline upon them. The blueprint for a hierarchy of secret paramilitary cells, basic to the Blanquists' conception of their organization in the late 1860s, was discarded.[28] In its place, the leaders of the Central Revolutionary Committee sought to erect a more loosely organized political apparatus. In this way, the inner circle of veterans (those whom Arthur Ranc once labeled "Blanquists of the first degree") hoped to extend their influence over the outer circle of sympathizers (the burgeoning ranks of Blanquists of the second degree), which earlier had remained apart from the Blanquist organization.

Blanquist groups fitted easily into the informal club life so characteristic of left-wing politics in Paris in that era. Caucusing in neighborhood cafés, these local committees filled a social as well as a political function. The Blanquists acknowledged that most individuals who followed the political scene regularly preferred the intimacy and direct exchange possible in small groups whose members knew one another well. The resistance of some members of the Blanquist subcommittees to a more disciplined organization was ordinarily matched by the willingness of the leaders of the Central Revolutionary Committee to shape their party around these informal groups. The degree to which such independence was accommodated is illustrated by the experience of the subcommittees of the thirteenth arrondissement. There the local chieftain, François Winant, held his band at a distance from the activities of the parent organization and several times threatened to secede. He also busied himself with the creation of anarchist groups which had no ties with the Blanquists. At the same time, Winant remained proud of his Blanquist identification and expressed considerable disappointment when his aspirations for a larger role in the Central Revolutionary Committee were spurned.[29] Such an arrangement was easily tolerated for its mutual benefits: the subcommittees retained a sense of spontaneity of association; the Central Revolutionary Committee extended its field of political activity. The underlying revolutionary faith of all the groups was assumed.

Yet it was no longer clear what such faith implied. The politics of anniversary remembrance prepared the way for the Blanquists' entry into mass politics, but the realities of mass politics in turn forced them to project their hopes for a revolutionary upheaval into a remote future whose relevance to present tasks was vague. If they heeded Roche's advice about the need for an intensified ritual remembrance of their revolutionary past—a sentiment Blanqui had so admired—their use of the politics of anniversary remembrance seemed to draw them toward Vaillant's proposal for a greater public role for their group in left-wing politics, a viewpoint of which Blanqui had been quite suspicious. If the Blanquists extolled revolution with renewed fervor, they likewise opened the way for more promising, pragmatic alternatives. In favoring these in their political practice during the 1880s, they tacitly admitted that, for the present at least, they would have to be content with smaller victories and lesser rewards.

It was in this spirit that the Blanquists became involved in all manner of political causes which were likely to capture public attention. If some Blanquist subcommittees seemed to enjoy a surprising amount of autonomy, the independence displayed by the satellite organizations was greater still. Among the first of these ventures was the League for the Abolition of Permanent Armies, designed to merge opposition to the government's imperialist policy in Tunisia with the favorite Blanquist cause of arming the people. It was founded in 1883 exclusively under Blanquist auspices and drew a number of Parisian and provincial groups into its orbit.[30] The League for the Defense of the Republic, on the other hand, was sponsored jointly with a number of left-wing groups to sustain the popular protest generated by the presidential crisis of 1887.[31] The League for the Abolition of Private Employment Agencies, founded in 1884, is an example of a practical effort to infiltrate the labor movement, whereas the Blanquists' connection with the Republican Society for Social Economy provides evidence of their simultaneous concern to remain fully in touch with discussions of the social question on a more intellectual plane.[32] The Blanquists also played a role in the founding of the Knights of Labor, a workers' wing of the Freemasons, of which Emmanuel Chauvière was for a time grand master.[33]

The indirect influence of the Blanquists extended well beyond this organizational complex. The party enjoyed the vigorous support of many celebrated left-wing militants of the day. Louise Michel, the heroine of the Commune, rarely missed a major Blanquist banquet or rally. More important still were the praise and publicity received by the party from Henri Rochefort, the most successful left-wing newspaper editor in Paris. Too much the maverick to affiliate with any group, Rochefort nonetheless saved his deepest sympathies for the Blanquists, who had shared his campaign against the Second Empire. His newspaper, *L'intransigeant*, was the principal medium through which the Blanquists reported their activities during the 1880s, and Rochefort was not averse to adding needy Blanquist militants to his staff even if they had previously displayed no special journalistic ability. Ernest Roche, for example, who could not find work as an engraver in Paris, was able to remain there because of Rochefort's generosity. Several of the older Blanquists drew personally close to him in the years following the amnesty. Eudes especially admired his qualities as a writer and asked him to be tutor to his children.[34]

Rochefort's talents as a popular tribune were admirably suited to the new mass politics. Not only was his newspaper among the most widely read of the day, but he personally was the unrivaled favorite of the Parisian crowd at any public demonstration he attended. Upon his triumphant arrival in Paris following the amnesty, he was cheered and pursued by his admirers as a returning hero.[35] Some of the most remarkable displays of popular adulation for Rochefort, moreover, were associated with Blanquist memorial demonstrations. At Blanqui's funeral the fanfare for Rochefort was a noticeable distraction. He was acclaimed all along the parade route to the cemetery, and at the burial he was for a time unable to deliver his eulogy because of the unrelenting press of the crowd. As he prepared to leave the cemetery gates, he was again mobbed by well-wishers and was finally forced to jump into his coach to flee the scene.[36] At the funeral of Albert Theisz, a few days later, he pacified the crowd only by repairing to a café which adjoined the cemetery in order to toast the revolutionary cause.[37]

In a study of French socialism in the mid-1880s, the political observer Mermeix suggested Rochefort as the most likely figure to provide unifying leadership for the incipient socialist movement.[38] Judging Rochefort to be a living symbol of the revolutionary tradition, many Blanquists were prepared to accept him as a surrogate for Blanqui and exhorted him to become part of their entourage. On his deathbed in 1885 Frédéric Cournet is reported to have pleaded with Rochefort in these terms to cast his support to the Blanquists:

Citizen Rochefort, you are a force, a great force, that is undeniable; but remember well what I must now tell you: you will be completely defeated and you will be of no service to the revolution if you do not rely upon a group which is seriously organized, and which will endure whatever comes to pass.

Rochefort answered evasively, but he departed visibly moved.[39]

Despite the availability of Rochefort's newspaper, the leaders of the Central Revolutionary Committee attached considerable importance to publishing one of their own. Such a venture presented enormous financial difficulties, and only for brief periods were the Blanquists able to find sufficient resources. *Ni Dieu, ni maître*, founded in late 1880, circulated for only a year because of inadequate funding. Not until the Boulangist crisis did the Central Revolutionary Committee again have a newspaper of its own at Paris, and then only because of Rochefort's financial support.

Strike action, which proliferated throughout France in the

1880s, was another obvious field for Blanquist agitation, although the party responded to it slowly. Only upon the most unsettled labor situations were the Blanquists willing to concentrate their efforts. Through the Blanquist-inspired League for the Abolition of Private Employment Agencies, founded to fan the grievances of a fast-growing reservoir of unemployed workers in the building trades and food service industries, the Blanquists established connections with the militant wing of the trade union movement at Paris. Agitation in that quarter culminated in the construction workers' strike in the summer of 1888, one of the most volatile expressions of labor protest in that era. For nearly three months, Blanquist militants led by Winant mingled daily with strikers in the cafés and workyards of the eastern quarters of Paris to sustain their resolve.[40]

The 1880s also marked the beginning of sustained contact between the Blanquists in Paris and their sympathizers in the provinces. Blanqui had long enjoyed the personal devotion of some militants in the far reaches of the country. His longtime friend Etienne Susini, physician, activist, and Communard at Marseilles, kept the aging Blanqui apprised of events in that city.[41] At Narbonne, Emile Digeon, who had been one of Blanqui's youthful disciples of the 1860s, likewise remained in personal correspondence with his mentor during his last years, as did Casimir Bouis at Toulon (who had edited a book of Blanqui's articles from *La patrie en danger* shortly after the Commune).[42] But not until Blanqui's death did his followers turn their attention to the problem of provincial committees to further revolutionary agitation. This, of course, was the policy which Vaillant, during the exile, had urged upon his comrades as the most promising approach to the renewal of the revolutionary movement.

Following the amnesty, Vaillant tried to set an example by returning to his native Vierzon rather than to Paris. There he began work to establish a revolutionary organization. By 1884 he had launched a newspaper, *Le républican socialiste du centre*, through which he hoped to publicize the activities of revolutionary groups at Bourges, Nevers, and Vierzon.[43] Similar efforts at organization were initiated by J. Montaron at Chalons sur Saône, by Adrien Farjat at Lyons, and by Frédéric von Stackelberg at Nice. Indeed, it is worth noting that while the Blanquists had no newspaper in Paris for most of the decade of the 1880s, they did found a succession of ephemeral newspapers in these provincial cities.[44]

Yet this endeavor was little more than a missionary effort. The editors of these newspapers made some effort to publicize local issues, but Blanquist journalists in Paris contributed most of the columns. True to their Hébertist traditions, the Blanquists looked upon revolutionary agitation in the provinces as little more than a chorus for the unfolding drama in Paris. Nor was there much system in the selection of cities for Blanquist activity beyond sentiment or historical ties. Vierzon was a sound choice in terms of Vaillant's larger strategy; but it was also his birthplace. Chalons sur Saône was selected because of its proximity to Le Creusot, the scene of a metal workers' strike in 1870 which the Blanquists believed had assumed potentially revolutionary proportions. Le Creusot continued to interest the Blanquists in the 1880s because of the large concentration of Creusotin workers in the fifteenth arrondissement of Paris, where Chauvière was a candidate for public office. Indeed, the newspaper *La tenaille* appears to have been founded with Chauvière's electoral campaign in mind.[45] It was appropriate for the Blanquists to seek to establish their influence at Lyons, but again the choice was dictated by personal contact (notably with Eudes's son-in-law, Adrien Farjat) rather than by some strategy of linking key cities in a national organization.

Moreover, militants engaged in these ventures in the hinterlands were more often than not drawn back to Paris out of ambition or a distaste for life in the provinces. Ernest Roche, who had been effectively building a revolutionary party at Bordeaux in the aftermath of the campaign for Blanqui, willingly heeded the "old one's" call to Paris despite much unfinished business in his native city.[46] Etienne Susini, who for many years had styled himself as a key organizer of the revolutionary cause at Marseilles, likewise abandoned his post by the mid-1880s in order to stand for election in Paris.[47] Frédéric Cournet, dispatched to Lyons to edit a newspaper in 1882, endured his sojourn for only a few months.[48] Alexandre Girault, Vaillant's editorial secretary at Vierzon for *Le républicain socialiste du centre* in 1884, also found his way to Paris by the end of the decade.[49] Even Vaillant, who had so fervently espoused a national strategy of revolutionary agitation, found the lure of Paris too compelling to resist. The Blanquists' interest in mass politics, while genuine, was still conceived in terms of the sans culottes of Paris, and the notion of Paris as the hearth of revolution proved impossible to overcome. The Blanquists had established a network of contacts throughout France, but one with little coherence and little hint of a popular following.

What drew these disparate activities in Paris and the provinces together was a special interest in political elections. There was a certain irony in the newfound enthusiasm with which the Blanquists took up this activity, given their professed scorn for the parliamentary process as a procedure favoring the "legal world." Yet after the amnesty, the Blanquists were willing to believe Vaillant's claim that the ballot box was an important means of publicizing the revolutionary movement which had to be pursued. By the mid-1880s, electoral campaigns for the Blanquists had become an interest which surpassed all others. If the Blanquists claimed that electioneering was but one weapon of protest in the revolutionary arsenal, it in fact became the focal point upon which all of their other activities converged. In the process, their energies were for all practical purposes transferred from revolutionary agitation to political participation.

For the legislative elections, the Blanquists could claim that they were merely engaged in a form of protest, as they stood little chance of victory. It was in this spirit that the Central Revolutionary Committee contributed the names of its best-known leaders, Eudes, Vaillant, Granger, Chauvière, and Susini, to Rochefort's coalition list for the legislative elections of 1885; and they were more than content with the moral support which tallies as high as 39,490 signified.[50] Moreover, the support they were capable of generating in the midst of a political crisis was genuinely impressive. It was therefore fitting that Ernest Roche, who had managed Blanqui's electoral campaign in Bordeaux in 1879, should have been chosen as the candidate of a left-wing coalition protesting governmental policy during the Decazeville strike of 1886. In a special legislative election in Paris in May of that year, Roche received more than 100,000 votes. Roche's candidacy dramatized the cause of the strikers, but the identification of a Blanquist with that cause, like the identification of Blanqui with the issue of amnesty in 1879, reinforced the image of the Blanquists as guardians of the revolutionary tradition.[51]

From the municipal elections in Paris the Blanquists hoped for a great deal more. By mid-decade they were presenting tangible evidence of solid electoral support in some quarters. In 1884 Edouard Vaillant, as a candidate in the Père-Lachaise ward of the twentieth arrondissement, became the first Blanquist since the Commune to win a seat on the Paris Municipal Council. He was joined three years later by Emmanuel Chauvière, who had gathered a strong following in the Javel ward of the fifteenth arrondissement on the Left Bank. The performance of Cournet, Eudes, and Granger in a number of other municipal electoral contests raised the prospect in the minds of the Blanquists that their contingent at City Hall would continue to grow.[52]

It is in this context that the bitter animosity between the Blanquists and a rival faction, the Possibilists, is more adequately understood. The two groups were divided by irreconcilable differences over the meaning and matter of political action. The demonstrative tactics which the Blanquists considered essential elements of their approach to politics were dismissed by the Possibilists as self-indulgent concessions to revolutionary romanticism. Correspondingly, the Blanquists construed the reformist politics of the Possibilists as the accommodation of ambitious men to the corruptions of the parliamentary style of politics. These differences concerning tactics took on special meaning in the practical struggles of left-wing politics in Paris in the closing years of the decade. Neither party could realistically aspire to place in national politics, but each judged that it was in a position to steer if not dominate the Left on the Parisian scene: the Possibilists through their substantial support in the moderate wing of organized labor, the Blanquists through their capacity to rally the industrial workers of the eastern districts of the city. Each hoped to use its strength to gain greater influence over the policies of the Paris Municipal Council—the Possibilists to further projects for the reform of municipal services, the Blanquists to prepare the way for a restoration of the Commune. The fervor with which this struggle for place in municipal politics was waged reveals the degree to which the Blanquists had come to understand themselves in a parliamentary rather than a revolutionary image.[53]

One might have expected that the politics of anniversary remembrance would have produced a renaissance of the Hébertist sentiment from which the Blanquists had earlier derived sustenance. But the Hébertist conception of revolution in the political world of the Third Republic appeared abstract without an archenemy, religious or political, which conformed to its definitions. The Second Empire, so closely associated with the Church, had been easily marked as a reactionary regime to be dismantled. But the moderate republic, for all its inadequacies, could not be totally disclaimed, for republicanism had been the core of the revolutionary movement during the formative years of the Blanquists' youth. Like themselves, the Opportunist leaders of the new republic were tough-minded, unsentimental politicians committed to science and secularism, men who opposed clerical influence in public affairs and despised authoritarianism. Opportunism was by comparison with Bonapartism a sorry substitute against which to try revolutionary courage. The immediate consequence for the Blanquists was a certain demoralization. The name chosen for a newspaper of theirs published briefly at Lyons in 1883, *Le branle-bas* (Clearing the decks), suggests the Blanquists' need to fight the inertia which sometimes plagued their efforts during the early years of the decade. Once-dauntless militants became discouraged—Ernest Granger so much so that in 1887 he voluntarily retired from revolutionary politics and set off to Algeria to sell machinery. He returned to the cause in Paris the following year, but only at the insistence of his comrades, who cornered him at a funeral at Asnières.[54]

Drawn openly into present-day politics, the Blanquists explained current conditions in terms which might better be described as populist in their preoccupation with issues far refrom their traditional concern with clericalism and authoritarianism. Whereas Hébertism in the 1860s had been almost exclusively a Blanquist ideology, populism in the 1880s appealed to a large number of left-wing groups who wished to revitalize radical politics. Populism was an expression of protest against the current trend toward large-scale economic organization. Its common denominator was an anxiety about the social implications of rapid industrial concentration in a country in which artisan industry had long been the predominant mode of economic organization. The populists were not hostile to industrial growth as such, but they feared the baneful effects of the concentration of wealth in the hands of a few capitalists, who, they believed, might manipulate the economy to their own advantage.[55]

For the Blanquists, the populist critique provided insight into how the trend toward mass production in the economic sphere paralleled the trend toward mass movements in the political sphere. One could say that the Blanquists were at last roused to an interest in economic questions, an interest which their exposure to the new socialism had never really promoted. To their pursuit of the new politics they now joined a new economics.

The populist argument enabled them to clothe the Hébertist doctrine of the "two nations" in a modern garb which emphasized material realities rather than a philosophy of materialism. The great entrepreneur now replaced the landed notable as the representative of the "legal world," yet for the Blanquists he bore certain similarities in method and manner to his more genteel predecessor, and he was held to be equally corrupt. If his spokesman, the Opportunist politician, was the neo-Girondin villain of the present age, he was that for his misuse of economic power rather than for his religious or political convictions.[56]

The populist argument appealed to the Blanquists as well for the hard pessimism with which it analyzed the dynamics of capitalism in the 1880s, a pessimism which distinguished it from the Marxist argument to which the Blanquists had found it so difficult to subscribe. At a time when the Guesdists were reformulating the Hébertist vision of willful revolution upon new foundations of scientific predictability, the populists voiced skepticism that capitalist society would eventually wither away. In contrast with the Marxists, they argued that the concentration of wealth was not a necessary stage of economic development, but a retrogression toward a "new feudalism," in which industrial overlords would carry on their private economic wars immune from public accountability and oblivious to the public interest in a more even distribution of national wealth. The gravity of the trend was documented with statistics about stock swindles, rising unemployment, and impending financial disaster. Tales of collusion between financiers and public officials were offered as further evidence of a trend toward economic chaos, a state of affairs from which, the populists contended, there was no easy escape. What this meant in practical terms was a preoccupation with problems of power in contemporary politics. While the Guesdists optimistically awaited the collapse of capitalism, the populists preached political *engagement* to reverse the trend toward "bourgeois anarchy."[57]

The populist focus on the present realities of power appealed to the Blanquists' longstanding inclination to place the emphasis upon struggle rather than victory in any discussion of revolution. In their explanation of the scope and complexity of the existing struggle, the populists confirmed the Blanquists' assessment of the difficulty of making a revolution in the present age. Since Tridon's formulation of an archetypal model of revolutionary struggle, the Blanquists had adhered to the proposition that revolution involved a conflict between opposing viewpoints out of which there could be no dialectical synthesis. The initial Blanquist commitment to the crusade for atheism had been informed by the sense that any victory was likely to be short-lived, as it had been historically, because the visible victor would soon have to deal with the visible vanquished on some new level of subterranean opposition. The sense that the struggle, win or lose, was of value for its own sake, implicit in Tridon's Hébertist ideology, now became explicit in its populist restatement as the odds against a political revolution mounted.

In the shift from the use of religious imagery (the two esprits) of the 1860s, to the political imagery (the two nations) of the 1870s, to the economic imagery (the new feudalism) of the 1880s, the Blanquists gradually abandoned their salvationist approach to the social question and began to formulate solutions which stopped short of revolutionary reconstruction. The possibility of a revolution was projected into a receding future and thus became a topic as devoid of passion for the present-minded Blanquists as the revolutionary past which had once fired their youthful imaginations. The present task was to join in the ordeal of opposition to the legal world with other groups which shared their populist sympathies. Comradeship in the making of a revolutionary movement, once viewed as the incipient form of a future community, was now only a consolation in an otherwise capricious world.[58]

The Blanquists were drawn to populism for its affinities with Hébertism, yet they alluded only rarely to this historical source of their values in their public statements in the 1880s. The present-mindedness with which they dealt with issues as veteran journalists contrasted sharply with their preferences as young journalists of the 1860s to weave each present event into the historical fabric of the revolutionary tradition. But a party which had staked its commitments upon a promise of revolution revealed in past precedents risked a great deal in devoting itself exclusively to contemporary concerns. In reformulating Hébertism as populism, the Blanquists desacralized the radical atheism which had contributed so powerfully to their faith in revolution in the 1860s.

Their relations with the Free Thought movement illustrate this point. Though Henri Place and a few companions played a modest role in the renewal of Free Thought journalism in the early 1880s, the movement escaped their influence as it broad-

ened and democratized. By 1883, an estimated fifteen thousand
people were inscribed in Free Thought groups, of which only a
small number belonged to the Blanquist-inspired Socialist Feder-
ation of the Free Thought movement.[59] A once-explosive issue
(such as the cause of lay schools) was in the 1880s an essential
aspect of the moderate republican program. Lay burial, in the
1860s an act of iconoclasm, was the accepted format for nearly
20 percent of the funerals in Paris in 1883.[60] Indeed, at the
International Congress of Free Thinkers in Paris in 1889, no
Blanquist delegate was present save Albert Regnard, who had
long since severed ties with the companions of his youth. There
was a ritual pilgrimage to Père-Lachaise to commemorate the
Communards, but no reference was made to the role of the
Blanquists in the founding of the Free Thought movement in
France. The Blanquists were no longer mindful of the degree to
which Free Thought had formed their revolutionary convictions;
and the Free Thought movement had shed its revolutionary
origins to become instead a sensible, moderate group promoting
a rational code of secular morality. Whereas Free Thinking intellectuals of the late 1860s had been somewhat embarrassed by
their academic stance and looked to the Blanquists as their revolutionary arm, the Free Thinkers of the late 1880s preferred the
philosophical posture.[61] But both groups had moved far from the
initial ground. While the Free Thinkers had domesticated radical
atheism, the Blanquists had secularized it. Having done so, they
lost touch with the quasi-religious source of their commitment
to revolution.

The populist vision with which the Blanquists justified their
involvement in the new politics meant that it was increasingly
difficult for them to make sense of the rituals of anniversary
remembrance. It was not that they valued the revolutionary
tradition less. On the contrary, they had become ever more scrupulous in the formal observance of the calendar of anniversary
remembrances. But it was not always clear how this witness
related to their present concerns. The commemoration of revolutionary precedents had originally been intended to reawaken
revolutionary ardor for the present. But in the 1880s the Blanquists acted as if they wished to enshrine their revolutionary
tradition in static terms, a vestige of the past too pure to sully
with the petty passions of contemporary politics.

This attitude was evident in the sentimental self-conscious-
ness in which they reminisced about the meaning of anniversary

remembrance. Henri Place wrote a series of articles about the didactic value of revolutionary festivals.[62] Albert Regnard analyzed the symbolic use of ritual in a full systematic study of the cult of the revolutionary tradition.[63] Alfred Breuillé fondly traced the history of pilgrimages to Blanqui's tomb by relating stories of the turmoil which had accompanied them.[64] Thus the rites and legends of revolution acquired central significance while the actual revolutionary events and personalities receded into the background. The Blanquists' transfer of emotional involvement from past revolutions to current festivals was symptomatic of their loss of faith in the prospect of revolution. As young men the Blanquists claimed to be demythologizers of religion in the name of the new science. Now they demythologized their own revolutionary tradition in the name of the new politics. The irony was that, as their belief in revolution waned, they simultaneously made of their revolutionary creed a formalized cult, systematized through intricate rites and legends. In the exchange of inspired activism for passive witness, the Blanquists followed

22. A republican ceremony honoring the anniversary of Baudin's death at his monument in the Montmartre cemetery: the taming of the legend of Baudin. Phot. Bibl. Nat.

the route once traveled by Auguste Comte, for which they had once ridiculed him so thoroughly.

The waning appeal of the politics of anniversary remembrance as a means of reawakening revolutionary sentiment became apparent in a ceremony marking the transfer of the remains of Alphonse Baudin from the Montmartre cemetery to the Pantheon in 1889.[65] His legend, too, had been made respectable. Once the symbol of the inspired rebel for the outcasts of the Second Empire, Baudin had at last become a symbol of the moderate republican consensus for the Establishment of the Third Republic. The revolutionary rhetoric had not changed, but it was time-worn—so much so that it was no longer clear what his admirers were trying to remember.

CHAPTER VII

The Boulangist Movement and the Death of Blanquist Ideology

The politics of anniversary remembrance led the Blanquists into new causes; it also lured them into a lost cause, specifically, that of Gen. Georges Boulanger. Apologists for the Blanquists still betray uneasiness when discussing Blanquist involvement in the Boulangist movement. The movement was narrowly identified by its critics with the thwarted ambitions of its leader, whose campaign, it was revealed in the aftermath of the legislative elections of the fall of 1889, had been secretly and lavishly funded by a monarchist camarilla which hoped to use it to prepare the way for restoration of the Orleanist dynasty. Its left-wing participants, whatever their motives for affiliation, were all to some degree tainted by the scandal and became easy targets for censure by comrades who prided themselves on their republican orthodoxy.[1] Historians sympathetic to the Blanquists, accepting rather uncritically this interpretation of Boulangism as a right-wing conspiracy, have minimized the Blanquists' involvement in an effort to preserve an image of their integrity as a revolutionary party. Ernest Granger's biographer, Wladimir Martel, therefore draws a distinction between Boulangists and Rochefortists, contending that Granger and his band campaigned with the Boulangists in the legislative elections of 1889 only out of loyalty to Rochefort.[2]

Such casuistry only obscures the facts, which are not in dispute. From June 1888 through January 1889, Granger, Vaillant, and a Blanquist staff edited two newspapers, first _L'homme libre_ and subsequently _Le cri du peuple_, with Rochefort's funds. In the autumn of 1889, Granger and the Blanquist faction which remained loyal to him divided the electoral districts of Paris with the Boulangists in preparation for the legislative elections. Five Blanquist candidates stood for the Chamber of Deputies (Granger, Roche, Place, Eli May, and Susini), of whom two (Granger and Roche) were elected. The campaign was conducted with the benevolent approval of the Committee of National Protest, the Boulangist headquarters.[3]

Blanquist allegiance to Boulangism, therefore, is not at issue. What has been called into question is the interpretation of the Boulangist movement as a monarchist front. Recent scholarship has revealed that the popular movement which rallied behind Boulanger was initially one of left-wing protest against the failings of the moderate republican regime, and as such pursued objectives which transcended the personal cause of General Boulanger. The Boulangists called for revision of the Constitution of 1875 in a vague-sounding nationalist program, but their actual grievances were more obviously economic, stemming from the high levels of unemployment which attended stagnating industrial production in many French cities during the mid-1880s. With its radical republican leadership and urban popular following, the Boulangist movement in fact appeared to many contemporary observers to be a configuration of protest not unlike those which had preceded the révolutions of 1830 and 1848. The Blanquists, like other groups on the Left, were therefore disposed to view the movement as a prelude to a more far-reaching revolutionary upheaval.[4]

Moreover, as the Boulangist movement developed, it was conspicuous for its use of techniques of political campaigning which anticipated political practices of the twentieth century. From this perspective, the Boulangist campaign represented France's first experience with the formation of a mass political movement. The Blanquists had been experimenting with new methods for crowd mobilization. But the Boulangists surpassed these efforts by demonstrating not only how the Parisian populace could be momentarily roused but also how its interest might be sustained in broader patterns of political involvement. The distinguishing feature of the Boulangist movement was the capacity of its leaders to channel popular unrest into a powerful political organization capable of challenging the moderate republican Opportunists on their own parliamentary ground.[5] The Boulangist campaign thus clarified Blanquist conceptions about the changing character of the political process, conceptions toward which the Blanquists had only been groping, and forced them to confront the problem of the ambiguous relationship between the new tactics and the old rituals which they had incongruously conjoined in the politics of anniversary remembrance. It was the very prob-

lem which would soon bring Blanquist leaders to the impasse in
which their party was to disintegrate.

It is not especially surprising, therefore, that the Blanquists
should have found the Boulangist movement so intriguing. First,
there were populist affinities. Blanquists and Boulangists borrowed from the same ideological sources. The themes of attack
upon Opportunist politicians loudly voiced by the Blanquists—
for ill-advised imperialist adventures, pork-barrel politics, and
financial conflicts of interest—were essentially the same as those
now pronounced by Boulangist leaders, who emerged out of the
ranks of left-wing radicalism. The Blanquists, therefore, genuinely sympathized with the causes championed by the Boulangist
leaders, for they had themselves backed the same causes for the
better part of the decade: rejection of the selfish and at times
venal practices of parliamentary government, defense of the republic against royalism at home and abroad, and demands for
constitutional revision to promote national unity and a more
democratic republic. The fact that these issues were now presented under the Boulangist banner did little to change the character of a struggle in which radicals and Blanquists had joined
forces in strikes, electoral campaigns, and protest demonstrations countless times before. In some instances, Boulangist leaders had even provided the Blanquists with direct support. Alfred
Naquet, Boulanger's principal advisor, had been a leading figure
in the campaign for amnesty for the Communards. Georges
Laguerre, a talented young lawyer who figured prominently in
Boulanger's entourage, had defended Blanquist workers and
other left-wing dissidents under indictment for political crimes.[6]
Blanquists and Boulangists may have found their way into the
republican opposition of the 1880s by different routes, but they
sounded the same populist themes of protest.[7]

Second, the Blanquists were less interested in Boulanger the
man than in his legend, whose political appeal was surprisingly
similar to that of Blanqui. Both names evoked wide acclaim as
symbols of radical republican protest. From the Blanquist viewpoint, the electoral campaign on behalf of Boulanger in 1888
bore a certain resemblance to that on behalf of Blanqui in 1879, a
resemblance all the more striking as revisionism replaced revolution as the watchword of Blanquist politics. In each case, an
urban protest movement campaigned under the banner of an
aggrieved hero to promote a larger issue: in 1879, with Blanqui
for amnesty for the Communards; in 1888, with Boulanger for

constitutional reform. Both movements singled out a moderate
republican statesman for vilification: in the former instance Léon
Gambetta; in the latter, Jules Ferry. Both movements mounted
campaigns of electoral protest which promoted solidarity among
a broad array of radical, socialist, and revolutionary groups, a
solidarity made possible by an overriding vision of the republic
transformed. Both enjoyed the tacit support of right-wing parties, and both launched frontal attacks upon parliamentary government in the hope of remodeling it to serve a democratized
political process. Whatever Boulanger's personal ambitions, his
radical subalterns made of him a folk hero, and the Blanquists
were genuinely impressed with the popular enthusiasm which
was engendered by his name. Lionized by the Paris crowd, he
presented an embarrassment to the Opportunists and, given the
proper circumstances, a potential force in a broader challenge to
Opportunist political domination. It was not apparent to the
Blanquists at the outset that his personal cause might outrun
the populist one for which he was a figurehead.[8]

Nor did the Blanquists believe they had changed their goals in
supporting Boulanger. Boulanger's campaign seemed but one
response to a potentially revolutionary situation, evidence of
which was readily apparent in the wave of strikes and other
disturbances which had proliferated since the Decazeville uprising of 1886. Involvement in Boulangist politics promised to
give the Blanquists one more access route to popular agitation.
Even at the height of Boulanger's electoral plebiscite in the summer of 1888, the Blanquists preferred to see the strike of the
Parisian construction workers as the more serious threat to the
government's power, and it was upon that agitation that the
Central Revolutionary Committee concentrated its efforts.[9]

From the Blanquist vantage point, the makings of a revolutionary situation had been more obviously present in the crisis
surrounding the election of the president of the Republic in late
November 1887. There the Blanquists rather than the Boulangists had played the decisive role. More important, the presidential crisis enabled the Blanquists to revisit the fantasies of revolution of their youth, which had to some degree been overshadowed by the reformist requirements of populist politics. In all its
ingredients, the presidential crisis conformed to the Blanquists'
expectations of what a revolutionary situation could be. It presented a moral issue of seemingly vast proportions in the Wilson
scandal, the egregious example of Opportunist corruption which

had necessitated the special election. In the leading aspirant for office, Jules Ferry, it also presented the villain of the siege of 1870—whom the Blanquists had held responsible then for the famine at Paris and whom they held accountable now for France's subservience to Germany in European affairs. With senators and deputies gathering at Versailles to elect the new president, the setting itself recalled for the Blanquists the confrontation between the "two nations" represented by Paris and Versailles on the eve of the Commune.[10]

Under the circumstances, the Blanquists harked back to an interpretation of the probable course of events which they had not invoked since 1871. With a sense of the imminence of "revolutionary days," the Central Revolutionary Committee laid plans to proclaim the Commune at Paris once again, should Ferry be chosen. A round-the-clock vigil was maintained by the Blanquists to monitor the deliberations at Versailles. Socialists and left-wing radicals from all quarters of the city offered their support, and a Blanquist-inspired vigilance committee, the League for the Defense of the Republic, was established to coordinate resistance among these groups. Even left-wing members of the Paris Municipal Council endorsed the cause. The Blanquists gathered arms and explosives at the committee's headquarters and advised revolutionary groups in Paris and some provincial cities to be ready to go out into the streets on signal from the league. The keystone of the operation was a plan for the occupation of City Hall by Emile Eudes and select Blanquist militants if Ferry should be chosen.[11]

When Ferry was passed over for another candidate, Eudes claimed that the Opportunists' designs had been thwarted by their fear of a Blanquist-inspired insurrection.[12] Yet his remarks convey an air of the mock-heroic nostalgia for barricades which had pervaded the frenetic activities of the Blanquists from the outset. The Blanquists' capacity to rouse public opinion did indirectly affect the outcome of the crisis through the pressure it brought to bear on the delegates at Versailles. But this last day of the revolutionary days of the nineteenth century only underscored the distance between the highly ritualized tactics of the revolutionary tradition and the highly experimental practices of modern politics, which could no longer rely exclusively upon the drama of an uprising at Paris. Rather, the preparations of November 27 provided the most grandiose festival of anniversary remembrance of the decade, and it is in this context that its relevance to the Boulangist movement becomes clear. The central significance of Blanquist vigilance in the presidential crisis was to alert Boulangist leaders to the prominent role played by the Blanquists as guardians of the revolutionary tradition in left-wing politics in Paris. The Boulangists began to court Blanquist leaders in the hope that their sympathy would lend support to the Boulangist cause within those circles. The Blanquists, on the other hand, believed they could use the Boulangists to further their own cause.

It was the Boulangists who in the spring of 1888 made the first overtures. Rochefort, now Boulanger's stalwart supporter and most effective propagandist, acted as intermediary. In early March 1888, Eudes and Boulanger dined together, and a deal for a joint political strategy was negotiated. The terms of the compact appeared to offer the Blanquists considerable advantages without demanding a great deal in return. Rochefort placed funds at their disposal to launch the newspaper they had so long coveted. All that was required of the Blanquist editors was a promise that they refrain from criticizing General Boulanger. Such a condition appeared to the Blanquists to present no special difficulty. They expected to use the paper to carry on their quarrel with the Possibilists with more sustained venom, an enterprise they assumed could be undertaken without addressing the Boulangist question directly.[13]

Time was to show that this seemingly harmless fellow-traveling would cost considerably more than anticipated. As Boulanger worked his political magic across France in the spring and summer of 1888, the hitherto diffuse currents of unrest polarized around him. Under the circumstances it became difficult for the Blanquists to draw the line between benevolent neutrality and complicity in Boulanger's campaign. With Boulanger's stunning electoral victory at Paris in January 1889, it was clear that the man had outdistanced the movement. At that point, Edouard Vaillant, who had long expressed reservations about the Boulangist venture, voiced his fears about the Caesarist dangers inherent in the Boulangist cause.[14] It was ironic that the most ardent advocate among the Blanquists of the new politics should have been the first to recoil from its implications when these were revealed in the Boulangist movement. In a curious way, Vaillant's behavior invites comparison with Gustave Tridon's nearly two decades before. In the last days of the Commune, Tridon, the ideologist, had been repulsed by the political excesses of comrades who claimed to be invoking his creed. Now, in the last days of the Boulangist crisis, Vaillant the pragmatist was shocked that his call for political experimentation could have caused his comrades to lose all sense of proportion concerning the kind of politics a revolutionary could authentically support.

With the coming of the legislative elections of 1889, the fiction of a parallel but separate campaign became impossible to maintain. When Henri Rochefort announced his candidacy in the Père-Lachaise ward of the twentieth arrondissement of Paris, the Central Revolutionary Committee was forced to make a decision. The Blanquist debt to Rochefort was substantial, but official support for Rochefort could only be interpreted as an overt endorsement of the Boulangist movement. That far some Blanquist leaders, notably Vaillant and Chauvière, were unwilling to go. Unable to find a basis for compromise, the party split into independent factions on the eve of the election. Vaillant's group retained the title Central Revolutionary Committee (CRC). But most of the old guard followed Granger into the Socialist Revolutionary Central Committee (Comité Central Socialiste Révolutionnaire)—CCSR—and the majority of the subcommittees remained loyal to them.[15] There was a final irony in the fact that the quarrel which dissolved the Blanquist confraternity arose over an election in the most sacred space of the revolutionary hearth, the Père-Lachaise quarter.

It was fitting, therefore, that the schism should have been made manifest in a last ritual confrontation at the Père-Lachaise cemetery on the occasion of the commemoration of Bloody Week, May 25, 1890. As Granger and his band approached Blanqui's grave that morning, Vaillant and his contingent barred their path. Across Blanqui's tomb, the former comrades glared at each other, until Granger diverted his group to the wall of the *fédérés*. But there another CRC contingent awaited them. The standoff became a scuffle, and in the ensuing melee Emile Rouillon, one of Granger's aging subordinates, was struck so forcefully with a cane that he had to be carried from the field.[16] Rouillon lay incapacitated for three months, then died, CCSR leaders claimed, from the blows he had received at Père-Lachaise.[17] Rouillon had been a relatively obscure member of the Blanquist party, but his companions decided to pay him a hero's tribute by erecting a monument to his memory.[18] Their mourning, it was clear, was not only for Rouillon, but also for the Blanquist traditions whose death knell had been sounded in the "battle of Père-Lachaise."

The Blanquists had embarked upon the Boulangist adventure hoping it would be a prelude to a larger revolutionary crisis. Instead, it signaled the demise of the revolutionary consensus upon which the politics of anniversary remembrance had been predicated. In its origins, the Boulangist movement promised to rekindle revolutionary fervor by restating Jacobin values in a populist idiom. Yet, in its denouement, the movement proved to be less an extension of the revolutionary tradition than a response to its decline. In ideology it adumbrated a new, more aggressive brand of nationalism than that identified with the revolutionary movement earlier in the century. In methods it provided a new kind of political experience which offered an alternative not only to parliamentary elitism but also to popular insurrection. The Boulangist campaign thus revealed the limits of the politics of anniversary remembrance in an age of mass politics. It suggested that the popular insurrection upon which Blanquists of both factions had based their hopes was unlikely to materialize in the foreseeable future. At the same time, it made clear that parliament need not be dominated by oligarchies, as it had been historically, but was capable of being adapted to the needs of democratic political movements.[19]

The Boulangist crisis, therefore, was the crucial event for the Blanquists in their transition from a style favoring popular agitation to one favoring political participation. The Blanquist involvement in the Boulangist campaign thus served as a model for the taming of the revolutionary movement at large to the parliamentary process. But that involvement also brought to the surface fundamental differences among Blanquist militants over the meaning and matter of revolutionary action, differences which became evident in the exchange between Vaillant and Granger following the schism. Granger argued that the political insight which had led the Blanquists to make common cause with the Boulangists was essentially sound. Despite Boulanger's questionable ambitions, he asserted, the Boulangist movement did represent a genuine expression of popular discontent with Opportunist political oppression; and, in light of the tactics pursued by the Blanquists since the founding of the CRC, it was appropriate for them to associate themselves with that agitation. In Granger's mind, the Blanquists' participation in the Boulangist crisis had answered Vaillant's plea that revolutionary agitation be conducted on a broader plane, even though a popular revolution had not followed from it in the manner they had originally anticipated.[20]

Vaillant, in contrast, contended that the Boulangist crisis made manifest the inadequacy of the Blanquist mode of agitation in the modern age. He challenged the assumption upon which their rituals of remembrance and all the activities extending from them had been founded: namely, that the values of the revolutionary movement were best rejuvenated, and its objectives best pursued, by more demonstrative tactics. For some time he had been growing less patient with what he considered the quaint obsession of Granger and other veteran militants with anniversary marches, solicitations for memorial monuments, and other theatrical activities which served to deepen the mythology of the revolutionary tradition. After five years of experience with the day-to-day realities of municipal government in Paris, he was disposed to find questions of political reform more practical than festive. Hence one of the first acts of the CRC reconstituted was to declare an end to all demonstrations of anniversary remembrance, save two to commemorate the founding and the fall of the Commune.[21]

The exchange between Vaillant and Granger goes to the heart of the dilemma of the Blanquists in seeking to reconcile ritual and improvisation in a politics which could link past and present conceptions of revolution. Vaillant correctly observed that, despite the democratization of the Blanquist party, the principles upon which its activities were based remained rooted in an earlier age when urban riot still had efficacy. But in disassociating his faction from the ritualism of the Blanquist movement, he tacitly abandoned the Hébertist ideology it symbolized. Granger, on the other hand, accurately surmised that Boulanger's electoral campaign offered a means of challenging the elitist style of parliamentary politics which had so long frustrated the ambitions of the revolutionary movement. Through its participation in the Boulangist electoral campaign, however, his group was for all practical purposes absorbed into the Boulangist cause. Thus Vaillant and Granger drew conclusions about the nature of revolutionary action which proved to be incompatible as the twentieth century drew nearer. Their acrimonious dialogue revealed in microcosm the disintegration of the revolutionary tradition and set the stage for the realignment of the Left in social democratic and radical nationalist groupings.

In this respect, the debate between Vaillant and Granger is as important for what went unstated, as each chose to emphasize what the other preferred not to discuss. It was in this unspoken domain that each guarded his deeper hopes for the future of revolutionary politics. Granger did not mention ritualism because it was an essential means for expressing his belief in the primacy of ideological renewal as a prerequisite for revolutionary action. For him, the principal legacy of the Boulangist movement was its quest for a coherent vision upon which to found political opposition. If Boulanger's legend no longer inspired popular confidence, if Blanqui's legend might eventually be forgotten, Granger continued to hope for the rebirth of some noble social myth which could inspire revolutionary heroism. The Blanquist creed had already been metamorphosed from Hébertism into populism, and Granger was willing to believe that it could undergo still one more transmutation. Thus he and his followers passed into the nationalist camp in the 1890s with the assurance that they were remaining true to the ethical impulse of Blanquist ideology.

Vaillant, in comparison, was unwilling to acknowledge the lessons he had learned from the Boulangist experience about tactics for radical political action in an urban, industrial society. Despite his attraction to Marxism, he conceived of politics increasingly in terms of practical measures, the efficacy of which the Boulangist movement had revealed. In the course of the decade, he had come to doubt the value of the holistic vision upon which the Blanquists had founded their politics, bound up as it was in fantasies of impending popular insurrection. By the late 1880s, with Blanqui and Eudes gone, he sensed that the distance between himself and the remaining veterans of the early Blanquist combats was so great that he would have to disassociate himself from them.

The Boulangist crisis persuaded Vaillant that Blanquist ideology had become a needless accessory. He still considered himself a Blanquist and a revolutionary, but his position was heretical in its departure from the Blanquist precept that revolutionary action is grounded in the moral energy which ideology inspires. Vaillant rejected this idealist thinking in favor of a determinism which counted less upon human will and more upon the long-range logic of economic change. Shrewdly opportunistic about dealing with immediate problems on a practical basis, he was naively fatalistic in believing that long-range trends pointed inexorably toward the coming of the good society. In this his position was close to that of Jules Guesde and the French Marxists. Vaillant thus charted a revisionist course analogous to that of Eduard Bernstein in Germany, gravitating toward Guesde and Jaurès as part of that convergence of left-wing militants in the Socialist party which began to take shape in the 1890s.

In terms of popular sympathy, Vaillant's dissident CRC met with greater acceptance and electoral success than did Granger's more orthodox faction. In 1893 Vaillant and Emmanuel Chauvière moved from City Hall to the Chamber of Deputies, thus avenging the electoral defeat by their rivals four years before. They were joined there by Eugène Baudin of Vierzon, who had run for office under the sponsorship of the CRC. Moreover, it was Vaillant's group which received the approval of the other socialist organizations. The CRC became a constituent element of the Socialist Union, by which the CCSR was pointedly snubbed.[22] The price of this immersion in the emerging socialist coalition was a loss of the strong sense of moorings which Blanquist ideology had provided. But Vaillant was determined to preserve his reputation as a revolutionary. His departure from the inner circle of the initiated was not so different from that of other militants who had exited before him: Longuet, Rey, Humbert, Casse, Villeneuve, Jaclard, Léonce Levraud, Viette, and Regnard, most of whom resurfaced as radical republicans. His case was exceptional, however, in his decision to take as many of the newcomers to the party with him as he could—a fateful decision, as only his faction ultimately survived to speak for the Blanquists in the unified socialist movement at the turn of the century.

The transformation of Blanquism into a protosocialist sect was given intellectual sanction in Vaillant's writings on the history of the movement. Unable to free his older comrades from their allegiance to the past, he chose to wrest the past from them by redefining the Blanquist heritage in terms of present tasks which, he argued, had passed his former comrades by. Vaillant offered his followers, and the Left generally, a new version of the history of the Blanquist movement, one which minimized the significance of the pantheon of eighteenth-century materialists, the neo-Hébertist atheism of the 1860s, and the youthful sect of the Second Empire which had apotheosized Blanqui. Instead, the Blanquist movement was viewed as a stepping stone from the primitive communism of Blanqui to the scientific communism of Marx, a vision of the past which placed hallowed traditions in the broader perspective of the collectivist cause. Blanqui, who in Tridon's version of the revolutionary movement in the nineteenth century had been cast as the aging sage of a perennial philosophy, was remembered in Vaillant's account as a youthful pioneer of the new socialism.[23]

The surviving Blanquist veterans of the 1860s never forgave him for this. "He was never one of ours," Gaston Da Costa commented derisively. Vaillant, Da Costa claimed, lacked the esprit of French youth formed by the revolutionary tradition, for his youth had been spent in German universities imbibing alien social doctrines.[24] Da Costa's brother Charles was more condemnatory still, accusing Vaillant of having demoralized and divided the Blanquists during the early years of the Third Republic and thereby of having accelerated the decline of their cause.[25] Thus Vaillant was relegated by his former comrades to that lengthening list of infamous Girondins who out of personal ambition had betrayed the revolutionary movement. The most insidious example of the enemy within, it seems, had at last appeared in their own midst. There had been a time when the Blanquists had prided themselves upon their intellectualism above all else. Now they scorned Vaillant as a cunning and deceitful intellectual who had shattered the harmony of the Blanquist vision. To emphasize this point, CCSR leaders drew a contrast between Vaillant and the late Emile Eudes, who was depicted as a simple man of action whose courage and personal magnetism had preserved the Blanquist alliance through many years of trial.[26] But Eudes in death could not provide for the Blanquists what he had provided in life. The mystique of Blanquist comradeship had vanished.

Militants of the CCSR met with little success in the electoral campaigns of the 1890s upon which the Boulangist movement had launched them. The defeat of all thirteen CCSR candidates in the Parisian municipal elections of April 1890 was their first intimation that they were destined to share in Boulanger's downfall, as they had earlier shared in his rise to fame.[27] Discredited by the financial scandal which closed the Boulangist episode, shunned by Vaillant and the Marxist socialists, the CCSR was unable to reestablish its reputation as a revolutionary party and passed into political oblivion before the turn of the century. Granger and Roche served out their terms in the Chamber of Deputies. Indeed, Roche was elected for several consecutive terms of office.[28] But as his party's sole representative, he was essentially an isolated figure, viewed by his colleagues as a maverick.

Some CCSR militants did play a modest role in Parisian municipal politics in the 1890s. David and Breuillé were elected to the City Council in 1893; the latter served for a time as second vice-president. There they supported some of the proposals for urban renewal which had emanated from their populist rhetoric: expanded public transportation, improved hospital services and care for the aged, public housing, public charities, and labor reforms. Once youthful revolutionaries dedicated to civil disobedience, they entered public office in middle age as moderate reformers with a strong sense of civic responsibility.[29]

To refill its depleted ranks, the CCSR tried valiantly for a few years to build a new youth organization, called the Blanquist Youth of Paris. Granger and other militants regularly lectured the recruits on the traditions of their party and the legend of Blanqui.[30] But what had been inspiration for one generation was only inculcation for the next. The Blanquist Youth of Paris was not destined to tap the wellsprings of Hébertist energy anew, and the remnants of the CCSR soon began to scatter. By mid-decade, party leader Ernest Granger was ready to retire to his family's country estate to take up life as a gentleman farmer.[31] In his spare time, he "edited" the papers, correspondence, and manuscripts of his beloved mentor, which he bequeathed to the National Library in 1899. The secret history of the Blanquist movement, once feared by officialdom as a subversive influence, thus became a public record. But so badly did Granger muddle the organization of the documents, on the pretext of editing them, that historians have yet to sort them out adequately.[32] One cannot say that the availability of Blanqui's writing clarified the nature of the movement in the late nineteenth century.

However marginal its political role, the CCSR continued to make its influence felt through journalism. *Le ralliement*, published in Lyons in 1890, followed by *Le réveil du peuple*, published in Paris from 1892 through 1894, featured articles by Granger, Place, Roche, Breuillé, Adrien Farjat, and Alexandre Girault. These writers sometimes addressed themselves to contemporary issues, but they were increasingly given to self-conscious and nostalgic reverie about former glories. Reminiscences of Blanqui were overshadowed by sketches of the companions of their youth, especially those who had given their lives in the revolutionary

combats of the Commune. Duval, Genton, Ferré, even the notorious Raoul Rigault were subjects of sympathetic reflection.[33]
Vivid descriptions of the last moments of these martyrs emphasized their courage in facing death as the final test of their commitment. Such recollections seemed to renew the authors' hopes
for the immortality of a movement which appeared to be dying.

It is in this context that Gaston Da Costa presented the series
of articles on Blanquist Communards which would later serve as
the basis of his history of the Commune.[34] And in these circumstances the writings of Gustave Tridon enjoyed a renaissance.
Tridon's essay Les Hébertistes was well-known, having been serial-
ized frequently in the Blanquist press over the years, but much
of his work remained unpublished until the 1880s. His last and
deepest tract, Du Molochisme juif, a study of the roots of Christianity in Semitic religious thought, first appeared in 1884. An anthology of Tridon's political essays, Oeuvres diverses, was published
in 1891 by Dr. Louis Watteau, the old friend who had provided
him and Blanqui asylum in Belgium. Albert Regnard, Tridon's
youthful companion and faithful admirer, edited an essay by
Tridon on political theory, "La Force," for publication in the Revue
socialiste in 1889. About the same time, he offered a ponderous
tome of his own on religious anthropology, Aryens et Sémites: Le
bilan du Judaïsme et du Christianisme, as an exegesis of Tridon's seminal insights on the subject.[35]

In promoting the cult of Tridon's ideology, the leaders of the
CCSR claimed to be acting as guardians of the authentic Blanquist traditions. But Blanquist ideology as expressed by these
militants in the 1890s had clearly undergone some modifications.
If Vaillant turned Blanquist ideology in a Marxist direction, Granger and his companions deflected it onto a nationalist course.
What passed for Blanquist ideology in its CCSR guise in the
1890s was an exaggeration of the populism of the 1880s, a caricature of the Hébertism of the 1870s, and a travesty of the
atheism of the 1860s of which Tridon's authorship had been the
essential formulation.

Nationalism, of course, was not a new idiom for the expression
of Blanquist thought. It had been the first medium for the translation of the young Blanquists' atheist thought into political
terms. On the eve of the Commune, nationalism for the Blanquists had been essentially a doctrine of national liberation, at
one with republicanism and popular democracy, as a basic ideal
of the revolutionary movement. Blanquist nationalism in that

era expressed a genuine sympathy for and solidarity with oppressed people everywhere. The Blanquists regarded the Commune of 1871 as a nationalist uprising which could serve as a model for other peoples. But by 1890, nationalism had acquired more particularistic connotations.

The Blanquists' initial understanding of consciousness as rational insight into material realities, insight presumably open to all men, had been replaced by an appreciation of consciousness as the unique character of the French mind. The revolutionary consciousness manifested in the French revolutionary tradition was not the expression of a universal urge for freedom, but of one peculiar to the French people. Thus the Blanquists of the CCSR formulated an interpretation of their revolutionary heritage not unlike that of German nationalists who described the unification movement in Germany as the liberation of the *Volk*, whose power was derived from its rootedness in the German landscape. Willfulness, once perceived to be a quality of courage, was now conceived as an unconscious psychological imperative, a unique combination of the privileged attributes of the French mind—superior especially, one Blanquist claimed, for its "clarity and gaiety."[36] Such a judgment enabled the Blanquists of the CCSR to contribute to the xenophobic chorus of French nationalists who called for legal restrictions on the number of foreign workers in France.[37] Alfred Gabriel, a leftist deputy from Nancy who had championed this cause during the Boulangist campaign, joined the staff of *Le réveil du peuple* in 1892. Thus the CCSR drifted into a new coalition of radical nationalists including elements of the League of Patriots, the Anti-Semitic League, and populist refugees from the revolutionary movement.[38]

The redefinition of Blanquism as a new nationalism is reflected in the remarks by CCSR spokesmen about Marxist socialism—a subject about which they had, in deference to Vaillant, previously been politely silent. His pride wounded for having been ostracized from the Socialist Union, Granger with his comrades in 1890 for the first time explicitly condemned Marxism as a foreign doctrine alien to the French revolutionary tradition. "Marx and Blanqui were equally great men," Granger conceded, "but as distinct as their two races in their temperaments, their antecedents, and their methods."[39] The rejection of Marxism as an alien German ideology was embarrassingly at odds with the young Blanquists' profession of faith in the German philosopher Ludwig Büchner, whom they had praised as the most important modern theorist of philosophical materialism. But Granger and his comrades were determined to restrict French socialism to its indigenous sources.[40] Their once narrow preoccupation with the Hébertist strand of the revolutionary heritage was now broadened to accommodate their newfound interest in a variety of political and social theories contributing to what they believed was France's unique brand of national socialism, and of which they believed their own party to be a natural expression.

In keeping with the nationalist model, the Blanquists of the CCSR stressed the organic unity of the French revolutionary's conception of community. The essential task, they claimed, was not to engage in class conflict, but to suppress the notion of class altogether. For this reason, they expressed preference for the concept of the "people," as opposed to that of the "working class," in identifying participants in the revolutionary movement. The Blanquists tolerated the term "worker" provided it was used to connote a state of mind rather than a mode of labor. "It is not the métier which makes the worker," Henri Place explained, "but his brain as it moves the tool."[41] Thus the Blanquists of the CCSR reiterated their belief in the didactic role of an intelligentsia in the process of consciousness-raising.

The notion of a French consciousness, initially a cultural concept, was soon to receive a racialist formulation. At a banquet in 1890, Ernest Granger called for solidarity among the Latin races to ward off the threat of Germanization.[42] Yet the more common symbol of the enemy employed by the Blanquists in the 1890s was not the German but the Jew. Anticlericalism had been the cause of contention of the 1860s; anti-Semitism served as its counterpart in the 1890s.

Anti-Semitism was a latent prejudice throughout the history of the Blanquists. From the time of their initial association, their personal correspondence contained occasional and usually offhand comments reflecting hostility toward Jews.[43] But the character of Blanquist anti-Semitism became explicit only with the posthumous publication of Tridon's *Du Molochisme juif* in 1884. Tridon's interest in the Jewish prophetic writings was an extension of his inquiry into Christian origins. He believed that Semitic culture was the source of the religious monotheism which had shaped the pattern of Western civilization for two thousand years. In attacking Judaism as a pernicious cultural force, he thought he was coming to terms with the theodicy problem. Judaism was the deeper source of the evil resulting from the triumph of the Christian world-view in the West. This argument was rather academic even in the 1860s, as only Tridon among Blanqui's followers was sufficiently motivated to deal with the problem of atheism in a larger philosophical context. That, together with the Blanquists' declining interest in the religious question, explains why anti-Semitism failed to assume a prominent place in their vocabulary in the era of the Commune. But the rise of populism in the 1880s cast the Jewish question in a new light for them. In the populist argument, the social question replaced the religious question as the central topic of interest. In its vocabulary, the Jewish financier replaced the Catholic priest as the most convenient personification of evil. The cult of Blanqui had been used by the Guesdists to further the new socialism; the cult of Tridon was similarly employed by the populist anti-Semites to promote the new nationalism. Thus Albert Regnard's *Aryens et Sémites* was not simply an exposition of Tridon's argument, as Regnard claimed, but rather an attempt to redefine Tridon's theology of culture as a science of racism.

Other populist anti-Semites contributed to this reinterpretation of Tridon's thought. Edouard Drumont, the chief apostle of anti-Semitism in France at the end of the nineteenth century, had high praise for Tridon as the only left-wing thinker who understood the relationship between the "social question" and the "Jewish question."[44] Drumont's interpretation was one with which Granger and his staff found themselves surprisingly comfortable, and they fell easily into his mode of parlance. Hence Granger sometimes praised the Aryan genius rather than the French mind when speaking of revolutionary consciousness.[45] The forming of the radical nationalist coalition, moreover, permitted Granger to point out the degree to which Blanquists and anti-Semites pursued a common cause, and even to praise Drumont, Guérin, and Morès as "true socialists and revolutionaries" because of their use of combative rhetoric to win favor among the urban populace.[46] But to reduce revolutionary consciousness to combativeness emptied Blanquist ideology of its intellectual content and reduced it to a simple and highly relativistic doctrine of power. As Gaston Da Costa expressed it so confidently: "Power, in the service of minorities, is the shock force for progress, it is the Revolution; in the service of majorities, it is Reaction. All of Blanquism is contained in this aphorism."[47]

The Blanquists' racialism was reinforced by their susceptibility to the vitalist philosophy so prevalent in France. One could say that the Blanquists of the CCSR moved from a preoccupation with the new politics to an obsession with the new biology. They readily accepted the arguments of those social scientists who tried to derive a model of social change from Darwin's theory of natural selection. The power of a natural life-force in shaping the course of events had considerable appeal to this sect, which anxiously sensed its powerlessness to deal with current political realities. It was easy to immerse the revolutionary movement in a vitalistic determinism. The capacity for revolutionary action, Gaston Da Costa argued, was rooted in a larger life-force.[48]

This stress on external energy as opposed to internal will might appear to have been a betrayal of the Blanquists' earlier insistence upon willful courage. Yet the theme of cosmic energy as the ground of human will had been a muted one in early Blanquist thought; and it was to Tridon's writings that the Blanquists again turned for the necessary text. His essay "La Force" emphasized the correspondence between human and cosmic energy.[49] Tridon envisioned no conflict between human will and the will of nature because from his perspective the essential task of the revolutionary was to overcome the religious illusions which obscured the reality of this correspondence. For Tridon, writing in 1870, the propagation of the doctrine of the energy inherent in the material world was itself an inspiration to activism. But by 1890 his doctrine served rather as an excuse for Blanquist failings. Its discussion by the Blanquists was linked closely to the theme of the decadence of the present age. The Blanquists apologized for their ineffectualness by claiming that the age lacked passion. For the moment, they claimed, they could only wait for revolutionary fervor to be born anew.[50] Thus the Blanquists, once committed to taking advantage of any circumstance which favored revolutionary agitation, now claimed that they had little scope for revolutionary initiative. Such an attitude infused into Blanquist nationalism of the 1890s a brooding pessimism about future prospects. Their image of the 1890s as an age of decline contrasted sharply with Vaillant's confident image of ascent toward a bright socialist future. Militants of the CCSR even lost their confidence in the revolutionary past. Gaston Da Costa, for example, questioned whether the French Revolution had in fact brought about any real change, since it had resulted in the substitution of a bourgeois aristocracy for the feudal one.[51]

As for Blanqui, the passion surrounding his legend had practically disappeared. The Blanquists continued to pay him homage on the anniversary of his death; but the police ceased to monitor these proceedings after 1885, so little was their expectation that the ceremony would inspire a mass gathering.[52] Blanqui's life was commented upon less frequently by his followers. His legend in the 1890s became largely the property of academic literary critics, who discarded his image as a realist in favor of a lyric image, one more likely to inspire reflection than activism. The celebrated biography by Gustave Geffroy was written in this vein.[53] Geffroy portrayed Blanqui as a Promethean figure, the eternal rebel doomed to defeat. Thus Blanqui, who for his followers had been godlike in his power, was in the end characterized by his more distant admirers as a god who died for his ineffectualness.

For Camille Mauclair, reviewing Geffroy's biography in 1897, Blanqui's asceticism was more important than his activism. Mauclair portrayed Blanqui as an essentially spiritual figure whose personal suffering epitomized the suffering of the French people through the ages. He concluded that Blanqui's life was a pilgrimage from struggle to contemplation, with *L'éternité par les astres*, written during his incarceration at Taureau in 1871, his culminating meditation.[54] It was a strange judgment upon a man whose life had been given to active and unrelenting struggle against political oppression. The legend of Blanqui which had inspired a generation of his disciples to accept the ordeal of revolutionary commitment whatever the personal cost came to a disturbingly serene ending. It is on this note that the meaning and legacy of the Blanquist experience must be considered.

CHAPTER VIII

The Blanquists and Style in Revolutionary Politics

This book has traced the fortunes of Auguste Blanqui's followers from the elitist fraternity of their youth to the more democratic, if less cohesive, organization of their maturity. More than the history of a party, it has been a history of the comradeship of a generation of radicals whose revolutionary consciousness was formed through their devotion to the nineteenth century's most dedicated champion of the revolutionary movement in France. Their discipleship was to the man Blanqui, but even more so to his legend, a legend which enabled them to participate vicariously in the historical creation of the revolutionary tradition. Their goal was to translate the ideal of fraternity which they had experienced in their own circle into a wider vision of community, first for the people of Paris, eventually for the people of France. The source of their inspiration was the Revolutionary Commune of 1793, cast in their memories as a community forged through heroic struggle.

In the experience of Hébert, Chaumette, Ronsin, and their followers, the Blanquists discovered an ideal of revolutionary solidarity to which they were determined to return. The revolutionary tradition for these militants was not a historical experience upon which to build but a timeless consciousness waiting to be reawakened. The Blanquists' return to revolutionary precedent, therefore, was also a return to archaic time, where change was measured in terms of recurrent cycles of consciousness recalled out of a primordial golden age. The past, the Blanquists believed, could be relived as well as remembered. The task was to reenter the passions, hopes, and anxieties of revolutionaries who had gone before. To the extent that these emotions could be recaptured, timebound experience could be transcended. More than a method for fomenting popular insurrection, Blanquism was a commitment to revolutionary struggle as a means of consciousness-raising to this timeless plane.

Few contemporary observers outside the Blanquist entourage

appreciated their ideology on this level. For most the Blanquists were simply inveterate conspirators, impatient with doctrine, instinctively conditioned to action. The first commentator to view their ideology with more critical insight was the German Marxist theoretician Eduard Bernstein, who wrote about the Blanquist movement in 1893, around the time of its demise. Bernstein was a "revisionist" Marxist, close to Vaillant in his thinking, and one could have expected that he would laud the course chosen by Vaillant. Instead, he focused on the ideology of the young Blanquists, which he treated with considerable sympathy. He sought to show that they were more than a coterie of conspirators and that there was a deeper, more tendentious purpose beneath their activism. He explained that elemental combativeness for the Blanquists was a source of creativity and praised this capacity in them. In taking advantage of any potentially explosive situation, he claimed, the Blanquists believed they were stimulating an infectious awareness that a sense of community is given to those who engage in revolutionary struggle. Bernstein accurately appraised Blanquist intentions, but with a certain condescension. Like Vaillant, he believed that willfulness counted for little in comparison with larger historical trends. As a paradigm of history, Blanquism in Bernstein's view was theoretically deficient in its neglect of economic considerations. Other facets of the model—the need for some decisive turning point, for example—were for him obviated by the practices of mass politics. The Blanquists might claim to espouse a perennial philosophy, but their doctrine had in fact been rendered obsolete by changing historical necessities.[1]

Bernstein dismissed Blanquist ideology because it failed to conform to the requirements of the Marxist model of development. Yet the Blanquist conception of revolutionary creativity invites an interesting comparison with the young Marx's conception of praxis, a conception with which Bernstein was unfamiliar but which has attracted much attention on the part of Marxist intellectuals in the twentieth century. These theorists have reintroduced into their discussions the heroic dimension of Marx's early writings, carefully excised by nineteenth-century admirers who wanted to make of his doctrine a science of society.[2] The Blanquists never grasped the Hegelian principle of dialectical change upon which Marx's theory of revolution was based, but they were close to the young Marx in their interest in the relationship between willfulness and creativity. Both Marxists and Blanquists shied away from provisional statements about the specific characteristics of the good society toward which they were striving, preferring instead to depict their hopes for its coming in aesthetic images. Hence, the problem of aesthetics counted for a great deal in both ideologies.

It is in their contrasting conceptions of the use of aesthetics that the differences of the two groups concerning the role of creativity in revolutionary change become clear. Whereas the Marxists stressed the importance of creative improvisation in the formation of social consciousness, the Blanquists ascribed to creative endeavor the task of objectifying a preexisting ideal of social harmony. For the Blanquists believed they had discovered the principles governing the social order in the interplay between energy and matter in the natural order. For this reason, they were especially concerned with aesthetic effect as the leaven of revolutionary agitation. Intellectual statement alone was insufficient. The need was to move men to a deeper awareness of the meaning of an idea. Tridon was revered by his companions not because of the force of his intellectual argument (which they believed had been developed by the eighteenth-century materialists), but because of the power of his style. His essay *Les Hébertistes* they judged a masterpiece of literature as well as history because of his ability to create a poetic image of radical revolution which could draw readers to sense its reality. In his friend Regnard's mind, Tridon's greatest achievement was the success of his hard-won striving after stylistic effect.[3] His benefactor, Louis Watteau, likened him to the sixteenth-century critic La Boétie for his capacity to write history in a classical literary idiom.[4]

The Blanquists' passion for great style was not limited to literature. The idea of style was more broadly conceived as an ability to give aesthetic definition to one's values through the quality of one's life experience. Blanqui's life was valued not for his specific accomplishments, but for the authenticity of the style in which he had pursued his ideological commitments. His lifestyle was likened by his followers to a work of art. Herein lies the deeper meaning of his legend, which enshrined his pilgrimage through life as a way of life worthy of imitation. In this sense, revolution for Blanqui's followers was a calling to change the world by first changing themselves. Duval, Ferré, Rigault, and Eudes, the "immortals" of the Blanquist circle, were honored by their comrades for the style with which they had persevered in their commitments, even in the face of death. Because of their reverence for style, the Blanquists needed not only to project their vision whole, but also to experience it concretely. This accounts for their determination through the years to give their ideology a ritual expression: ritual was a means of making explicit in aesthetic images the style of their revolutionary calling. The Blanquists engaged in rituals from the outset of their association, at first in simple ceremonies almost unknowingly, in time in elaborate festivals quite self-consciously. The forms varied, depending upon the occasion. But in the ensemble of their imagery they provided a typology of revolutionary experience. Whether associated with festivals of victory, the pageantry of revolutionary combat, or the elegy of martyrdom and defeat, all were designed to satisfy their unstated need for graphic tableaux with which to appeal to popular emotions.

The irony was that the more stylized these rites became, the less ideological conviction they seemed to convey. Blanquist ideology was predicated on a belief in the transparent interchange of idea and action, and the Blanquists never abandoned their conviction that ceremony was for that reason valuable and renewing. In the early years following the Commune, the rituals commemorating the revolutionary tradition exercised great power of appeal, and the Blanquists, thoroughly involved in orchestrating them, briefly enjoyed a stature disproportionate to their numbers. But the creative energy the group sought to unleash for the revolutionary cause through ceremonial gesture was eventually diminished in this exchange of content for form, enthusiasm for routine, improvisation for imitation. For an ideology which inspired its adherents to seek revolution as if it were a rendezvous with the apocalypse, Blanquism through the years suffered a steady attenuation.

Eduard Bernstein and other Marxist critics blamed this trend on the intellectual inadequacy of Blanquist ideology, the principles of which were undermined by the popularization of the scientific principles of Marxist socialism.[5] But to give the Blanquists their due, their ideology must be evaluated not only in terms of the model of linear progress of the Marxist historians, but also in terms of the cyclical view of history from which their own idea of revolution was derived. For this reason, this book has been concerned not only with the Blanquists' efforts to enliven their ideology, but also with their changing perception of its meaning. Not only did they advance a cyclical interpretation of history; their understanding of their own ideology developed full circle. They repeatedly returned to the same mythic paradigm in their periodic restatement of their revolutionary ideal, an ideal whose evolution has been traced here from its first expression as a philosophy of atheism to its final elaboration as a theory of biological determinism.

The Blanquists' conception of revolution assumed many forms as their interests changed and as new realities forced new considerations upon them. With some ingenuity, they transformed their initial philosophical interest (radical atheism) into a political interest (Communard nationalism), then into a socioeconomic interest (Boulangist populism), and finally into a biological interest (vitalist determinism). Through each metamorphosis, the Blanquist paradigm of the revolutionary struggle conformed to the same conceptual structure; but each time it was adorned with a fresh vocabulary and publicized with diminished confidence. By the 1870s, Blanquist ideology had acquired a decorative appeal for a substantial portion of the French Left. But as the vocabulary of the Blanquists grew ever more remote from their initial insight into the revolutionary implications of atheism, their model of revolution became less useful as a basis for practical action in the world. Hence they retreated from enthusiastic participation in the present world to the formalized imitation of past experience in an artificial world of their own making.

Determined initially to project the Parisian revolution outward upon France and Europe, the Blanquists finally internalized their conception of revolution to such an extent that it hardly touched anyone beyond their own circle. At the time of the Boulangist crisis, a major faction of the party decided to discard Blanquist ideology altogether because of the illusionary spell with which it obscured present problems. In keeping with the Blanquists' fondness for cyclical history, it was appropriate for them to hope that 1893, the centennial of the birth of Hébertist ideology, would also mark its revival. But by the turn of the century, the power of the legend of Blanqui to command respect for the revolutionary tradition appears to have been spent. The new socialism, the issue of a new paradigm, had clearly won the day.

It was in this setting that another Marxist critic, Georges Sorel, offered his judgment of Blanquist ideology. Sorel was close in attitude to the Blanquists of the CCSR in his preoccupation with the power of social myth. He might have been expected to view Blanquist ideology sympathetically, given his interest in the creative sources of revolutionary activism. Yet he had surprisingly little use for the Blanquists as mythmakers. He denied not only the present power of their revolutionary ideology, but even its historical source, their mythology of the French Revolution of 1793. Sorel was skeptical that the legend of the revolutionary tradition had inspired real political or social change during the nineteenth century and scoffed at the Blanquists, its leading apostles, for their worship of a revolution he claimed had never taken place.[6]

Eduard Bernstein believed in the coming of a classless society through the inexorable logic of historical development. With special attention to Blanquist beginnings, he criticized Blanquist ideology because it did not serve the needs of the Marxist conception of history. Sorel believed in the coming of a new social myth born of present necessities which would move men to revolutionary fervor anew. With a disdainful survey of the Blanquists' decline, he judged them harshly for their inability to translate their rituals of revolution into effective political action. Each judged Blanquist ideology to be a perennial philosophy, and therefore lacking as a conception of revolutionary change. But Blanquist ideology can also be evaluated as a movement of belief in light of the historical experience of those revolutionaries who chose to commit themselves to it.

If there is a pattern to the evolution of the Blanquist vision, it is to be discovered in this religious context. The Blanquists' journey through a generation of revolutionary activism was a passage from faith in their revolutionary calling to skepticism about its efficacy. Its stages are easily plotted: from the enthusiastic convictions of the youth of the 1860s, to the piety of the young men of the 1870s, to the ceremonial formalism of the middle-aged men of the 1880s, to the doubts of the old men of the 1890s. In the beginning, the Blanquists spoke as skeptics yet silently behaved as believers in the revolutionary power of their materialist cosmology; in the end, they vaunted their belief in the coming of revolution yet in their hearts questioned their own power to achieve even reformist ends. In this way, they did live out their cyclical vision of history. It was not in the logic of a law of history, but in the logic of their self-conceptions that their revolutionary activity came full circle; for their vision of revolution evoked not a state of affairs but a state of mind. In the ideal of fraternity to which they held fast through all the transmutations of their doctrine, they sought a timeless ground of revolutionary consciousness which it would always be possible, given the will and the courage, to recall. Their quest for community was at its deepest level a quest for immortality.

This quest reveals the essentially religious character of the Blanquists' revolutionary endeavor. A group which dedicated itself to such a complete and unrelenting attack on Christian religious doctrine could not avoid imitating its conceptual structure. Blanquist atheism in Tridon's writings was not unlike a profane inversion of the Augustinian doctrine of grace and election. The rituals of the politics of anniversary remembrance, especially the rites of passage, were strikingly close in format to those of Catholic religious observance.[7] Yet not only in its rituals and dogmas did the religious character of Blanquist ideology reside. It was derived especially from the call to courage—the risk toward self-transcendence—which was the inspiring purpose behind the legend of Blanqui.[8] The appeal of Blanqui to the republican youth of the 1860s who chose to follow him was in the challenge of a heroic and idealistic way of life and accounts for the martial tone in which they tried to convey its meaning. The revolutionary commitment, however, proved to be an especially difficult act of faith, with its open-ended demands for perseverence in a relentless crusade.

Herein lies the source of the erosion of the Blanquists' revolutionary conviction. The problem was not their disenchantment with their model of revolution considered as an intellectual construct. To the contrary, they proved resilient in their capacity to restate their conception of revolution in new vocabularies designed to address new problems. Bernstein's charge that the Blanquist model lacked a basis for theoretical elaboration underestimated its possibilities. Rather, it was the Blanquist goal of inspired community which was extreme and unyielding. In their claim that revolutionary will alone could make such a community a reality, the Blanquists set themselves a task which promised adventure in a high calling but which was vulnerable to great disappointment. The crucial test for the Blanquists in this respect was the Siege of Paris of 1870, in which they and other advocates of a staunch defense were overwhelmingly outmatched militarily by the Prussians and excluded politically by moderates within the provisional government.

Historians have praised Blanqui's daily call to battle in the columns of *La patrie en danger* and have not ceased to speculate about the difference his participation in the Commune might have made in promoting more energetic combat and in inspiring moral courage.[9] But there is a point at which the call to courage becomes a temptation to fantasy. In clinging to a myth of the Commune's enduring viability in the face of its obvious failings, the Blanquists passed the frontier into that imaginary land wherein they could fulfill the aspirations of their aesthetic reverie free of the intrusion of harsh realities.[10] Such fantasies were far from innocuous, as the arbitrary and capricious looting and executions carried out in the name of the Hébertist ideal by Rigault, Ferré, and their subordinates in the last days of the Commune attest. The evil worked by the pursuit of religious illusion had been a cardinal tenet of the Blanquists' indictment of Christianity. The fact that they failed to recognize evil's presence in their pursuit of their own illusions does not lessen its reality. What had begun as a risk toward self-transcendence eventually became a denial of its possibility. It was this glorification of violence in the name of highly abstract, internalized ideals which provides the analogy between Blanquist ideology and fascist doctrines in the twentieth century—as much as the specific points of "national socialist" doctrine which the Blanquists extolled in their declining years.[11]

The nature of the Blanquists' pursuit placed them not only on the extreme fringe of revolutionary politics, but also on the extreme fringe of social understanding. It is in this context that their ideal of fraternity must be evaluated. In their conceptions of the good society, most men settle for the comic mean of sociable relations, where obligations are often ambiguously understood yet easily satisfied. The Blanquists preferred the tragic extreme of social virtue, where commitments are clearly defined but difficult to fulfill. Like the artist David, whose sketches of 1793 they valued so much, the Blanquists wanted images which were pure and sharply etched. Whereas such images seemed a sound basis for comradeship in the well-defined world of Second Empire realism, they became an impossible foundation for community amid the blurred forms of Third Republic impressionism, where political realities were more complex and ideological issues more confusing.

The disintegration of the Blanquist party in the face of the new politics in the late nineteenth century does not mean that Blanquist ideology was without a legacy for French politics in the twentieth. Just as the legend of Blanqui still appeals to a wide

audience with only the most tenuous identification with his commitments, so too has Blanquist ideology continued to exercise
varied if increasingly diffuse influences. It is a legacy which has
been felt at both ends of the political spectrum. Most of the early
historical writing on the Blanquist legacy focused on the assimi-
lation of the Blanquists into the socialist movement at the end of
the nineteenth century. Blanquist ideology was treated as one
among many historical sources blended in modern French socialist thought. The expectation underlying these histories was
that the various revolutionary factions of the nineteenth century
would fuse into a unified movement in the twentieth as the
principles of Marxism were amalgamated with those of the
French Jacobin inheritance.[12] Accordingly, Edouard Vaillant's
role as theorist received far more attention than did that of
Tridon or other intellectuals identified with the Blanquist
cause.[13] But the contribution of Vaillant to the theory and practice of the Socialist party in the early twentieth century, as important as it may have been on its own terms, was but a pale and
diluted version of anything the Blanquists had actually advocated in their heyday.

The long-range significance of the Blanquist contribution to
the socialist movement, moreover, can be questioned, given the
deep and enduring split of the revolutionary movement into
socialist and communist branches since 1920. Insofar as Blanquist thought has continued to influence this milieu, its impact
has been upon the Communist, not the Socialist, party. The
Socialist party since 1920 has followed a course toward parliamentary social democracy which has little to do with Blanquist
ideology. It is not surprising that Léon Blum, leader of the Socialist party during the interwar years, often referred to the
communists pejoratively as latter-day Blanquists.[14] The influences of the Blanquists upon the French Communist party are,
of course, somewhat remote, in that they were transmitted via
the Bolsheviks and the experience of the Russian Revolution of
October 1917. Still, the revolutionary methods of Blanqui and
his youthful entourage of the 1860s did in the 1920s and 1930s
find resonances in the methods of the French Communist party,
which likewise valued the elitist comradeship of the revolutionary party and which adopted many of the trappings of secrecy
and sectarianism characteristic of the Blanquist organization.[15]

In this respect, the Communist party's ambition to become a
"countersociety in miniature" is close to the Blanquist concep-

tion of the revolutionary party as an expanding fraternity of like-minded members. Parallels can also be drawn between the Blanquists of the 1880s and the communists of the 1930s in their common determination to maintain their autonomy as close-knit parties while exerting their influence upon broader popular movements. The communists' role in the Popular Front of 1936, like the Blanquists' role in the Boulangist movement of 1889, was based on a strategy designed to free them of their sectarianism without requiring them to sacrifice their identity to the larger cause.[16] Poignant, too, is the way the Communist party looked upon the Bolshevist Revolution as a moral touchstone, much as the Blanquists looked upon the Commune a half-century before.[17]

In terms of direct influences, however, Blanquist ideology made its most immediate impact on the political Right. Granger and his faction popularized a doctrine which remained revolutionary in its extremist rhetoric and combative methods but which had become thoroughly conservative in its values. The intellectual evolution of Granger, Place, Breuillé, and the Blanquist old guard from the Hébertism of their student years to the nationalism of their mature years reveals a pattern of thought through which many Jacobins passed in their migration from the revolutionary Left to the revolutionary Right in the late nineteenth century. As fellow travelers with Rochefort, Paul Déroulède, Maurice Barrès, and the Boulangist radicals, the Blanquists became spokesmen for a point of view which sustained the radical Right during the Dreyfus affair and which anticipated fascist thought in the twentieth century.[18] As a contribution to revolutionary thought, this legacy of the Blanquists, unsavory as it may be, ought not to be minimized. For in many ways, it was the Right, refurbished with a militant nationalist ideology and a belligerent political style, which emerged as the more revolutionary force in France in the years between the first and second world wars. Nationalism, more than Marxism, was the ideology which threatened French democratic political institutions during this era.

Blanquist ideology, therefore, has bequeathed a mixed legacy to the present age. Yet the lasting significance of Blanquist thought is derived not only from its legacy but also from the insights it offers into the workings of the archaic revolutionary mentality. That mentality, as shown here, exhibited a profound fascination with pristine origins and hence drew deeply upon the values identified with the birth of the revolutionary movement in France in the late eighteenth century. As long as these values remained a vital resource for the revolutionary movement, as they did well into the nineteenth century, the Blanquists were able to identify with forces seeking to change French political institutions. But as the French revolutionary tradition ceased to inspire revolutionary action in a practical way after the fall of the Commune, the Blanquists were obliged to internalize these values in the rituals of anniversary remembrance, and to pursue a politics which depended less upon changing political institutions than upon manipulating mass emotions. The Blanquist conception of revolution, therefore, passed from a creative to a destructive expression in the midst of the changing realities of the late nineteenth century. As the French Left lost interest in its revolutionary heritage as a model for change, the Blanquists lost sight of the essential insight of their youth into the paradox of revolutionary leadership: that the authentic leader must serve rather than direct the people he hopes to inspire.

Despite the declining influence of the Blanquists in French revolutionary politics, their very effort to resist that decline accounts for the enduring relevance of their conception of revolution in the contemporary age beyond the French frontier. For Blanquist politics was intimately tied to the problem of renewing and sustaining revolutionary zeal, and, in the twentieth century, this has often been the most pressing problem facing revolutionary leaders. The need to keep alive the élan of the revolutionary experience in the aftermath (or sometimes the absence) of the revolutionary event has prompted many twentieth-century revolutionaries to revisit the historical circumstances which first defined their struggle. The Cultural Revolution of Mao Tsetung is a conspicuous example of such endeavor, as are the attempts of leaders of various nations of the Third World to resurrect their deep cultural heritage as a foundation, first for revolt against colonialism, and subsequently for postrevolutionary reconstruction.[19]

From this perspective, the movement of national liberation of the "real country" from the "legal country" championed by the Blanquists in nineteenth-century France has prefigured the movements of national liberation of the peoples of Africa and Asia from their colonial overlords in the twentieth century.[20] The power of such movements to appeal to tradition as a basis for change belies the argument that Blanquist conceptions, in the longings they express for a past of primordial simplicity, have since been transcended by more sophisticated ones. Blanquist attitudes were derived from an archaic revolutionary mentality; but they have nonetheless been restated in the contemporary world in even more strident terms.[21] The Blanquists, like many of their present-day counterparts, were idealists—at once simple, naive, and credulous—driven to despair by their experiences with the complexities of the modern world. If the archaic revolutionary mentality from which such idealism was derived is destined eventually to disappear from the earth, it promises to do so slowly, and with the same determined resistance once exhibited by the followers of Blanqui.

Notes

Chapter I

1. André Siegfried, *Tableau des partis en France* (Paris, 1930), pp. 57-80; David Thomson, *Democracy in France since 1870*, 5th ed. (Oxford, 1969), pp. 9-18; Alice Gérard, *La Révolution Française: Mythes et interprétations, 1789-1970* (Paris, 1970), pp. 11-64; Patrick H. Hutton, "Vico's Theory of History and the French Revolutionary Tradition," *Journal of the History of Ideas*, 37 (1976), 253-256; Jean Touchard, *La Gauche en France depuis 1900* (Paris, 1977), pp. 20-24.

2. Robert R. Palmer, *The Age of the Democratic Revolution* (Princeton, 1964), II, 30, 49-50; Isser Woloch, *Jacobin Legacy: The Democratic Movement under the Directory* (Princeton, 1970), pp. 11-14; Claude Mazauric, "Quelques voies nouvelles pour l'histoire politique de la Révolution Française," *Annales historiques de la Révolution Française*, 47 (1975), 149-163.

3. Ferdinand Brunot, *Histoire de la langue française des origines à 1900* (Paris, 1937), IX, 654-656, 813-815, 832; Jean Dubois, *Le vocabulaire politique et social en France de 1869 à 1872* (Paris, 1962), pp. 105-106, 327-328.

4. Carlton J.H. Hayes, *The Historical Evolution of Modern Nationalism* (New York, 1931), p. 44; Louis Girard, *Etude comparée des mouvements révolutionnaires en France en 1830, 1848 et 1870-71* (Paris, 1969), p. 51; Albert Soboul, "Tradition et création dans le mouvement révolutionnaire français au XIXᵉ siècle," *Le mouvement social*, 79 (April-June 1972), 22-27; Mazauric, "Quelques voies nouvelles," 162.

5. These remarks are limited to the political meaning of Jacobinism. But Jacobinism had an influence upon various forms of early nineteenth-century French social thought as well; see esp. Leo Loubère, *Louis Blanc: His Life and His Contribution to the Rise of French Jacobin-Socialism* (Evanston, Ill., 1961), pp. 15-21; and George Lichtheim, *The Origins of Socialism* (New York, 1969), pp. 3-82.

6. Hayes, *Historical Evolution of Modern Nationalism*, pp. 43-83; Raoul Girardet, *Le nationalisme français, 1871-1914* (Paris, 1966), pp. 11-14.

7. André-Jean Tudesq, *La démocratie en France depuis 1815* (Paris, 1971), pp. 14-19.

8. *Ibid.*, pp. 29-45; Georges Weill, *Histoire du parti républicain en France, 1814-1870* (Paris, 1928), pp. 403-407; John Plamenatz, *The Revolutionary Movement in France, 1815-71* (London, 1952), pp. 39-41, 48; René Rémond, *La Droite en France de la première restauration à la Vᵉ République* (Paris, 1963), pp. 75-94.

9. Albert Mathiez, "Notes inédites de Blanqui sur Robespierre," *Annales historiques de la Révolution Française*, 5 (1928), 305-321; Soboul, "Tradition et création," 27-28.

10. Soboul, "Tradition et création," 30.

11. Palmer, *Age of the Democratic Revolution*, II, 232-244; R.B. Rose, *Gracchus Babeuf: The First Revolutionary Communist* (Stanford, 1978), pp. 306-328.

12. David Thomson, *The Babeuf Plot: The Making of a Republican Legend* (London, 1947), pp. 52-59.

13. Eduard Bernstein, *Socialisme théorique et social-démocratie pratique*, trans. Alexandre Cohen (Paris, 1900), pp. 47-63.

14. Roger Garaudy, *Les sources françaises du socialisme scientifique* (Paris, 1949), pp. 218-272.

15. André Marty, *Quelques aspects de l'activité de Blanqui* (Paris, 1951), pp. 19-28.

16. Paul Louis, *Les étapes du socialisme* (Paris, 1903), pp. 223-234; Alexandre Zévaès, *De l'introduction du Marxisme en France* (Paris, 1948), pp. 161-169; Maurice Dommanget, *Auguste Blanqui: Des origines à la révolution de 1848* (Paris, 1969), p. 7.

17. Maurice Dommanget, *Les idées politiques et sociales d'Auguste Blanqui* (Paris, 1957), p. 403.

18. Edouard Vaillant, "Les Blanquistes," in Léon de Seilhac, *Le monde socialiste* (Paris, 1904), pp. 83-86; cf. Jolyon Howorth, "La propagande socialiste d'Edouard Vaillant pendant les années 1880-1884," *Le mouvement social*, 72 (July-September 1970), 83-119, and "Edouard Vaillant," *International Review of Social History*, 17 (1972), 408-420.

19. Dommanget, *Les idées politiques*, pp. 397-398; Bibliothèque Nationale: Nouvelles acquisitions françaises, papiers philosophiques d'Auguste Blanqui, 9588(2), fo. 678, Lafargue to Blanqui, June 12, 1879 (hereafter cited as Blanqui MSS).

20. Maurice Duverger, *Les partis politiques*, 2d ed. (Paris, 1954), pp. 1-16.

21. Jacques Rougerie, *Procès des Communards* (Paris, 1964), pp. 235-249; Charles Rihs, *La Commune de Paris, 1871: Sa structure et ses doctrines* (Paris, 1973), pp. 7-21.

22. Patrick H. Hutton, "Popular Boulangism and the Advent of Mass Politics in France, 1886-90," *Journal of Contemporary History*, 11 (1976), 85-106; Zeev Sternhell, *La Droite révolutionnaire, 1885-1914: Les origines françaises du fascisme* (Paris, 1978), pp. 33-60.

Chapter II

1. Blanqui MSS, 9578-9598; Gustave Geffroy, *L'Enfermé* (Paris, 1926), II, 6.

2. Among the biographies of Blanqui, see esp. Alexandre Zévaès, *Auguste Blanqui* (Paris, 1920); Maurice Dommanget, *Blanqui* (1924, reprinted Paris, 1970); Sylvain Molinier, *Blanqui* (Paris, 1948); Alan Spitzer, *The Revolutionary Theories of Louis-Auguste Blanqui* (New York, 1951); and Samuel Bernstein, *Auguste Blanqui* (Paris, 1970).

3. Peter H. Amann, *Revolution and Mass Democracy: The Paris Club Movement in 1848* (Princeton, 1975), pp. 33, 119-122.

4. Georges Duveau, *1848: The Making of a Revolution*, trans. Anne Carter (New York, 1967), pp. 84, 117-124.

5. Gustave Tridon, "Le roman à la mode," *La patrie en danger*, October 15, 1870, p. 1; Arthur Ranc, *Souvenirs, correspondance, 1831-1908* (Paris, 1913), p. 31; Spitzer, *Revolutionary Theories*, p. 8.

6. Maurice Dommanget, *Un drame politique en 1848: Blanqui et le document Taschereau* (Paris, 1948); cf. Maurice Paz, "Clemenceau, Blanqui's Heir: An Unpublished Letter from Blanqui to Clemenceau Dated 18 March 1879," *The Historical Journal*, 16 (1973), 606, n. 8.

7. Maurice Dommanget, *Auguste Blanqui: Des origines à la révolution de 1848* (Paris, 1969), p. 7, has calculated that Blanqui spent a total of forty-three of his seventy-six years in prison or under direct penal surveillance.

8. On the origins of the Blanquist youth movement, see esp. Charles Da Costa, *Les Blanquistes* (Paris, 1912), pp. 6-8; Geffroy, *L'Enfermé*, II, 10-16; Maurice Dommanget, *Blanqui et l'opposition révolutionnaire à la fin du Second Empire* (Paris, 1960), pp. 51-54; Bernstein, *Auguste Blanqui*, pp. 246-254.

9. Wladimir Martel, *Mes entretiens avec Granger* (Paris, 1939), pp. 19-24; Auguste Scheurer-Kestner, *Souvenirs de jeunesse* (Paris, 1905), pp. 80-86; Geffroy, *L'Enfermé*, II, 45; Dommanget, *Blanqui et l'opposition révolutionnaire*, pp. 49-54. See also the interesting study by Bruce Mazlish, *The Revolutionary Ascetic* (New York, 1976), esp. pp. 3-43, which analyzes the psychological appeals of the revolutionary leader. Although Mazlish does not discuss Blanqui, his model of an ideal type of revolutionary ascetic could easily be applied to Blanqui.

10. Geffroy, *L'Enfermé*, II, 47-48.

11. Paul Lafargue, "Auguste Blanqui: souvenirs personnels," *La Révolution Française*, April 20, 1879, p. 1.

12. Louis-Auguste Blanqui, *Aux étudiants en médecine et en droit* (Paris, 1830).

13. Alexis de Tocqueville, *Recollections*, trans. George Lawrence, ed. J.P. Mayer and A.P. Kerr (1893; reprinted Garden City, N.Y., 1971), pp. 147-148.

14. Martel, *Mes entretiens*, p. 24; *Candide*, May 3-27, 1865.

15. Gaston Da Costa, *La Commune vécue* (Paris, 1903-1905), I, 428; open letter, Albert Regnard to Blanqui, *La patrie en danger*, October 25, 1870, p. 1.

16. On the legend of Blanqui in relation to the amnesty campaign of 1878-1880, see Alexandre Zévaès, *De la Semaine Sanglante au congrès de Marseille* (Paris, 1911), pp. 102-113; Jean T. Joughin, *The Paris Commune in French Politics* (Baltimore, 1955), I, 160-181; II, 245-269; and Maurice Dommanget, *Auguste Blanqui au début de la IIIᵉ République, 1871-1880* (Paris, 1971), pp. 39-118.

17. Ranc, *Souvenirs*, pp. 20-21.

18. Louis-Auguste Blanqui, *Critique sociale*, 2 vols. (Paris, 1885); Martel, *Mes entretiens*, pp. 19-20.

19. Benoît Malon, "Blanqui socialiste," *La revue socialiste*, 2 (1885), 586-597; and 9 (1889), 153-170, 288-301.

20. Louis-Auguste Blanqui, *L'éternité par les astres* (Paris, 1872); Louis Combes, *Portraits révolutionnaires: Blanqui* (Paris, 1872), p. 2.

21. Martel, *Mes entretiens*, pp. 150-154.

22. Ranc, *Souvenirs*, p. 27.

23. Jean Maitron, ed., *Dictionnaire biographique du mouvement ouvrier français* (Paris, 1964-1977), V, 19. Maitron provides valuable biographical sketches of nearly all the principal Blanquist militants.

24. Iouda Tchernoff, *Le parti républicain au coup d'état et sous le Second Empire* (Paris, 1906), pp. 286-362.

25. Blanqui MSS, 9589, liasse vi, fo. 325, Losson to Emile Gois, April 21, 1866; Martel, *Mes entretiens*, pp. 24-29.

26. Martel, *Mes entretiens*, pp. 21-24; Geffroy, *L'Enfermé*, II, 16-20.

27. Maitron, *Dictionnaire biographique*, V, 19-20; VI, 347; VIII, 344-345.

28. Da Costa, *La Commune vécue*, III, 361.

29. Much of this correspondence has been preserved in the Blanqui MSS, esp. 9592(2), liasse ix, fo. 49-51 (Jaclard), fo. 52-54 (Villeneuve), fo. 55-316 (Tridon); and 9594, liasse xi, fo. 214-248 (Villeneuve), fo. 329-380 (Genton, Losson, Chollet), fo. 397-465 (Edmond Levraud). For a more complete guide, see the inventory by Maurice Paz, "Auguste Blanqui: Le révolutionnaire professionnel" (thesis, doctorat ès lettres, University of Aix-en-Provence, 1974), pp. 161-260, a copy of which is available in the Salle des Manuscrits at the Bibliothèque Nationale.

30. Blanqui MSS, 9587, fo. 4-167, 420-430 (Biographies commandées par Blanqui).

31. Blanqui to Watteau, April 18, 1866, in Maurice Paz, ed., *Lettres familières d'Auguste Blanqui et du Docteur Louis Watteau* (Marseilles, 1976), pp. 213-215; Blanqui MSS, 9592(2), fo. 95-97, Tridon to Blanqui, March 26, 1866; fo. 98-100, Tridon to Blanqui, April 25, 1866.

32. Da Costa, *Les Blanquistes*, pp. 17-25; Maurice Paz, "Présentation des inédits," in *Lettres familières d'Auguste Blanqui*, pp. 19-20.

33. Geffroy, *L'Enfermé*, II, 57-59; Da Costa, *La Commune vécue*, III, 339; *La patrie en danger*, September 16 and 17 and November 4, 1870.

34. Dommanget, *Blanqui et l'opposition révolutionnaire*, pp. 105-106, 159-160, 163.

35. Archives de la Préfecture de Police, Paris (hereafter cited as APP), Ba/1098 (Gois), doc. 6; Ba/1238 (Regnard), newsletter "Les hommes d'aujourd'hui: Albert Regnard," (n.d. [ca. 1881]).

36. APP, Ba/1287 (Tridon), biographical report (n.d.), reports November 8, 1866, and November 18, 1876; Louis Watteau, *Préface*, in *Oeuvres diverses*, by Gustave Tridon (Paris, 1891), pp. v-xxiv; Maurice Dommanget, *Hommes et choses de la Commune* (Marseilles, 1937), pp. 120-130.

37. Blanqui MSS, 9592(2) fo. 67-68, Tridon to Blanqui, October 13, 1864.

38. APP, Ba/1287, report November 8, 1866.

39. Blanqui MSS, 9592(2), fo. 58-59, 62, 69-70, 76-78, 95-97, 113-167, Tridon to Blanqui, April 1864-March 1866.

40. APP, Ba/885 (Granger), biographical reports October 8, 1880, and January 30, 1882; Martel, *Mes entretiens*, pp. 11-48.

41. Blanqui MSS, 9592(2), fo. 168-169, Tridon to Blanqui, March 30, 1867.

42. Dommanget, *Hommes et choses,* pp. 149-165; APP, Ba/1067 (Eudes), docs. 30, 38, 156, 311-312.

43. APP, Ba/1177 (Mégy), biographical report September 1871; for Genton, see Dommanget, *Hommes et choses,* pp. 183-193.

44. Dommanget, *Hommes et choses,* pp. 174-182; Institut Français d'Histoire Sociale, Paris, 14 AS 99 bis: Papiers d'Emile Eudes (hereafter cited as Eudes MSS), Emile Eudes, "Note sur Duval," April 9, 1873, 14 pp.

45. Blanqui to Tridon [Bonnieux], n.d. (1866), Paz, *Lettres familières,* pp. 201-203; Georges Weill, *Histoire du mouvement social en France, 1852-1910,* 3d ed. (Paris, 1924), pp. 117-120; F.F. Ridley, *Revolutionary Syndicalism in France* (Cambridge, England, 1970), pp. 29-32, 36; Max Nomad, *The Anarchist Tradition,* in *The Revolutionary Internationals, 1864-1943,* ed. Milorad M. Drachkovitch (Stanford, 1966), pp. 59-62.

46. James Guillaume, *L'Internationale: Documents et souvenirs, 1864-1878* (1905; reprinted New York, 1969), I, 6, n. 2.

47. Blanqui MSS, 9591(2), fo. 362-363, Blanqui to Pierre Denis, September 14, 1868; fo. 473-498 (Notes sur le congrès de Genève); Dommanget, *Blanqui et l'opposition révolutionnaire,* pp. 203-213.

48. Dommanget, *Blanqui et l'opposition révolutionnaire,* pp. 213-216; Guillaume, *L'Internationale,* I, 75-76, 214-215; Julius Braunthal, *History of the International,* trans. Henry Collins and Kenneth Mitchell (New York, 1967), I, 136-139.

49. Braunthal, *History of the International,* I, 139; Ridley, *Revolutionary Syndicalism,* pp. 38, 41; Nomad, *The Anarchist Tradition,* p. 67; E.H. Carr, *Michael Bakunin* (1937; reprinted New York, 1961), pp. 150-152.

50. APP, Ba/1123 (Jaclard), report October 31, 1871; Jacques Freymond, ed., *Etudes et documents sur la Première Internationale en Suisse* (Geneva, 1964), pp. 205, 220.

51. Eudes MSS, Emile Eudes, "Note sur Duval."

52. Eudes MSS, Eudes to Vaillant, May 14, 1874.

53. Da Costa, *Les Blanquistes,* pp. 26-27; Geffroy, *L'Enfermé,* II, 42-45; Martel, *Mes entretiens,* pp. 43-46; Dommanget, *Blanqui et l'opposition révolutionnaire,* pp. 150-159.

54. Martel, *Mes entretiens,* pp. 233-234; Dommanget, *Hommes et choses,* pp. 149-165.

55. Martel, *Mes entretiens,* p. 46; Geffroy, *L'Enfermé,* II, 45; Bernstein, *Auguste Blanqui,* p. 274; Dommanget, *Blanqui et l'opposition révolutionnaire,* p. 158.

56. Da Costa, *Les Blanquistes,* pp. 26-27.

57. *Ibid.,* p. 31; Martel, *Mes entretiens,* pp. 46-48; Zévaès, *Auguste Blanqui,* p. 214.

58. Geffroy, *L'Enfermé,* II, 61.

59. Blanqui MSS, 9589, liasse vi (Affaire de société secrète, étudiants et ouvriers, 1866-67); 9591(2), liasse viii, fo. 182-273 (Procès de la Renaissance); Tchernoff, *Le parti républicain,* pp. 356-358; Da Costa, *Les Blanquistes,* pp. 17-25.

60. Blanqui MSS, 9592(2), fo. 82-85, Tridon to Blanqui, January 17, 1866; fo. 105-109, Tridon to Blanqui, December 25, 1866.

61. Maurice Paz, in his doctoral thesis "Auguste Blanqui," has decoded the pseudonyms of about twenty of the most important Blanquists.

62. APP, Ba/892 (Rigault), biographical reports June 29, 1872, and November 17, 1874; Alfred Breuillé, "Raoul Rigault," *Le branle-bas*, May 25 and June 1, 1884; Da Costa, *Les Blanquistes*, pp. 16, 27-28; Charles Prolès, *Les hommes de la révolution de 1871: Raoul Rigault* (Paris, 1898); Georges Laronze, *Histoire de la Commune de 1871* (Paris, 1928), pp. 31-47.

63. Da Costa, *La Commune vécue*, II, 250.

64. Prolès, *Les hommes . . . Raoul Rigault*, p. 18.

65. Da Costa, *La Commune vécue*, II, 122-123; Blanqui MSS, 9594, fo. 440, Edmond Levraud to Blanqui, November 3, 1868; 9592(2), fo. 170-171, Tridon to Blanqui, April 8, 1867.

66. For Blanqui's correspondence with Lacambre, see Dommanget, *Blanqui et l'opposition révolutionnaire*.

67. APP, Ba/1135 (Lafargue), biographical report November 1891; Blanqui MSS, 9592(2), fo. 510-513, Watteau to Blanqui, April 26, 1866; fo. 514-515, Lafargue to Blanqui, April 22, 1866; Tchernoff, *Le parti républicain*, pp. 338, 350-352; Dommanget, *Blanqui et l'opposition révolutionnaire*, pp. 50-51, 71-73, 111-114.

68. Blanqui MSS, 9593, fo. 286-287, Denis to Blanqui, September 5, 1868; Geffroy, *L'Enfermé*, II, 27-28; Paz, *Lettres familières*, p. 234; Paz, "Clemenceau, Blanqui's Heir," 604-615.

69. Da Costa, *Les Blanquistes*, pp. 17-25.

70. Eudes MSS, Emile Eudes, "Note sur Duval."

71. Maitron, *Dictionnaire biographique*, V, 19-20; VI, 347; VII, 155; IX, 321.

72. Laronze, *Histoire de la Commune*, p. 190.

73. Eudes MSS, letter from Emile Eudes concerning the organization of the Blanquist party as a secret society (n.d.).

Chapter III

1. André Lefèvre, *La renaissance du matérialisme* (Paris, 1881), pp. 115-134; Iouda Tchernoff, *Le parti républicain au coup d'état et sous le Second Empire* (Paris, 1906), pp. 303-315; Georges Weill, *Histoire de l'idée laïque en France au XIXe siècle* (Paris, 1925), pp. 348-361.

2. Henri Place [Henri Verlet], *1793-1869: Le peuple et la révolution; l'athéisme et l'Être suprême* (Paris, 1869), pp. 10-15; Place, "Rapport sur les origines de la 'pensée libre,'" *La pensée libre*, September 4, 1880, p. 2 (all references in the footnotes to Place's writings before the Commune will be to his pseudonym, Henri Verlet). See also Lefèvre, *La renaissance*, p. 127; Albert Regnard, Preface to *Force et matière*, by Ludwig Büchner, ed. and trans. Albert Regnard, 6th ed. (Paris, 1884), pp. xxv-xl.

3. Blanqui MSS, 9587, fo. 434-455 (Congrès de Liège). Albert Regnard, *Etude de politique scientifique: l'état* (Paris, 1885), p. 81; Tchernoff, *Le parti républicain*, pp. 316, 354; Charles Da Costa, *Les Blanquistes* (Paris, 1912), pp. 11-13.

4. Blanqui MSS, 9590(2), liasse vii, fo. 406-429 (Affaire des écoles); 9592(2), fo. 78-81, 89-90, 95-97, Tridon to Blanqui, December 20, 1865-March 26, 1866; APP, Ba/1123 (Jaclard), docs. 25-26, Jaclard to Charles Robert, secretary general of the Ministry of Education (n.d.); Albert Regnard, "M. Husson, les hôpitaux, et les médecins," *La patrie en danger,*

October 30, 1870, p. 1; Raoul Rigault, "Le service des garnis à la préfecture," *La patrie en danger*, November 10, 1870, p. 2. For the Blanquist demonstration of January 21, 1866 (l'affaire de la rue des Amandiers), see Wladimir Martel, *Mes entretiens avec Granger* (Paris, 1939), pp. 36-42.

5. Albert Regnard, Preface, pp. xxv-xl; APP, Ba/1238 (Regnard), newsletter "Les hommes d'aujourd'hui: Albert Regnard," (n.d. [ca. 1881]).

6. Henri Verlet, "Murmures," *L'excommunié*, October 30, 1869, pp. 3-4, offers the following estimates of the total circulation of Blanquist and Free-Thought newspapers during the Second Empire: *Candide* (1865) —18,000; *La libre pensée* (1867)—4,000; *Le démocrite* (1869)—6,000.

7. Raoul Rigault, "De la tolérance," *Le démocrite*, December 10, 1868, pp. 1-2; Auguste Vitu, *Les réunions publiques à Paris, 1868-1869* (Paris, 1869), pp. 16-17, 22-24, 34, 43, 46-47, 83.

8. Archives Nationales (cited hereafter as AN), BB[24] 742, dossier 2522 (Place).

9. For the Naples Anti-Council, see the articles by Henri Verlet in *La libre pensée*, January 24 and 29, 1870, and by Verlet, Denis Brack, Charles Le Balleur-Villier, and Giuseppe Ricciardi in *L'excommunié*, November 6, 13 and December 11, 18, 1869, also January 22, 1870; and Henri Place, "Rapport sur les origines de la 'pensée libre,'" *La pensée libre*, September 4, 1880.

10. Jehen Frollo, "Murmures," *La libre pensée*, January 24, 1870 pp. 3-4.

11. *La libre pensée*, February 5, April 23, May 28, June 4, 12, 25, and July 16, 1870; *Le réprouvé*, September 1872.

12. In *La libre pensée*: Jehen Frollo, "Murmures," January 24, 1870, pp. 3-4; Albert Goullé, "Les curés de campagne," February 19, 1870, p. 2; Goullé, "Le prêtre," April 2, 1870, p. 3; J.E. Loiseau, "Simeon Stylite," April 23, 1870, p. 3; A. Barbarreux, "Alexandre VI Borgia," May 14, 1870, p. 1; Henri Verlet, "Les hommes noirs," June 25, 1870, p. 1.

13. Alfred Breuillé, "Les églises de Paris," *La libre pensée*, January 28 and February 19, 1870.

14. Raoul Rigault, "MM. Dupanloup et Louis Veuillot," *Le démocrite*, January 15, 1868, p. 2; also, in *La libre pensée*: Alfred Breuillé, "La liberté de l'enseignement supérieur," April 16, May 21, and June 4, 1870; Casimir Bouis, "Le Jésuitisme," May 14, 1870, p. 1; Henri Verlet, "On les sifflera tous," June 4, 1870, pp. 1-2; Paule Mink, "Les vertus catholiques," July 9, 1870, p. 1.

15. Baron Antoine de Ponnat, *La croix ou la mort* (Brussels, 1862); Ponnat, *Histoire des variations et contradictions de l'Eglise Romaine* (Paris, 1882), 2 vols. See Tridon's comments on Ponnat in Blanqui MSS, 9592(2), fo. 63-64, Tridon to Blanqui, October 3, 1864.

16. Gustave Tridon, *Du Molochisme juif: Etudes critiques et philosophiques* (Brussels, 1884), pp. i-vii; Tridon, "La Force," *Revue socialiste*, 9 (1889), 41-53; Verlet, *1793-1869*, p. 3; Verlet, "Chronique d'un réprouvé," *La libre pensée*, April 30, 1870, pp. 1-2.

17. Tridon, "La Force," 42-43; Tridon, *Les Hébertistes*, 2d ed. (Paris, 1871), pp. 35-36, 40; Tridon, "Les martyrs de l'humanité," *Candide*, May 10, 1865, pp. 1-2.

18. Tridon, *Les Hébertistes*, p. 36.

19. Tridon, "La Force," 42; Tridon, *Du Molochisme juif*, ix, xii; Albert Regnard, "Sur l'existence de Jésus," *La libre pensée*, April 30, 1870, p. 1; Albert Goullé, "L'abnégation," *La libre pensée*, June 12, 1870, p. 1; open letter, Henri Verlet to Denis Brack, *L'excommunié*, May 22, 1869, p. 3.

20. Tridon, *Du Molochisme juif*, pp. xi-xii, xix-xx; Henri Verlet, "Un tournoi de Libres-Penseurs," *L'excommunié*, May 15, 1869, p. 2.

21. Concerning Comte, see the articles by Verlet, Regnard, and Célestin de Blignières in *La libre pensée*, February 12, 26 and March 5, 19, 26, 1870; see also Regnard, Preface, p. xxx.

22. Regnard, Preface, pp. xxxiv-xxxvi; Tridon, "La Force," 41; Henri Verlet, "Force et matière," *La libre pensée*, June 18, 1870, p. 1.

23. Regnard (Preface, p. xxxii) called Büchner's work "the catechism of youth" and credited him with sparking the materialist renaissance at the University of Paris in the early 1860s. See also Büchner's letter to his French admirers in *La libre pensée*, November 11, 1866.

24. Henri Verlet, "Force et matière," *La libre pensée*, April 16, 23, May 7, 14, 21, June 18, 25, and July 2, 1870.

25. *La libre pensée*, April 16, 1870, p. 4.

26. Tridon, *Du Molochisme juif*, pp. v-vi; Tridon, "La Force," 48.

27. Tridon, *Du Molochisme juif*, pp. xii-xvi, 5-48, 209-214. Tridon's concern with the significance of Christian origins sheds light upon Blanqui's obsessive polemic against the fourth-century Church fathers. See Blanqui [Suzamel], "Annales chrétiennes: Un père de l'Eglise au IVᵉ siècle, 340-420," *Candide*, May 6, 10, 1865.

28. Gustave Tridon, *Gironde et Girondins: La Gironde en 1869 et en 1793* (Paris, 1869), pp. 3-5; Tridon, "La Force," 41, 48; Tridon, *Du Molochisme juif*, pp. vi, xvii.

29. Tridon, "La Force," 46; Tridon, *Les Hébertistes*, pp. 18-19; Tridon, *Du Molochisme juif*, pp. ix-x, xvii; Regnard, Preface, pp. xxvi-xxvii; Regnard, *Le calendrier de l'ère révolutionnaire et sociale* (Paris, 1892), pp. 10-12; open letter, Regnard to Blanqui, October 31, 1870, *La patrie en danger*, November 2, 1870, p. 1.

30. François Viette, "Etienne Marcel," *Candide*, May 17, 1865; Gustave Tridon, "Servet et Giordano Bruno," *Candide*, May 17, 20, 1865; Albert Regnard, "Du rôle de la Commune de Paris," *L'affranchi*, April 3, 1871; Regnard, "Ce que nous sommes," *Le réprouvé*, September 1872.

31. Gustave Tridon, "Charlotte Corday," *Candide*, May 3, 1865; Tridon, *Les Hébertistes*, pp. 14-15, 26-27.

32. Tridon, *Les Hébertistes*, pp. 15-19.

33. *Ibid.*, pp. 42-44; Regnard, Preface, p. xxviii; Raoul Rigault, "Le spiritualisme et l'histoire," *Le démocrite*, January 11, 1868; Verlet, *1793-1869*, p. 7; Albert Mathiez, "Notes inédites de Blanqui sur Robespierre," *Annales historiques de la Révolution Française*, 5 (1928), 305-321.

34. Tridon, "Charlotte Corday"; Tridon, *Gironde et Girondins*, pp. 3-32; Raoul Rigault, "L'athéisme chez les Girondins," *Le démocrite*, December 3, 1868.

35. Tridon, *Du Molochisme juif*, pp. i-xxii.

36. Tridon, *Les Hébertistes*, pp. 20-23, 29, 31, 45, 55-69; Rigault, "L'armée révolutionnaire," *Le démocrite*, December 17, 1868.

37. Tridon, *Les Hébertistes*, pp. 18, 40.
38. Tridon, "La Force," 46-47, 50-51.
39. Tridon, *Les Hébertistes*, pp. 19, 39-54.
40. *Ibid.*, p. 47; Verlet, *1793-1869*, pp. 4-5.
41. Tridon, *Gironde et Girondins*, pp. 24-32; Regnard, *Le calendrier*, p. 12; Verlet, *1793-1869*, p. 4.
42. Regnard, *Le calendrier*, p. 19; Tridon, *Les Hébertistes*, pp. 33-34.
43. Raoul Rigault, "Le 21 janvier," *Le démocrite*, January 22, 1868.
44. Tridon, *Les Hébertistes*, p. 47; Verlet, *1793-1869*, p. 4.
45. *Les Hébertistes*, pp. 19, 31-32, 47-49.
46. *Ibid.*, p. 48.
47. Regnard, Preface, p. xxix; Tridon, "La Force," 46; Albert Goullé, "Des hommes nouveaux," *La patrie en danger*, November 11, 1870, p. 2.
48. Tridon, *Du Molochisme juif*, p. x.
49. Verlet, *1793-1869*, pp. 3-8.
50. *Ibid.*, pp. 5-6; Tridon, *Les Hébertistes*, pp. 18, 41, 46, 49; Albert Regnard, *Chaumette et la Commune de 93* (Paris, 1889).
51. For the Blanquists' attitudes concerning the significance of the Civil Burial movement, see the articles by Henri Verlet, Charles Le Balleur-Villiers, Denis Brack, and Benjamin Gastineau in *L'excommunié*, August 21, September 11, 25, October 23, and November 6, 1869; also the letter from Antony Jeunesse to Verlet in *La libre pensée*, May 14, 1870.
52. Verlet, "Le testament du libre penseur," *La libre pensée*, July 16, 1870, p. 3; Blanqui MSS, 9592(2), fo. 80-81, Tridon to Blanqui, January 3, 1866.
53. Da Costa, *Les Blanquistes*, p. 15.
54. Blanqui MSS, 9589, liasse vi, fo. 198-379 (Dossiers des prévenus).
55. "Un enterrement sans prêtres à Paris," *La libre examen* (Brussels), May 10, 1867, p. 3.
56. Regnard's eulogy is reprinted in Henri Verlet, "Un anniversaire," *La libre pensée*, January 24, 1870, p. 4.
57. Eugène Tenot, *Paris in December 1851*, trans. S.W. Adams and A.H. Brandon (New York, 1870), p. 168.
58. AN, BB[18]1780, dossier 9565 (l'affaire Baudin); Tchernoff, *Le parti républicain*, pp. 526-31; Da Costa, *Les Blanquistes*, pp. 29-30.
59. A. Brun, "Le premier duel de Victor Noir," *La libre pensée*, May 14, 1870, p. 4.
60. Ernest Granger, "L'oeil de la police," *Le réveil du peuple*, May 12, 1894, p. 2; Tchernoff, *Le parti républicain*, pp. 583-585; Da Costa, *Les Blanquistes*, p. 31.
61. *La libre pensée*, February 19 and April 2, 1870.
62. Henri Place, "Le quartier," *L'excommunié*, April 10, 1881, p. 1; Alfred Breuillé, "Raoul Rigault," *Le branle-bas*, June 1, 1884, p. 4.

Chapter IV

1. Robert Wolfe, "The Parisian Club de la Révolution of the 18th Arrondissement, 1870-1871," *Past and Present*, 39 (April 1968), 99; also

the following articles in *La patrie en danger*, 1870: Gustave Flourens, open letter, September 13; Gustave Tridon, "Angoisses," October 8; Tridon, "Pourquoi nous attaquons le gouvernement," October 9; Tridon, "Nouvelles provocations à la guerre civile," October 11; Tridon, "Ordre et liberté," October 13; Alfred Breuillé, "Vive la Commune de Paris!," October 8; Breuillé, "La Commune," October 10; Henri Verlet, "Vive la Commune!," October 12; Verlet, "La fête est terminée," November 9. All references to *La patrie en danger* in this chapter are for 1870.

2. Blanqui, Breuillé, Gaston Da Costa, Albert Goullé, Albert Regnard, Raoul Rigault, Tridon, and Verlet wrote for both newspapers.

3. See the following articles in *La patrie en danger*: Tridon, "La chouannerie bonapartiste," September 14; Tridon, "Vive la république et vive la France!," September 18; Tridon, "Angoisses," October 8; Tridon, "Un jeu de mot réactionnaire," September 15; Goullé, "Les partis," October 13; Breuillé, "Gouvernement provisoire et Commune de Paris," October 9; Blanqui, "Le commencement de la fin," October 18; Blanqui, "Alliance ouverte de la réaction," November 25.

4. *La patrie en danger*: Regnard, "Enfin," September 2; Regnard, "Le réveil du lion," September 15; Regnard, "L'opposition actuelle et son but," September 23; Verlet, "La fête est terminée," November 9; Blanqui, "Point d'assemblée," November 19.

5. Blanqui, *Instructions pour une prise d'armes*, ed. Georges Bourgin, in *Archiv für die Geschichte des Sozialismus und der Arbeiterbewegung*, 15, 2 (1930), 272-300, esp. 275-276, 298.

6. *La patrie en danger*: Breuillé, "La faim," September 14; Breuillé, "La ration," September 25; Breuillé, "Gouvernement provisoire et Commune de Paris," October 9; Breuillé, "La Commune," October 10; Goullé, "La question des vivres," September 14; Goullé, "Ambulances et sociétés de secours," September 16; Goullé, "Imprévoyance," October 19; Tridon, "La faim," September 19; Tridon, "Le terme," October 4; Gois, "Les barricades," November 5; Blanqui, "Les nécessités de la défense," September 28; Blanqui, "Conservons le gouvernement," October 14; Regnard, "Les subsistances et la taxe des riches," September 28; Kavanagh, "La ration," October 6; Verlet, "Les approvisionnements," October 3; Verlet, "Les boucheries municipales," October 8.

7. Rigault, "MM Dupanloup et Louis Veuillot," *Le démocrite*, January 15, 1868.

8. Gustave Tridon, "La France malheureuse," in *Oeuvres diverses*, ed. Louis Watteau (Paris, 1891), pp. 171-177, 181-182; also, in *La patrie en danger*: Tridon, "L'empire c'est la Prusse," September 2; Léonce Levraud, "La trahison de Bonaparte," September 12; Emile Villeneuve, "Comment on détruit une nation," September 15; Villeneuve, "Les deux frères," September 16; Frédéric Charrassin, "Les espions prussiens," September 16; Verlet, "Aux armes!" September 17; Verlet, "Les héros d'armistice," November 15; Casimir Bouis, "La réaction," September 25.

9. Eudes MSS, Eudes, "Les fautes du gouvernement de la défense nationale" (n.d.); also, in *La patrie en danger*: Blanqui, "La réaction," September 19; Blanqui, "Du fer et du plomb," September 22; Blanqui, "La dictature militaire," October 4; Blanqui, "Le péril grandit," October 5; Blanqui, "La défense nationale," September 23 and October 22, 23, 25; Verlet,

"L'ultimatum du peuple," September 21; Tridon, "Les Prussiens sont contents de nous," October 27; Tridon, "La Place du Panthéon," October 31; Goullé, "Des hommes nouveaux," November 11.

10. Tridon, "La France malheureuse" (in *Oeuvres diverses*), pp. 183-187; in *La patrie en danger*: Blanqui, "1792-1870," October 30; Blanqui, "L'abdication d'un peuple," November 14; Blanqui, "Le sort des peuples qui abdiquent," November 28; Goullé, "Un mot d'histoire," November 9.

11. *La patrie en danger*: Regnard, "Le rôle du clergé," September 13; Regnard, "La première aux catholiques," October 2; Tridon, "Le triomphe de Loyola," October 20; Verlet, "Matérialisme et matériallisme," October 31; Verlet, "Association des libres penseurs," November 16; Léon Lébéhot, "Troisième aux Corinthiens," November 25.

12. Verlet in *La patrie en danger*: "Association des libres penseurs," November 16; and "La Libre Pensée," November 20.

13. *La patrie en danger*: Tridon, "Obsèques des citoyens Lapie et Baudot," October 29; Verlet, "Faits et nouvelles," November 25.

14. Flourens, "Funérailles des tirailleurs de Belleville," *La patrie en danger*, December 2. Civil funerals conducted as revolutionary pageants continued to be sponsored during the Commune. See the vivid account of one of them by Maxime Vuillaume, *Mes cahiers rouges au temps de la Commune* (1909; reprinted Paris, 1971), pp. 168-188.

15. *La patrie en danger*: "Ecoles laïques," September 17; "L'enseignement laïque," October 11; "Le IIIe arrondissement," October 25.

16. *La patrie en danger*: Tridon, "Les agents de Bismarck," October 7; Tridon, "Le complot orléaniste," October 18; Verlet, "Vive Louis-Philippe II!" October 16; Blanqui, "Condamnation à mort de la république," November 7; Blanqui, "La fin d'une nation," November 8; Blanqui, "La dernière comédie," November 11; Blanqui, "Les trahisons," November 26.

17. Gaston Da Costa, *La Commune vécue* (Paris, 1903-1905), II, 134-135; Guillaume Cresson, *Cent jours du siège à la préfecture de police* (Paris, 1901), pp. 46-50.

18. Rigault, "Les agents secrets," *La patrie en danger*, November 15, 20, 25, 27.

19. Da Costa, *La Commune vécue*, III, 66, 368.

20. Blanqui in *La patrie en danger*: "Affaire de La Villette," September 16, 17; "La vérité sur le 31 October," November 4.

21. Da Costa, *La Commune vécue*, III, 313-357; Wladimir Martel, *Mes entretiens avec Granger* (Paris, 1939), pp. 51-59.

22. Summaries of the speeches at the Club Blanqui were reported daily in *La patrie en danger*. See also Vuillaume, *Mes cahiers rouges*, pp. 229-231; Gustave de Molinari, *Les clubs rouges pendant le siège de Paris* (Paris, 1871), pp. 9, 11, 15, 21-23, 27-30, 35-42; Charles Rihs, *La Commune de Paris, 1871: Sa structure et ses doctrines* (Paris, 1973), pp. 51-62.

23. *La patrie en danger*, September 13, 18, 19 and October 12. For Ferré's role in the clubs of Montmartre, see Wolfe, "The Parisian Club de la Révolution," pp. 91-99.

24. Auguste Vitu, *Les réunions publiques à Paris, 1868-1869* (Paris, 1869), pp. 10-24, 37-66, 83.

25. Molinari, *Les clubs rouges*, p. 22.

26. Cited in Samuel Bernstein, *Auguste Blanqui* (Paris, 1970), p. 274.

27. *La patrie en danger*: Tridon, "Le terme," October 4; Tridon, "Nouvelles provocations à la guerre civile," October 11; Verlet, "Vive la Commune," October 12; Verlet, "La nuit d'avant-hier," November 3; Breuillé, "Gouvernement provisoire et Commune de Paris," October 9; Regnard, "Le parti blanquiste," November 9.

28. Tridon, *Gironde et Girondins: La Gironde en 1869 et en 1793* (Paris, 1869), pp. 7, 14; Tridon, *Les Hébertistes*, 2d ed. (Paris, 1871), p. 14; Tridon, "La patrie en danger," *La patrie en danger*, September 3; Regnard, "L'abîme," *La patrie en danger*, November 14; Eudes MSS, Eudes to Vaillant, May 14, 1874.

29. *La patrie en danger*: Giuseppe Garibaldi, open letter, September 15; Tridon, "Le roman à la mode," October 15; Tridon, "Et Garibaldi," November 5; Da Costa, *La Commune vécue*, I, 358-365.

30. *La patrie en danger*: Kavanagh, "Restauration bonapartiste," September 22; Verlet, "Le deux decembre," December 3; Bouis, "La réaction," September 25; Tridon, "Angoisses," October 8; Tridon, "Nouvelles provocations à la guerre civile," October 11; Breuillé, "Vive la Commune de Paris!" October 8.

31. Tridon in *La patrie en danger*: "Vive la république et vive la France!" September 18; and "Ordre et liberté," October 13; Tridon, *Les Hébertistes*, p. 50; Eudes and Granger, "Truc réactionnaire," *La patrie en danger*, October 18.

32. Gaston Da Costa, *La Commune vécue*, III, 60; Charles Da Costa, *Les Blanquistes* (Paris, 1912), p. 41.

33. Gustave Geffroy, *L'Enfermé* (Paris, 1926), II, 57-59; Maurice Dommanget, *Blanqui, la guerre de 1870-71 et la Commune* (Paris, 1947), pp. 10-13; Ernest Granger, "L'oeil de la police," *Le réveil du peuple*, May 12, 1894, p. 2.

34. Granger, "L'oeil de la police," p. 2; Tridon, "La France malheureuse" (*Oeuvres diverses*), pp. 170-172; Iouda Tchernoff, *Le parti républicain au coup d'état et sous le Second Empire* (Paris, 1906), pp. 585-587; Charles Prolès, *Les hommes de la révolution de 1871: Gustave Flourens* (Paris, 1898), pp. 48-51; Prosper-Olivier Lissagaray, *Histoire de la Commune de 1871* (1896; reprinted Paris, 1970), pp. 40-45, 51; Flourens, *Paris livré* (Paris, 1871), pp. 7-12; APP, Ba/1177 (Mégy), report September 9, 1871.

35. Emile Gois and Raoul Rigault, *Le grand complot: Mélodrame plébiscitaire à grand spectacle* (Paris, n.d. [1870]).

36. Vuillaume, *Mes cahiers rouges*, p. 141; Dommanget, *Blanqui, la guerre . . . et la Commune*, pp. 13-15; Blanqui, "Affaire de La Villette," *La patrie en danger*, September 16, 17; Gabriel Brideau, "A Escande," *La patrie en danger*, November 26; Granger, "L'oeil de la police."

37. Martel, *Mes entretiens*, pp. 51-55.

38. Granger, "L'oeil de la police."

39. *Ibid.*; Blanqui, "Affaire de La Villette," *La patrie en danger*, September 17; Eudes MSS, Emile Eudes, "Note sur Duval," April 9, 1873; Da Costa, *La Commune vécue*, III, 339.

40. Da Costa, *La Commune vécue*, III, 312-326; Martel, *Mes entretiens*, pp. 55-59; Georges Bourgin, *Histoire de la Commune* (Paris, 1907), p. 35.

41. *La patrie en danger*, September 14, 15, 21, October 3, 4, 14, and November 7, 21, 27; Edward S. Mason, *The Paris Commune* (1930; reprinted

New York, 1967), pp. 85-93; Georges Duveau, *Le siège de Paris,·septembre 1870-janvier 1871* (Paris, 1939), pp. 72-83.

42. Da Costa, *La Commune vécue*, III, 357; Eudes MSS, Eudes, "Note sur Duval."

43. Jean Dautry and Lucien Scheler, *Le Comité Central Républicain des vingt arrondissements de Paris* (Paris, 1960), pp. 35, 53, 147-148; Rihs, *La Commune de Paris*, pp. 25-27.

44. Regnard, "La journée du 31 octobre," *La patrie en danger*, November 3; Flourens, *Paris livré*, pp. 137-154; Charles Da Costa, *Les Blanquistes*, pp. 35-36; Gaston Da Costa, *La Commune vécue*, III, 330-347; Stewart Edwards, *The Paris Commune, 1871* (New York, 1971), pp. 76-89.

45. Dautry and Scheler, *Le Comité Central*, pp. 134-135, 147-156; Da Costa, *La Commune vécue*, III, 347-357.

46. Gaston Da Costa, *La Commune vécue*, III, 347-357; Henri Place, "'Gustave Chaudey," *Le réveil du peuple*, February 3, 1894; Charles Da Costa, *Les Blanquistes*, p. 37; Vuillaume, *Mes cahiers rouges*, pp. 233-234, 417-418.

47. Regnard, "Le parti Blanqui," *La patrie en danger*, November 9.

48. Da Costa, *La Commune vécue*, III, 313-314, 320, 326-329.

49. *Ibid.*, I, 431-448; Lissagaray, *Histoire de la Commune*, pp. 231-236; Georges Laronze, *Histoire de la Commune de 1871* (Paris, 1928), pp. 183-449.

50. Maurice Dommanget, *Hommes et choses de la Commune* (Marseilles, 1937), pp. 12-24; Dommanget, *Blanqui, la guerre . . . et la Commune*, pp. 111-21.

51. Rihs, *La Commune de Paris*, pp. 88-89.

52. *Ibid.*, pp. 192-194, 211-217; Da Costa, *La Commune vécue*, III, 36-40; Jacques Rougerie, "Mil huit cent soixante et onze," *Le mouvement social*, 79 (April-June 1972), 50; Jean Bruhat, Jean Dautry, and Emile Tersen, *La Commune de 1871* (Paris, 1970), pp. 139-146.

53. Note that Gaston Da Costa, *La Commune vécue*, III, 31-38, minimizes the significance of the Communal Assembly.

54. Eudes MSS, Eudes, notes for a speech entitled "17 mars 1871" (1881); Eudes, "Note sur Duval."

55. Maxime Du Camp, *Les convulsions de Paris* (Paris, 1879), I, 64-66.

56. *Ibid.*, I, 64-80; Paul Lidsky, *Les écrivains contre la Commune* (Paris, 1970), pp. 47, 57, 60-61, 68-70.

57. Du Camp, *Les convulsions*, I, 65-69; Charles Prolès, *Les hommes de la révolution de 1871: Raoul Rigault* (Paris, 1898), pp. 41-48; Laronze, *Histoire de la Commune*, pp. 31-48 and passim; Jules Clère, *Les hommes de la Commune* (1871; reprinted New York, 1972), pp. 148-153.

58. Mason, *Paris Commune*, pp. 195-196.

59. Eudes MSS, Levraud to Eudes, November 12, 1871.

60. Da Costa, *La Commune vécue*, II, 141-142; Clère, *Les hommes*, pp. 84-86; Laronze, *Histoire de la Commune*, pp. 297-300; Jean Maitron, ed., *Dictionnaire biographique du mouvement ouvrier français* (Paris, 1964-1977), VI, 38.

61. Da Costa, *La Commune vécue*, II, 122-137.

62. *Ibid.*, II, 137-143.

63. The following discussion of the Blanquists' role in internal security relies heavily upon the detailed study of the police system and

judicial institutions of the Commune by Laronze, *Histoire de la Commune*, pp. 183-449; see also Da Costa, *La Commune vécue*, II, 217-223; and Mason, *Paris Commune*, pp. 195-198.

64. APP, Ba/1024 (Gaston Da Costa), esp. docs. 1, 353; "Gaston Da Costa," *Le réveil du peuple*, April 14, 1894; Da Costa, *La Commune vécue*, II, 219; III, 358-362; Laronze, *Histoire de la Commune*, pp. 265-267; Maitron, *Dictionnaire biographique*, V, 216-217.

65. Da Costa, *La Commune vécue*, I, 461-474.

66. APP, Ba/1238 (Regnard), newsletter "Les hommes d'aujourd'hui: Albert Regnard" (n.d. [circa 1881]); Regnard, "Du rôle de la Commune de Paris," *L'affranchi*, April 3, 1871; Laronze, *Histoire de la Commune*, pp. 267-69; Maitron, *Dictionnaire biographique*, VIII, 308.

67. Eudes MSS, Breuillé to Eudes, March 30, 1872; APP, Ea/40 (Breuillé); Laronze, *Histoire de la Commune*, pp. 271-272; Maitron, *Dictionnaire biographique*, IV, 414-415.

68. Laronze, *Histoire de la Commune*, pp. 269-271; Maitron, *Dictionnaire biographique*, VII, 154.

69. Laronze, *Histoire de la Commune*, pp. 279-282; Du Camp, *Les convulsions*, I.

70. Da Costa, *La Commune vécue*, II, 249; Laronze, *Histoire de la Commune*, pp. 272-279.

71. Da Costa, *La Commune vécue*, I, 432.

72. Philippe Cattelain, *Mémoires inédits du chef de la sûreté sous la Commune* (Paris, 1900), pp. 52-67, 110-113; Eudes MSS, Breuillé to Eudes, March 30, 1872.

73. Eudes MSS, Breuillé to Eudes, March 30, 1872.

74. Vuillaume, *Mes cahiers rouges*, pp. 381-385; Da Costa, *La Commune vécue*, II, 245-248; Laronze, *Histoire de la Commune*, pp. 184-190; Maitron, *Dictionnaire biographique*, VIII, 254-255.

75. APP, Ba/1177, report September 9, 1871; Laronze, *Histoire de la Commune*, pp. 190-194.

76. Laronze, *Histoire de la Commune*, p. 194.

77. *Ibid.*, pp. 195-261; Frank Jellinek, *The Paris Commune of 1871* (1937; reprinted New York, 1965), pp. 197-198; Lissagaray, *Histoire de la Commune*, pp. 238-239.

78. Da Costa, *La Commune vécue*, I, 431; Laronze, *Histoire de la Commune*, pp. 347-374; Mason, *Paris Commune*, pp. 266-273; Bruhat et al., *La Commune*, pp. 225-227; Edmond de Pressensé, *Les leçons du 18 mars* (Paris, 1871), pp. 65-67.

79. Prolès, *Les hommes . . . Raoul Rigault*, p. 46; Laronze, *Histoire de la Commune*, pp. 353-357.

80. Laronze, *Histoire de la Commune*, p. 374; Du Camp, *Les convulsions*, I, 98-101; Lissagaray, *Histoire de la Commune*, p. 232.

81. Da Costa, *La Commune vécue*, II, 239; Laronze, *Histoire de la Commune*, pp. 347-361.

82. Da Costa, *La Commune vécue*, II, 237-242; Laronze, *Histoire de la Commune*, pp. 362-374; Lissagaray, *Histoire de la Commune*, pp. 232-233; Mason, *Paris Commune*, pp. 270-273.

83. Da Costa, *La Commune vécue*, II, 251-272; Vuillaume, *Mes cahiers rouges*, pp. 121-126; Cattelain, *Mémoires*, pp. 184-194.

84. Da Costa, *La Commune vécue*, I, 426-428; Martel, *Mes entretiens*, pp. 73-81.

85. Da Costa, *La Commune vécue*, I, 410-430; Prolès, *Les hommes . . . Raoul Rigault*, p. 68; Benjamin Flotte, *Blanqui et les otages en 1871* (Paris, 1885), pp. 5-31, quote p. 14.

86. Flotte, *Blanqui et les otages*, pp. 24-29; Lissagaray, *Histoire de la Commune*, pp. 233-234; cf. Vuillaume, *Mes cahiers rouges*, pp. 236-238.

87. Da Costa, *La Commune vécue*, I, 410, 430; Mason, *Paris Commune*, p. 191; Lissagaray, *Histoire de la Commune*, p. 200; Jellinek, *Paris Commune*, pp. 197-198.

88. Da Costa, *La Commune vécue*, I, 432-445, quote p. 445; Prolès, *Les hommes . . . Raoul Rigault*, pp. 63-66.

89. Da Costa, *La Commune vécue*, I, 446.

90. Albert Goullé, "La Semaine Sanglante," and Alfred Breuillé, "Correspondance parisienne," in *Le branle-bas*, May 25, 1884.

91. Mason, *Paris Commune*, p. 282; Edwards, *Paris Commune*, pp. 313-350; Louis Fiaux, *Histoire de la guerre civile de 1871* (Paris, 1879), pp. 487-559.

92. Lissagaray, *Histoire de la Commune*, pp. 305-371; Lissagaray, *Les huit journées de mai derrière les barricades* (Brussels, 1871), pp. 1-285; Jellinek, *Paris Commune*, pp. 338-363; Bruhat et al., *La Commune*, pp. 255-280; J.-P. Azéma and Michel Winock, *Les Communards* (Paris, 1964), pp. 155-156.

93. Da Costa, *La Commune vécue*, I, 447-448.

94. Vuillaume, *Mes cahiers rouges*, pp. 190-191, 245-251; Mason, *Paris Commune*, p. 238.

95. Mason, *Paris Commune*, pp. 234, 238-240; Da Costa, *La Commune vécue*, II, 242-245.

96. Dommanget, *Hommes et choses*, pp. 149-165; Mason, *Paris Commune*, pp. 278-282; Fiaux, *Histoire de la guerre civile*, pp. 513, 516, 519, 523; cf. Edith Thomas, *Les "Pétroleuses"* (Paris, 1963), pp. 179-183.

97. Laronze, *Histoire de la Commune*, p. 615.

98. This justification was offered by the Blanquist group in exile, the Revolutionary Commune, in its manifesto *Aux Communeux* (June 1874), reprinted in Jean Maitron, "Le parti blanquiste de 1871 à 1880," *L'actualité de l'histoire*, 6 (January 1954), 13-19.

99. Eudes MSS, Eudes to Vaillant, May 14, 1874.

100. Da Costa, *La Commune vécue*, I, 463.

101. For a brief summary, see Mason, *Paris Commune*, pp. 275-278.

102. Vuillaume, *Mes cahiers rouges*, pp. 415-419; Lissagaray, *Histoire de la Commune*, p. 334; Henri Place, "Gustave Chaudey," *Le réveil du peuple*, February 3, 1894.

103. Vuillaume, *Mes cahiers rouges*, pp. 302-304.

104. *Ibid.*, pp. 304-306; Lissagaray, *Histoire de la Commune*, p. 340.

105. Vuillaume, *Mes cahiers rouges*, pp. 85-88; Lissagaray, *Histoire de la Commune*, pp. 338-339; Da Costa, *La Commune vécue*, II, 223-234.

106. Vuillaume, *Mes cahiers rouges*, pp. 59-66.

107. *Ibid.*, pp. 66-83; Lissagaray, *Histoire de la Commune*, pp. 343-344.

108. Vuillaume, *Mes cahiers rouges*, pp. 108-115; Lissagaray, *Histoire de la Commune*, p. 364.

109. Vuillaume, *Mes cahiers rouges*, pp. 116-121; Lissagaray, *Histoire de la Commune*, pp. 363-364.

110. Vuillaume, *Mes cahiers rouges*, pp. 423-427; Breuillé, "Correspondance parisienne," *Le branle-bas*, May 25, 1884; Place, "Le mur des fédérés," *Le réveil du peuple*, May 5, 1894; Bruhat et al., *La Commune*, pp. 278-279. Twenty-five thousand executions is the estimate of Azéma and Winock, *Les Communards*, p. 165. Jacques Rougerie, *Paris libre, 1871* (Paris, 1971), p. 257, believes the figure could be as high as thirty-four thousand.

111. Lissagaray, *Histoire de la Commune*, pp. 409-423; Jacques Rougerie, *Procès des Communards* (Paris, 1964), pp. 63-64, 85-87.

112. The complete text of Ferré's remarks can be found in Rougerie, *Procès des Communards*, pp. 85-87.

113. Da Costa, *La Commune vécue*, II, 139; Lissagaray, *Histoire de la Commune*, pp. 416-417.

114. Dommanget, *Hommes et choses*, pp. 192-193; Gaston Da Costa, "Nos morts—Genton, ouvrier sculpteur sur bois," *Le réveil du peuple*, March 31, 1894.

115. APP, Ba/1024, docs. 45, 56, 87-106; Da Costa, *La Commune vécue*, I, 447-448.

116. Eudes MSS, dossier Etienne Balsenq, esp. Henri Place to Breuillé, February 16 and October 31, 1874. Balsenq's letters have been published by Jean Maitron, "A partir des papiers du Général Eudes," *L'actualité de l'histoire*, 5 (October 1953), 18-24.

117. Charles Da Costa, *Les Blanquistes*, p. 40.

Chapter V

1. Wladimir Martel, *Mes entretiens avec Granger* (Paris, 1939), pp. 83-113; Charles Da Costa, *Les Blanquistes* (Paris, 1912), pp. 40-54; Miklos Molnar, "A Londres: Quelques jalons," *International Review of Social History*, 17 (1972), 304-317.

2. Da Costa, *Les Blanquistes*, p. 43.

3. Pierre Vésinier, "Société des réfugiés de la Commune," *La fédération*, August 24, 31, 1872; "Société des réfugiés de la Commune," *L'union démocratique*, August 31, 1872; APP, Ba/1067 (Eudes), docs. 59, 67, 77, 137-138; Ba/1098 (Gois), docs. 33, 50. Jean Maitron, "Le parti blanquiste de 1871 à 1880," *L'actualité de l'histoire*, 6 (January 1954), 9-11, suggests that Caria was trying to cover up his own theft.

4. APP, Ba/1067, docs. 1-189; Eudes MSS, dossier "Famille" (correspondence with Blanquists during the exile), esp. Breuillé to Eudes, July 13, 1873.

5. APP, Ba/1287 (Tridon), biographical report (n.d. [circa 1871]); "Enterrement de Gustave Tridon," *La liberté* (Brussels), September 4, 1871; Eudes MSS, Eudes to Dr. Louis Watteau, September 23, 1871; Maurice Paz, *Lettres familières d'Auguste Blanqui et du Docteur Louis Watteau* (Marseilles, 1976), pp. 234-235.

6. APP, Ba/1238 (Regnard), police reports 1872-1883; Da Costa, *Les Blanquistes*, pp. 41-42. For Regnard's role in the popularization of Tridon's thought during the 1880s and 1890s, see Chapter VI, pp. 156, 159.

7. Albert Regnard, Preface, in *Force et matière*, by Ludwig Büchner, trans. Albert Regnard, 6th ed. (Paris, 1884), p. xxx.

8. Karl Marx, *The Civil War in France*, in *Selected Works* (New York, 1970), pp. 274-313, esp. 274-288, 301-305.

9. *Ibid.*, pp. 282-283, 288-300, 308; Da Costa, *Les Blanquistes*, p. 42; APP, Ba/1067, doc. 104.

10. Maurice Dommanget, *Blanqui et l'opposition révolutionnaire à la fin du Second Empire* (Paris, 1960), pp. 189-222.

11. Marx, *Civil War in France*, pp. 288-294, 307-308; Maurice Dommanget, "Les Blanquistes dans l'Internationale de la chute de la Commune à la conférence de Londres," in Ernest Labrousse, ed., *La Première Internationale* (Paris, 1968), pp. 142-143; Miklos Molnar, *Le déclin de la Première Internationale* (Geneva, 1963), pp. 64-68, 109.

12. Those elected, it should be noted, were newcomers to the Blanquists' ranks, won over by the fervor of their participation in the Commune but uninitiated in the groups of the late 1860s. The veterans of this earlier association endorsed the newcomers' participation in the International but remained themselves at a certain remove.

13. Marx, *Civil War in France*, pp. 284, 288-295, 299-300, 310-311.

14. For the Blanquist critique of the Marxist interpretation of the Commune, see Gaston Da Costa, *La Commune vécue* (Paris, 1903-1905), III, 63-76.

15. Dommanget, "Les Blanquistes dans l'Internationale," pp. 141-149.

16. Alexandre Zévaès, *De l'introduction du Marxisme en France* (Paris, 1947), pp. 52-55; Zévaès, *De la Semaine Sanglante au congrès de Marseille* (Paris, 1911), pp. 18-21; Hans Gerth, ed., *The First International: Minutes of the Hague Congress of 1872* (Madison, Wis., 1958), pp. 280-283.

17. *Internationale et révolution: A propos du congrès de La Haye*, in *Cahiers de l'Institut de Science Economique Appliquée*, ser. S, 8 (August 1964), 164-173.

18. Martel, *Mes entretiens*, p. 99; Eudes MSS, Eudes to Vaillant, May 14, 1874.

19. Reprinted in Maitron, "Le parti blanquiste," 13-19.

20. Reprinted in Alexandre Zévaès, *Le socialisme en France depuis 1871* (Paris, 1908), pp. 316-322.

21. Friedrich Engels, *Le programme des réfugiés blanquistes de la Commune*, June 26, 1874, reprinted in *Le mouvement ouvrier français*, ed. and trans. Roger Dangeville (Paris, 1974), II, 72-80.

22. Quoted in part in Jeannine Verdès, "Les délégués français aux conférences et congrès de l'Association Internationale des Travailleurs," *Cahiers de l'Institut de Science Economique Appliquée*, ser. S, 8 (August 1964), 163.

23. Jolyon Howorth, "La propagande socialiste d'Edouard Vaillant pendant les années 1880-1884," *Le mouvement social*, 72 (July-September 1970), 83-119.

24. Vaillant tried to convince Blanqui of the advantages of this strategy in a long letter of September 8, 1880. Blanqui MSS, 9588(1), liasse v, fo. 409-412.

25. Eudes MSS, Eudes to Vaillant, May 14, 1874.

26. Da Costa, *La Commune vécue*, III, 59.

27. Blanqui MSS, 9588(1), liasse v, fo. 409-412.

28. Da Costa, *La Commune vécue*, III, 56-57; Maxime Vuillaume, *Mes cahiers rouges au temps de la Commune* (1909; reprinted Paris, 1971), p. 227;

Maurice Dommanget, *Edouard Vaillant: Un grand socialiste, 1840-1915* (Paris, 1956), pp. 17-87.

29. For a typical expression of Blanquist praise for Vaillant during the 1870s, see Eudes MSS, Edmond Levraud to Eudes, November 12, 1871.

30. For Vaillant's correspondence with Marx during the exile, see Molnar, "A Londres," 308-312.

31. Gabriel Terrail [Mermeix], *La France socialiste* (Paris, 1886), pp. 1-10 (Terrail is hereafter cited by his pseudonym); Charles Mauger, *Les débuts du socialisme marxiste en France* (Paris, 1908), p. 10; Georges Weill, *Histoire du mouvement social en France, 1852-1910*, 3d ed. (Paris, 1924), pp. 210-248.

32. Alexandre Zévaès, *Jules Guesde* (Paris, 1928), pp. 5-31; Samuel Bernstein, "Jules Guesde: Pioneer of Marxism in France," *Science and Society*, 4 (1940), 29-56; Claude Willard, Introduction, in Jules Guesde, *Textes choisis*, ed. Claude Willard (Paris, 1959), pp. 7-38.

33. Benoît Malon, "Le collectivisme en France de 1875 à 1879," *La revue socialiste*, 4 (1886), 990-1016; Zévaès, *De la Semaine Sanglante*, pp. 25-29, 53-61; Zévaès, *De l'introduction du Marxisme*, pp. 76-77; Mermeix, *La France socialiste*, pp. 41-57, 63-65; Samuel Bernstein, *The Beginnings of Marxian Socialism in France*, rev. ed. (New York, 1965), pp. 112-125; Maurice Dommanget, *L'introduction du Marxisme en France* (Lausanne, 1969), pp. 121-132, 154-162; Claude Willard, *Les Guesdistes* (Paris, 1965), pp. 11-15.

34. Mermeix, *La France socialiste*, pp. 63-68; Zévaès, *De l'introduction du Marxisme*, pp. 92-95; Dommanget, *L'introduction du Marxisme*, pp. 153-160; Jacques Girault, "Les Guesdistes, la deuxième *égalité* et la Commune (1880)," *International Review of Social History*, 17 (1972), 421-430.

35. On the messianic aspect of Guesdist ideology, see Michelle Perrot, "Les Guesdistes: Controverse sur l'introduction du Marxisme en France," *Les annales: Economies, sociétés, civilisations*, 22 (1967), 701-710.

36. Mermeix, *La France socialiste*, pp. 153-163; Weill, *Histoire du mouvement social*, pp. 244-246. For succinct statements of the Guesdist view of history, see Jules Guesde, "Le collectivisme" (1879), in Guesde, *Collectivisme et révolution*, ed. Alexandre-Marie Desrousseaux [Bracke] (Paris, 1945), pp. 7-28; and Gabriel Deville, *Aperçu sur le socialisme scientifique*, in Karl Marx, *Le capital*, ed. Gabriel Deville (Paris, 1883), pp. 1-63.

37. Mermeix, *La France socialiste*, pp. 61-62; Malon, "Le collectivisme," p. 994; Zévaès, *De l'introduction du Marxisme*, p. 109; Blanqui MSS, 9588(1), liasse v, fo. 389-392, Etienne Susini to Blanqui, November 13, 1879.

38. Summaries of the campaign can be found in Zévaès, *De la Semaine Sanglante*, pp. 102-113; Jean T. Joughin, *The Paris Commune in French Politics* (Baltimore, 1955), I, 160-181; II, 245-269; and Maurice Dommanget, *Auguste Blanqui au début de la IIIe République, 1871-1880* (Paris, 1971), pp. 39-118. There is an important dossier of press clippings and police intelligence reports dealing with the campaign in APP, Ba/868 (Blanqui, 1870-1879). On Roche's background, see Raymond Lavigne to Guesde, August 29, 1885, in Adéodat Compère-Morel, *Jules Guesde: Le socialisme fait homme, 1845-1922* (Paris, 1924), pp. 288-289.

39. Blanqui MSS, 9588(1), liasse v, fo. 160-166, Deville to Blanqui, March 28 and April 8, 9, 1879.

40. Eudes MSS, Eudes to Blanqui, June 11, 1879; Blanqui MSS, 9588(1), liasse v, fo. 72-79 (Casimir Bouis to Blanqui, October 1, 2, 9, 1879); fo. 350-351 (Henri Place to Blanqui, September 2, 1879); 9593, liasse x, fo. 277 (Chauvière to Blanqui, n.d.).

41. Paul Lafargue, "Auguste Blanqui: Souvenirs personnels," *La Révolution Française*, April 20, 1879.

42. Gabriel Deville, *Blanqui libre* (Paris, 1878), pp. 3-33.

43. Zévaès, *De l'introduction du Marxisme*, p. 97; Willard, *Les Guesdistes*, pp. 15-17.

44. Mermeix, *La France socialiste*, pp. 93-101; Weill, *Histoire du mouvement social*, pp. 230-232; Zévaès, *De la Semaine Sanglante*, pp. 74-88; Benoît Malon, "Le congrès de Marseille," *La revue socialiste*, 4 (1886), 1065-1088.

45. Zévaès, *De l'introduction du Marxisme*, p. 98.

46. Willard, *Les Guesdistes*, pp. 39, 137, 154.

47. Blanqui MSS, 9588(1), liasse v, fo. 389-392, Susini to Blanqui, November 13, 1879.

48. Blanqui MSS, 9593, liasse x, fo. 363-364, Susini to Blanqui, October 25, 1879.

49. Blanqui MSS, 9588(2), fo. 678, Lafargue to Blanqui, June 12, 1879.

50. Blanqui MSS, 9588(1) liasse v, fo. 1-424 (Correspondance—lettres de divers à Blanqui, 1879); APP, Ba/869 (Blanqui, 1880), reports concerning speeches by Blanqui, 1880.

51. Blanqui MSS, 9593, liasse x, fo. 156-158 (Roche to Blanqui, March 11 and April 7, 1880); fo. 357-358 (Roche to Blanqui, December 20, 1879).

Chapter VI

1. Blanqui MSS, 9593, liasse x, fo. 162-163, Roche to Blanqui, September 5, 1879.

2. These letters have been preserved in Blanqui MSS, 9588(1), liasse v.

3. *La pensée libre*, July 24, 1880-January 23, 1881, esp. Henri Place, "Rapport sur les origines de la 'pensée libre,'" September 4, 1880; "Echos," *Le mot d'ordre*, February 25, 1881; APP, Ba/1493 (Libre pensée), summary report for 1881; Ba/1514 (Parti blanquiste, 1881-1888), report March 1886.

4. *Le pays*, December 4, 1872; Albert Petrot, "Les grands Libres-Penseurs—Baudin," *La libre-pensée*, September 5, 1880, pp. 5-6; APP, Ea/32 (Baudin).

5. Jean Maitron, ed., *Dictionnaire biographique du mouvement ouvrier français* (Paris, 1964-1977), IX, 235.

6. Blanqui MSS, 9588(1), liasse v, fo. 418-419, Vallès to Blanqui, November 4, 1879.

7. APP, Ba/1081 (Flourens), docs. 57-66, 101-170, 177, 190-197, 203-220, 244, 248.

8. *Ibid.*, docs. 103, 107, 150.

9. "Exhumation de Théophile Ferré," *La voix du peuple*, July 28, 1881.

10. "Les obsèques de Blanqui," *La pensée libre*, January 8, 1881; "Mort de Blanqui," *Ni Dieu, ni maître*, January 9, 1881.

11. APP, Ba/869 (Blanqui), dossier "Anniversaire de la mort de Blanqui, 1882-1885."

12. *Ibid.*, dossier "Souscription pour élever un monument à la mémoire de Blanqui," reports 1881-1885; "Un monument à Blanqui," *Ni Dieu, ni maître*, January-November 1881; *Le républicain socialiste du centre*, October 14 and November 4, 1883, and February 3, 1884; APP, Ba/1514, report April 28, 1882.

13. Alfred Breuillé, "Souvenir," *Le ralliement*, January 4, 1890.

14. Paris, 1885, 2 vols.; Wladimir Martel, *Mes entretiens avec Granger* (Paris, 1939), pp. 145-147.

15. Paris, 1885, esp. pp. 30-31.

16. Martel, *Mes entretiens*, pp. 150-154.

17. Auguste Coussillan [Jacques Hillairet], *Dictionnaire historique des rues de Paris*, 2d ed. (Paris, 1964), pp. 117-118.

18. APP, Ba/1514, report March 3, 1882; Ba/1300 (Winant), reports February 14 and September 12, 1886; Ba/201 (Socialisme en France, 1885-1892), report November 5, 1888; *Le branle-bas*, May 25 and June 1, 1884; *Le cri du peuple*, February 18 and May 27, 1885; Benoît Malon, "Nos Morts," *La revue socialiste*, 1 (1885), 515-522; Malon, "La journée de huit août," *La revue socialiste*, 8 (1888), 216-218.

19. "Comité pour le monument de Delescluze et des fédérés," *Le républicain socialiste du centre*, December 23, 1883.

20. APP, Ba/1300, report August 15, 1886; Emmanuel Chauvière, "Le comité révolutionnaire central," *La revue socialiste*, 4 (1886), 1105; Albert Goullé, "La Semaine Sanglante," *Le branle-bas*, May 25, 1884; Edouard Vaillant, "Le 18 mars," *Le républicain socialiste du centre*, March 16, 1884.

21. APP, Ba/869, dossier "Anniversaire de la mort de Blanqui, 1882-1885," docs. 154-183.

22. "La tombe de Ferré," *Ni Dieu, ni maître*, November 29, 1880; Alfred Breuillé, "Le 28 novembre et l'affaire Morphy," *Ni Dieu, ni maître*, February 8, 1881.

23. *L'intransigeant*, December 11, 1887; APP, Ba/1514, report November 12, 1887.

24. Michel Roy, "L'affaire du Père-Lachaise," *Le cri du peuple*, May 30, 1888; APP, Ba/1258 (Rouillon), report May 28, 1888.

25. APP, Ba/1067 (Eudes), dossier "Obsèques d'Eudes," doc. 893.

26. For the founding of the Central Revolutionary Committee, see the regular columns "Un monument à Blanqui" and "Le comité révolutionnaire central," in *Ni Dieu, ni maître*, January-November 1881; also APP, Ba/869, dossier "Souscription pour élever un monument à la mémoire de Blanqui."

27. *Le branle-bas*, May 25, 1884, p. 3; Martel, *Mes entretiens*, pp. 141-145; see also Blanqui's brochure on the topic, published just before his death, *L'armée esclave et opprimée* (Paris, 1880), pp. 3-32.

28. Police reports for October 13, 1881, and March 13, 1886, in APP, Ba/1514 provide detailed analysis of the Blanquist organization. Ba/200 (Socialisme en France, 1882-1884), doc. 20, provides a list of Blanquist militants, with data concerning their addresses, subcommittee affiliations, and, in some cases, their ages and professions.

29. Eudes MSS, Winant to Eudes, January 7, 1885; Winant to David, October 29, 1885; APP, Ba/1300, February 19, May 9, 14, June 3, and July 9, 1885; October 25, 1886; July 17, 1888.

30. APP, Ba/885 (Granger), reports January 30, 1884 and June 23, 1885; Ba/1020 (Cournet), report August 28, 1884; Ba/1514, July 28 and September 19, 1883; Le républicain socialiste du centre, July 22, 1883-March 2, 1884.

31. APP, Ba/1515 (Parti blanquiste, 1888-1893), dossier "Ligue de la défense de la république," esp. summary report, October 1, 1888.

32. Chauvière, "Le comité révolutionnaire central," 4:1106; "Société républicaine d'économie sociale," La revue socialiste, 3 (1886), 73-83.

33. Maitron, Dictionnaire biographique, XI, 191.

34. APP, Ba/1020, report August 17, 1880; Ba/620 (Election législative du 2 mai 1886), report April 28, 1886; Ba/1249 (Rochefort), report May 17, 1885; Alexandre Zévaès, Henri Rochefort: Le pamphlétaire (Paris, 1946), pp. 256-257.

35. Zévaès, Henri Rochefort, pp. 155-158.

36. APP, Ba/1249, reports January 5, 12, 1881.

37. Ibid., report January 15, 1881.

38. Mermeix, La France socialiste (Paris, 1886), pp. 241-250.

39. APP, Ba/1249, report May 17, 1885.

40. APP, Ba/1515, reports July 31 and August 27, 1888; Ba/1300, December 29, 1885, March 1887, July 19-September 22, 1888; L'homme libre, July 30 and August 6, 16, 1888; Le cri du peuple, August 30, 1888.

41. Blanqui MSS, 9588(1), liasse v, fo. 384-399; 9593, liasse x, fo. 150, 363-373.

42. Blanqui MSS, 9588(1), liasse v, fo. 72-79, 295-296 (Bouis); 9593, liasse x, fo. 285-290 (Digeon).

43. For an analysis of Vaillant's articles in this newspaper, see Jolyon Howorth, "La propagande socialiste d'Edouard Vaillant pendant les années 1880-1884," Le mouvement social, 72 (July-September 1970), 83-119.

44. These newspapers of the 1880s were: La voix du peuple, ed. E. Roche (Bordeaux, 1881-1882); La tenaille, ed. J. Montaron (Chalons sur Saône, 1882-1883); Le réveil des travailleurs, ed. F. von Stackelberg (Nice, 1883-1884); Le républicain socialiste du centre, ed. E. Vaillant (Vierzon, 1883-(1884); Le butte aux cailles, ed. F. Winant (Lyons, 1884); Le branle-bas, ed. A. Farjat (Lyons, 1884); and Le progrès du Loiret, ed. A. Farjat (Orléans, ?).

45. Alfred Breuillé, "Correspondance parisienne," Le branle-bas, May 4, 1884; Le républicain socialiste du centre, April 19 and May 3, 10, 1884.

46. Blanqui MSS, 9588(1), liasse v, fo. 369-370; 9593, liasse x, fo. 156-158, 357-358, Roche to Blanqui, 1879-1880.

47. Maitron, Dictionnaire biographique, IX, 163.

48. APP, Ba/1020, docs. 548-566.

49. Jean Jolly, ed., Dictionnaire des parlementaires français, 1889-1940 (Paris, 1960-1977), V, 1841.

50. Vaillant's 39,490 votes represented the second highest figure received by any socialist candidate on the first ballot, but the minimum tally among those candidates subsequently elected was 113,121. In all, 434,000 persons actually voted ("Les voix socialistes dans la Seine," Le cri du peuple, October 12, 1885).

51. APP, Ba/620, docs. 1-3, 25, 46, 51, 62, 76, 188. The victor received 146,060 votes, compared with Roche's 100,820.

52. APP, Ba/1067, docs. 202-206, 586-600; Ba/911 (Chauvière), reports December 12, 14, 1883, May 4-11, 1884, and May 17, 1887; "L'élection de Javel," *Le cri du peuple*, May 26, 1887; Maurice Dommanget, *Edouard Vaillant: Un grand socialiste, 1840-1915* (Paris, 1956), pp. 73-79, 87.

53. The development of the quarrel can be followed in the exchange between the Blanquist-directed newspaper *Le cri du peuple* (Granger, ed.) and the Possibilist newspapers *Le prolétariat* (Paul Brousse, ed.) and *Le parti ouvrier* (Jean Allemane, ed.), from September 1888 through January 1889.

54. Martel, *Mes entretiens*, pp. 158-160.

55. For the populist viewpoint, see Mermeix, *La France socialiste*, pp. 264-275; Auguste Chirac, *L'agiotage sous la Troisième République, 1870-1887* (Paris, 1888), 2 vols.; Numa Gilly, *Mes dossiers* (Paris, 1888); and Emmanuel Beau de Lomenie, ed., *Edouard Drumont: Ou l'anticapitalisme national* (Paris, 1968).

56. For the appeals of the populist critique to the Blanquists, see the articles by Edouard Vaillant and Alexandre Girault in *Le républicain socialiste du centre*, July 1883-May 1884.

57. Charles-Ange Laisant, *L'anarchie bourgeoise* (Paris, 1887), pp. 292-325. For the theoretical contrast between populism and Marxism, see Alfred Naquet, *Socialisme collectiviste et socialisme libéral* (Paris, 1890); and Francis Laur, *De l'accaparement* (Paris, 1900), pp. 283-295.

58. The populist restatement of the Blanquist theory of the two nations is suggested in Emmanuel Chauvière's articles on the Blanquist party in the 1880s in *La revue socialiste*, 4 (1886), 1104-1106; and 5 (1887), 167-170, 385-394.

59. APP, Ba/1493, summary report for 1881; Pierre Lévêque, "Libre pensée et socialisme," *Le mouvement social*, 57 (October-December 1966), 101-141.

60. "Echos," *Le mot d'ordre*, February 25, 1881.

61. *Congrès universel des Libres-Penseurs* (Paris, 1889), pp. 1-16, 98-101, 114-120, 209-224, 287-288.

62. *Le ralliement*, January 11, 1890; *Le réveil du peuple*, March 18, 1893; January 6 and May 5, 1894.

63. *Le calendrier de l'ère révolutionnaire et sociale* (Paris, 1892), pp. 7-109.

64. *La tenaille*, January 14, 1883; *Le branle-bas*, May 25, 1884; *Le ralliement*, January 4, 1890.

65. APP, Aa/435 (Panthéon), report July 23, 1889; "La manifestation du 2 decembre," *Le monde illustré*, December 7, 1888, pp. 363-364.

Chater VII

1. Mermeix, *Les coulisses du Boulangisme* (Paris, 1890).

2. Wladimir Martel, *Mes entretiens avec Granger* (Paris, 1939), pp. 174-180.

3. APP, Ba/639 (Elections législatives, 1889), docs, 5168-5265; Ba/885 (Granger), reports August 22 and November 10, 1889; Ba/1067 (Eudes), March 21, 24 and June 16, 1888; Ba/1300 (Winant), June 11,

1888; Ba/1515 (Parti blanquiste), March 30, May 19, June 12, August 20, 1888, and January 11, 21, May 9, July 27, and December 10, 1889.

4. Jacques Néré, "La crise industrielle de 1882 et le mouvement boulangiste" (thesis, doctorat ès lettres, University of Paris, 1958), 2 vols.

5. Patrick H. Hutton, "Popular Boulangism and the Advent of Mass Politics in France, 1886-90," *Journal of Contemporary History*, 11 (1976), 85-106.

6. *La tenaille*, October 22, 1882, pp. 2-4.

7. See Vaillant's articles attacking Opportunism in *L'homme libre*, esp. June 25 and August 27, 1888; and Granger's of June 23, 25 and July 11, 1888. Concerning the Blanquists' sympathy for revisionism in the early 1880s, see Adrien Farjat, "Discussions vaut injures," *Le ralliement*, February 1, 1890.

8. APP, Ba/497 (Boulangisme), summary report "Attitudes des socialistes devant le mouvement boulangiste," November 1888; Ba/1515, esp. reports March 21, 25, 30, April 2, 3, 21, 25, May 9, June 22, and July 31, 1888.

9. *L'homme libre*, July 30 and August 16, 1888; *Le cri du peuple*, August 30, 1888.

10. APP, Ba/1598 (Crise présidentielle, 1887), reports November-December 1887.

11. APP, Ba/1514 (Parti Blanquiste), reports November-December 1887.

12. Ba/1067, report December 5, 1887; Ba/1514, December 3, 1887; Henri Rochefort, *The Adventures of My Life* (London, 1896), II, 317-321.

13. APP, Ba/1067, reports March 21, 24 and June 16, 1888; Ba/1300, June 11, 1888.

14. Vaillant, "Le danger," *L'homme libre*, August 23, 1888; Eudes MSS, Vaillant to Breuillé, July 16, 1888.

15. APP, Ba/1515, dossier "Scission." Hereafter these factions will be cited as CRC and CCSR.

16. APP, Ba/1514, report May 26, 1890; Ba/1258 (Rouillon), May 26, 1890; "La blessure du citoyen Rouillon," *L'intransigeant*, May 30, 1890.

17. Henri Rochefort, "La mort de Rouillon," *L'intransigeant*, September 12, 1890; Henri Place, "Rouillon," *Le ralliement*, September 13, 1890.

18. APP, Ba/1515, dossier CCSR, reports September 9, 10, 1890.

19. Hutton, "Popular Boulangism," 95-96.

20. Letters of Granger in *L'intransigeant*, October 10 and November 10, 1889; Jean Picard, "Les blanquistes: Conversation avec le citoyen Granger," *La cocarde*, October 24, 1889; Granger, "Réponse au député Thivrier," *Le ralliement*, January 25, 1890; Granger, "Coup d'oeil en arrière," *Le réveil du peuple*, November 5, 1892.

21. "La scission blanquiste," *Le temps*, August 17, 1889; Letter from the CRC in *La bataille*, October 16, 1889; APP, Ba/1514, report December 29, 1890; Maurice Dommanget, *Edouard Vaillant: Un grand socialiste, 1840-1915* (Paris, 1956), pp. 112-113.

22. APP, Ba/1515, dossier "CRC—Vaillant," reports 1891-1893; Charles Da Costa, *Les Blanquistes* (Paris, 1912), p. 67; Aaron Noland, *The*

Founding of the French Socialist Party, 1893-1905 (Cambridge, Mass., 1956), pp. 57-58. See also the CRC newspaper *Le parti socialiste*, 1891-1895.

23. Vaillant, "Les Blanquistes," in Léon de Seilhac, *Le monde socialiste* (Paris, 1904), pp. 83-86; Vaillant, *Un programme*, in *Almanach de la question sociale et de la libre pensée*, ed. Paul Argyriadès (Paris, 1892), pp. 25-30.

24. *La Commune vécue* (Paris, 1903-1905), III, 56-60.

25. *Les Blanquistes*, pp. 64-65.

26. Adrien Farjat, "Emile Eudes," *Le ralliement*, August 9, 1890; Henri Place, "Le 10 août 90," *Le ralliement*, August 16, 1890.

27. *L'intransigeant*, April 13, 1890; *Le ralliement*, April 19, 1890.

28. Place, "L'union," *Le réveil du peuple*, February 18, 1893; "Paris et sa banlieue," *Le réveil du peuple*, September 2, 1893.

29. APP, Ea/40 (Breuillé); *Le réveil du peuple*, April 15, 1893, March 10 and April 14, 1894.

30. APP, Ba/1517 (La Jeunesse blanquiste de Paris, 1891-1895).

31. Martel, *Mes entretiens*, pp. 221-227.

32. Maurice Paz, "Présentation des inédits," in *Lettres familières d'Auguste Blanqui et du Docteur Louis Watteau*, ed. Paz (Marseilles, 1976), p. 12.

33. See esp. the articles by Henri Place in *Le ralliement*, August 16, 1890, and *Le réveil du peuple*, August 5 and September 16, 1893, January 6, 13 and May 5, 1894.

34. *Le réveil du peuple*, March 31-June 23, 1894.

35. Paris, 1890, vol. I.

36. Gaston Da Costa, "Socialisme français," *Le réveil du peuple*, September 30, 1893; Alfred Breuillé, "Socialisme et patriotisme," *Le réveil du peuple*, June 2, 1894.

37. Alfred Gabriel, "Ouvriers étrangers," *Le réveil du peuple*, September 2, 1893; "La défense du travail national," *Le réveil du peuple*, January 6, 1894; Ernest Granger, "Gaston Da Costa—candidat à Grenelle," *Le réveil du peuple*, April 7, 1894.

38. C. Stewart Doty, "Parliamentary Boulangism after 1889," *The Historian*, 32 (1970), 250-269.

39. Granger, "Les Blanquistes," *Le ralliement*, March 22, 1890. See also the anti-Marxist statements in *Le ralliement* by Farjat, "Trop de théories," August 23, 1890; and Place, "'Vive' la France," October 25, 1890.

40. Maurice Paz, "Auguste Blanqui: Le révolutionnaire professionnel" (thesis, doctorat ès lettres, University of Aix-en-Provence, 1974), p. 21, charges that Granger, in an effort to erase any record of solidarity between Marx and Blanqui, obliterated a portion of a letter Marx wrote to Louis Watteau on November 10, 1861 (Blanqui MSS, 9594, fo. 310-311) offering to help raise funds to engineer Blanqui's escape from prison. The letter was part of the collection bequeathed by Granger to the Bibliothèque Nationale in 1899.

41. Place, "La lutte des classes," *Le réveil du peuple*, September 30, 1893.

42. APP, Ba/1515, report March 19, 1890.

43. Eugène Gellion-Danglar, "Sémitisme," *La libre pensée*, January 20, 1867; Eudes MSS, Edmond Levraud to Eudes, February 1, 1872; Eudes, "Cri d'alarme," *Le républicain socialiste du centre*, July 22, 1883; Albert Regnard, *Aryens et Sémites: Le bilan du Judaïsme et du Christianisme* (Paris, 1890), I, 5-7.

44. Regnard, *Aryens et Sémites*, pp. 5-12; Edouard Drumont, *La fin d'un monde* (Paris, 1889), p. 185; Robert F. Byrnes, *Antisemitism in Modern France: The Prologue to the Dreyfus Affair* (New Brunswick, N.J., 1950), pp. 156-158.

45. Granger, "Morès et Guérin," *Le réveil du peuple*, February 25, 1893. See also the anti-Semitic articles by Farjat in *Le ralliement*, February 15, 1890, and Place and Girault in *Le réveil du peuple*, January 21, February 25, September 16, December 30, 1893, and January 6, 1894.

46. Granger, "Morès et Guérin," *Le réveil du peuple*, February 25, 1893.

47. Da Costa, *La Commune vécue*, III, 364.

48. *Ibid.*, III, 362-371.

49. *La revue socialiste*, 9 (1889), 41-53.

50. Gabriel, "Pessimisme," *Le réveil du peuple*, August 5, 1893; Granger, "Le rocher de Sisyphe," *Le réveil du peuple*, July 28, 1894; Da Costa, *La Commune vécue*, II, 143; III, 367.

51. Da Costa, *La Commune vécue*, III, 367.

52. *Le ralliement*, January 4, 11, 1890; *Le réveil du peuple*, December 30, 1893, and January 6, 13, 1894.

53. *L'enfermé* (Paris, 1926), 2 vols.

54. Camille Mauclair, "Blanqui et l'énergie présente," *Mercure de France*, 23 (September 1897), 440-449.

Chapter VIII

1. Eduard Bernstein, *Socialisme théorique et social-démocratie pratique*, trans. Alexandre Cohen (Paris, 1900), pp. 47-63.

2. Mark Poster, *Existential Marxism in Postwar France* (Princeton, 1975), pp. 36-71.

3. Albert Regnard, *Aryens et Sémites: Le bilan du Judaïsme et du Christianisme* (Paris, 1890), I, 4-7.

4. Louis Watteau, *Préface*, in *Oeuvres diverses*, by Gustave Tridon (Paris, 1891), p. vi.

5. Bernstein, *Socialisme théorique*, pp. 55-63; André Marty, *Quelques aspects de l'activité de Blanqui* (Paris, 1951), pp. 21-29; Henri Lefebvre, *La proclamation de la Commune* (Paris, 1965), pp. 155-160.

6. Georges Sorel, *The Decomposition of Marxism*, in *Radicalism and the Revolt against Reason*, ed. Irving Horowitz (Carbondale, Ill., 1961), pp. 225, 228, 241-248.

7. François-André Isambert, *Christianisme et classe ouvrière* (Paris, 1961), p. 77.

8. See Paul Tillich's discussion of the philosophy of courage for the Stoics and for Spinoza, whom the Blanquist intellectuals much admired: *The Courage To Be* (New Haven, 1952), pp. 9-24.

9. Maurice Dommanget, *Blanqui, la guerre de 1870-71 et la Commune* (Paris, 1947), pp. 128-131.

10. See George Mosse's study of the relationship between the use of myth and symbol in mass politics and the rise of fascism in Germany: *The Nationalization of the Masses: Political Symbolism and Mass Movements in Germany from the Napoleonic Wars through the Third Reich* (New York, 1975).

11. Ernst Nolte, *Three Faces of Fascism*, trans. Leila Vennewitz (New York, 1966), pp. 429-454.

12. See Chapter I, pp. 9-10.

13. Jolyon Howorth, "La propagande socialiste d'Edouard Vaillant pendant les années 1880-1884," *Le mouvement social*, 72 (July-September 1970), 83-119, traces Vaillant's efforts to push his Blanquist comrades toward a perspective which modified traditional Blanquist precepts with Marxist insights. In his article "The Myth of Blanquism under the Third Republic, 1871-1900," *Journal of Modern History*, 48 (1976), 31 pp. (IJ-00010), Howorth distinguishes Vaillant's viewpoint from that of the old-guard Blanquists and points to the proto-fascist orientation of Granger and his faction.

14. Jean Touchard, *La Gauche en France depuis 1900* (Paris, 1977), p. 166.

15. Annie Kriegel, *Les communistes français: Essai d'ethnographie politique*, 2d ed. (Paris, 1970), esp. chaps. 6, 9, 11; George Lichtheim, *Marxism in Modern France* (New York, 1966), pp. 17, 53, 64-65, 68-79.

16. Annie Kriegel, "Le parti communiste français et la question du pouvoir, 1920-1939," *Les annales: Economies, sociétés, civilisations*, 21 (1966), 1245-1258.

17. Lichtheim, *Marxism*, pp. 70-71.

18. Zeev Sternhell, *La Droite révolutionnaire, 1885-1914: Les origines françaises du fascisme* (Paris, 1978), pp. 47-50, 189-190.

19. Robert Jay Lifton, *Revolutionary Immortality: Mao Tse-tung and the Chinese Cultural Revolution* (New York, 1968).

20. Geoffrey Barraclough, *An Introduction to Contemporary History* (1964; reprinted Baltimore, 1968), pp. 153-198.

21. See the suggestive study by Eric J. Hobsbawm, *Primitive Rebels: Studies in Archaic Forms of Social Movement in the 19th and 20th Centuries*, 2d ed. (New York, 1963), pp. 150-174.

Bibliography

I. Unpublished Sources

A. *Bibliothèque Nationale, Paris*

Nouvelles acquisitions françaises 9578-9598: Papiers philosophiques d'Auguste Blanqui (21 bundles [liasses] in 8 cartons). Referred to in notes as Blanqui MSS.

B. *Institut Français d'Histoire Sociale, Paris*

14 AS 99bis: Papiers d'Emile Eudes (1 large carton). Referred to in notes as Eudes MSS.

C. *Institut Universitaire de Hautes Etudes Internationales, Geneva*

Papiers d'Ernest Granger (4 small dossiers).

D. *Archives de la Préfecture de Police, Paris.* Referred to in notes as APP.

Aa/435, Panthéon.
Ba/200, Socialisme en France, 1882-1884.
Ba/201, Socialisme en France, 1885-1892.
Ba/366, Commune de Paris, généralités.
Ba/494-496, Enterrements civils, 1870-1881.
Ba/497, Boulangisme.
Ba/620, Election législative du 2 mai 1886.
Ba/639, Elections législatives, 1889.
Ba/868, Auguste Blanqui, 1870-1879.
Ba/869, Blanqui, 1880-1881; Anniversaire de la mort de Blanqui, 1882-1885.
Ba/885, Ernest Granger.
Ba/892, Raoul Rigault.
Ba/911, Emmanuel Chauvière.
Ba/969-977, Mouvement boulangiste.
Ba/1001, Germain Casse.
Ba/1020, Frédéric Cournet.
Ba/1024, Gaston Da Costa.
Ba/1067, Emile Eudes.
Ba/1081, Gustave Flourens.

Ba/1098, Emile Gois.
Ba/1123, Victor Jaclard.
Ba/1125, Antony Jeunesse.
Ba/1135, Paul Lafargue.
Ba/1157, Maxime Lisbonne.
Ba/1177, Edmond Mégy.
Ba/1238, Albert Regnard.
Ba/1249-1250, Henri Rochefort.
Ba/1258, Emile Rouillon.
Ba/1287, Gustave Tridon.
Ba/1288, Alexis Trinquet.
Ba/1300, François Winant.
Ba/1482-1484, Parti guesdiste, 1882-1893.
Ba/1493, *Libre pensée*, 1879-1891.
Ba/1514, Parti blanquiste, 1881-1888, 1890.
Ba/1515, Parti blanquiste, 1887-1893.
Ba/1517, Jeunesse blanquiste de Paris, 1891-1895.
Ba/1598, Crise présidentielle, 1887.
Ea/32, Alphonse Baudin, anniversaire de la mort de, 1872-1889.
Ea/40, Alfred Breuillé.
Ea/46, Alphonse Humbert.

E. *Archives Nationales, Paris.* Referred to in notes as AN.
BB¹⁸ 1780, dossier 9565, Affaire Baudin, 1867-1869.
BB²⁴ 742, dossier 2522, Henri Place.
BB²⁴ 862, dossier 5145, Emile Gois.
_____, dossier 5148, Albert Goullé.
_____, dossier 5155, Victor Jaclard.
_____, dossier 5168, Emile Moreau.
_____, dossier 5763, Eugène Protot.

F. *Archives Historiques du Ministre de la Guerre, Vincennes*
Conseils de guerre: Dossiers des insurgés
    4ᵉ conseil, no. 1148, Alfred Breuillé.
    6ᵉ conseil, no. 189, Gustave Genton.
Sous-série Lʸ: Commune de Paris
    Lʸ/17-19, Commissariats des arrondissements de Paris.
    Lʸ/132, Rapports sur les exécutions d'otages.

G. *Unpublished Studies*
Néré, Jacques. "La crise industrielle de 1882 et le mouvement boulan-
    giste." Thesis, doctorat ès lettres, University of Paris, 1958, 2 vols.
Paz, Maurice. "Auguste Blanqui: Le révolutionnaire professionel."
    Thesis, doctorat ès lettres, University of Aix-en-Provence, 1974.

II. *Published Sources*

A. *Newspapers* (Paris unless otherwise indicated)

Affranchi (L'). 1871.
Blanquiste (le). Lyons, 1890.
Branle-bas (Le). Lyons, 1884.
Butte (La) aux cailles. Lyons, 1884.
Candide (Le). 1865.
Courrier (Le) français. 1866.
Cri (Le) du peuple. 1871, 1883-1889.
Démocrite (Le). 1868.
Egalité (L'). 1868.
Etudiant (L'). 1867.
Excommunié (L'). Lyons, 1869-1870.
Fédération (La). London, 1872-1873.
Homme (L') libre. 1888.
Intransigeant (L'). 1889-1890.
Journal (Le) du peuple. 1889.
Libre (La) pensée. 1870.
Libre pensée (La). 1866-1867.
Libre-pensée (La). 1880.
Marseillaise (La). 1869-1870.
Monde (Le) illustré. 1871, 1888-1889.
Montagne (La). 1871.
Ni Dieu, ni maître. 1880-1881.
Nouvelle (La) république. 1870, 1871.
Ouvrier (L') de l'avenir. 1871.

Parti (Le) socialiste. 1891-1895.
Patrie (La) en danger. 1870.
Pensée (La) libre. 1880-1881.
Pensée (La) nouvelle. 1867-1869.
Phare (Le) de la Loire. Nantes, 1866.
Prolétaire (Le). 1871.
Ralliement (Le). Lyons, 1890.
Renaissance (La). 1869.
Réprouvé (Le). 1872.
Républicain (Le) socialiste du centre.
    Vierzon, 1883-1884.
Réveil (Le) des travailleurs. Nice, 1883.
Réveil (Le) du peuple. 1892-1894.
Révolution (La) Française. 1879.
Revue (La) encyclopédique. 1866.
Rive (La) gauche. 1864-1866.
Temps (Le). 1889.
Tenaille (La). Chalons sur Saône,
    1882-1883.
Union (L') démocratique. London,
    1872.
Victoire (La). Bordeaux, 1879.
Voix (La) du peuple. Bordeaux, 1881.

B. *Books and Pamphlets*

Amann, Peter H. *Revolution and Mass Democracy: The Paris Club Movement in 1848.* Princeton, 1975.

Amouroux, Charles, and Henri Place. *L'administration et les Maristes en Nouvelle-Calédonie: Insurrection des Kanaks en 1878-1879.* 2d ed. Paris, 1882.

Arnould, Arthur. *Histoire populaire et parlementaire de la Commune de Paris.* 1878; reprinted New York, 1972.

Azéma, J.-P., and Michel Winock. *Les Communards.* Paris, 1964.

Barraclough, Geoffrey. *An Introduction to Contemporary History.* 1964; reprinted Baltimore, 1968.

Bayet, Albert. *Histoire de la libre-pensée.* 3d ed. Paris, 1970.

Beau de Lomenie, Emmanuel, ed. *Edouard Drumont: Ou l'anticapitalisme national.* Paris, 1968.

Bernstein, Eduard. *Socialisme théorique et social-démocratie pratique*, trans. Alexandre Cohen, Paris, 1900.

Bernstein, Samuel. *Auguste Blanqui.* Paris, 1970.

──────. *The Beginnings of Marxian Socialism in France.* Rev. ed. New York, 1965.

──────. *Essays in Political and Intellectual History.* New York, 1955.

Blanqui, Louis-Auguste. *L'armée esclave et opprimée.* Paris, 1880.

──────. *Critique sociale.* 2 vols. Paris, 1885.

──────. *L'éternité par les astres.* Paris, 1872.

──────. *Aux étudiants en médecine et en droit.* Paris, 1830.

──────. *Instructions pour une prise d'armes*, ed. Georges Bourgin. In *Archiv für die Geschichte des Socialismus und der Arbeiterbewegung*, 15, 2 (1930), 272-300.

──────. *La patrie en danger.* Paris, 1871.

Blum, Léon. *Les congrès ouvriers socialistes français.* 2 vols. Paris, 1901.

Bourgin, Georges. *Histoire de la Commune.* Paris, 1907.

Braunthal, Julius. *History of the International*, trans. Henry Collins and Kenneth Mitchell. 2 vols. New York, 1967.

Bruhat, Jean, Jean Dautry, and Emile Tersen. *La Commune de 1871.* Paris, 1970.

Brunot, Ferdinand. *Histoire de la langue française des origines à 1900.* 13 vols. Paris, 1937.

Brynes, Robert F. *Antisemitism in Modern France: The Prologue to the Dreyfus Affair.* New Brunswick, N.J., 1950.

Carr, E.H. *Michael Bakunin.* 1937; reprinted New York, 1961.

Cassirer, Ernst. *The Myth of the State.* New Haven, 1950.

Cattelain, Philippe. *Mémoires inédits du chef de la sûreté sous la Commune.* Paris, 1900.

Charlton, Donald G. *Positivist Thought in France during the Second Empire, 1852-70.* Oxford, 1959.

──────. *Secular religions in France, 1815-70.* New York, 1963.

Chauvière, Emmanuel. *L'histoire devant la Raison et la Vérité.* Paris, 1880.

Chirac, Auguste. *L'agiotage sous la Troisième République, 1870-1887.* 2 vols. Paris, 1888.

Cleemputte, Paul Adolphe van. *Paris de 1800 à 1900.* 3 vols. Paris, 1901.

Clère, Jules. *Les hommes de la Commune.* 1871; reprinted New York, 1972.
Combes, Louis. *Portraits révolutionnaires: Blanqui.* Paris, 1872.
Compère-Morel, Adéodat. *Jules Guesde: Le socialisme fait homme, 1845-1922.* Paris, 1924.
Congrès universel des Libres-Penseurs. Paris, 1889.
Coussillan, Auguste [Jacques Hillairet]. *Dictionnaire historique des rues de Paris.* 2d ed. Paris, 1964.
Cresson, Guillaume. *Cent jours du siège à la préfecture de police.* Paris, 1901.
Da Costa, Charles. *Les Blanquistes.* Paris, 1912.
Da Costa, Gaston. *La Commune vécue.* 3 vols. Paris, 1903-1905.
Dautry, Jean and Lucien Scheler. *Le Comité Central Républicain des vingt arrondissements de Paris.* Paris, 1960.
Delord, Taxile. *Histoire illustrée du Second Empire.* Rev. ed. 6 vols. Paris, 1880-1883.
Deville, Gabriel. *Aperçu sur le socialisme scientifique.* In Karl Marx, *Le capital,* ed. Gabriel Deville. Paris, 1883.
────── . *Blanqui libre.* Paris, 1878.
Dommanget, Maurice. *Auguste Blanqui: Des origines à la révolution de 1848.* Paris, 1969.
────── . *Auguste Blanqui au début de la IIIᵉ République, 1871-1880.* Paris, 1971.
────── . *Blanqui.* Paris, 1924.
────── . *Blanqui, la guerre de 1870-71 et la Commune.* Paris, 1947.
────── . *Blanqui et l'opposition révolutionnaire à la fin du Second Empire.* Paris, 1960.
────── . *Un drame politique en 1848: Blanqui et le document Taschereau.* Paris, 1948.
────── . *Edouard Vaillant: Un grand socialiste, 1840-1915.* Paris, 1956.
────── *Hommes et choses de la Commune.* Marseilles, 1937.
────── . *Les idées politiques et sociales d'Auguste Blanqui.* Paris, 1957.
────── . *L'introduction du Marxisme en France.* Lausanne, 1969.
Drumont, Edouard. *La fin d'un monde.* Paris, 1889.
Dubois, Jean. *Le vocabulaire politique et social en France de 1869 à 1872.* Paris, 1969.
Du Camp, Maxime. *Les convulsions de Paris.* 4 vols. Paris, 1879.
Duveau, Georges. *1848: The Making of a Revolution,* trans. Anne Carter. New York, 1967.
────── . *Le siège de Paris, septembre 1870-janvier 1871.* Paris, 1939.
Duverger, Maurice. *Les partis politiques.* 2d ed. Paris, 1954.
Edwards, Stewart. *The Paris Commune, 1871.* New York, 1971.
Engels, Friedrich. *Le programme des réfugiés blanquistes de la Commune,* June 26, 1874. Reprinted in *Le mouvement ouvrier français,* ed. and trans. Roger Dangeville. 2 vols. Paris, 1974.
Engels, Friedrich, Paul Lafargue, and Laura Lafargue. *Correspondance,* ed. Emile Bottigelli. 3 vols. Paris, 1956.
Fiaux, Louis. *Histoire de la guerre civile de 1871.* Paris, 1879.
Flotte, Benjamin. *Blanqui et les otages en 1871.* Paris, 1885.
Flourens, Gustave. *Appel de la "Rive gauche" à la jeunesse européenne.* Brussels, n.d.
────── . *Paris livré.* Paris 1871.

Freymond, Jacques, ed. *Etudes et documents sur la Première Internationale en Suisse.* Geneva, 1964.

Garaudy, Roger. *Les sources françaises du socialisme scientifique.* Paris, 1949.

Geffroy, Gustave. *L'Enfermé.* 2 vols. Paris, 1926.

Gérard, Alice. *La Révolution française: Mythes et interprétations, 1789-1970.* Paris, 1970.

Gerth, Hans, ed. *The First International: Minutes of the Hague Congress of 1872.* Madison, Wis., 1958.

Gilly, Numa. *Mes dossiers.* Paris, 1888.

Girard, Louis. *Etude comparée des mouvements révolutionnaires en France, en 1830, 1848 et 1870-71.* Paris, 1969.

———. *La garde nationale.* Paris, 1964.

Girardet, Raoul. *Le nationalisme français, 1871-1914.* Paris, 1966.

Gois, Emile, and Raoul Rigault. *Le grand complot: Mélodrame plébiscitaire à grand spectacle.* Paris, n.d. [1870].

Guesde, Jules. *Collectivisme et révolution,* ed. Alexandre-Marie Desrousseaux [Bracke]. Paris, 1945.

———. *Textes choisis,* ed. Claude Willard. Paris, 1959.

Guesde, Jules, and Paul Lafargue. *Le Programme du Parti ouvrier: Son histoire, ses considérants, ses articles.* Paris, 1883.

Guillaume, James. *L'internationale: Documents et souvenirs, 1864-1878.* 4 vols. 1905; reprinted New York, 1969.

Hayes, Carlton J.H. *The Historical Evolution of Modern Nationalism.* New York, 1931.

Hobsbawm, Eric J. *Primitive Rebels: Studies in Archaic Forms of Social Movement in the 19th and 20th Centuries.* 2d ed. New York, 1963.

Internationale et révolution: A propos du congrès de la Haye. In *Cahiers de l'Institut de Science Economique Appliquée,* ser. S, 8 (August 1964), 164-173.

Isambert, François-André. *Christianisme et classe ouvrière.* Paris, 1961.

Jean-le-Veridique. *Libre pensée et enterrements civils.* Paris, 1883.

Jellinek, Frank. *The Paris Commune of 1871.* 1937; reprinted New York, 1965.

Jolly, Jean, ed. *Dictionnaire des parlementaires français, 1889-1940.* 8 vols. Paris, 1960-1977.

Joughin, Jean T. *The Paris Commune in French Politics.* 2 vols. Baltimore, 1955.

Kranzberg, Melvin. *The Siege of Paris, 1870-71.* 1950; reprinted Westport, Conn., 1971.

Kriegel, Annie. *Les communistes français: Essai d'ethnographie politique.* 2d ed. Paris, 1970.

Labrousse, Ernest, ed. *La Première Internationale.* Paris, 1968.

Lafargue, Paul. *Textes choisis,* ed. Jacques Girault. Paris, 1970.

Laisant, Charles-Ange. *L'anarchie bourgeoise.* Paris, 1887.

Larchey, Lorédon. *Memorial illustré des deux sièges de Paris.* Paris, n.d.

Laronze, Georges. *Histoire de la Commune de 1871.* Paris, 1928.

Laur, Francis. *De l'accaparement.* Paris, 1900.

Lefebvre, Henri. *La proclamation de la Commune.* Paris, 1965.

Lefèvre, André. *La renaissance du matérialisme.* Paris, 1881.

Lefranc, Georges. *Le mouvement socialiste sous la Troisième République, 1875-1940.* Paris, 1963.

Lefrançais, Gustave. *Souvenirs d'un révolutionnaire*. 1902; reprinted Brussels, 1972.

Lichtheim, George. *Marxism in Modern France*. New York, 1966.

————. *The Origins of Socialism*. New York, 1969.

Lidsky, Paul. *Les écrivains contre la Commune*. Paris, 1970.

Lifton, Robert Jay. *Revolutionary Immortality: Mao Tse-tung and the Chinese Cultural Revolution*. New York, 1968.

Ligou, Daniel. *Histoire du socialisme en France, 1871-1961*. Paris, 1962.

Lissagaray, Prosper-Olivier. *Histoire de la Commune de 1871*. 1896; reprinted Paris, 1970.

————. *Les huit journées de mai derrière les barricades*. Brussels, 1871.

Loubère, Leo. *Louis Blanc: His Life and His Contribution to the Rise of French Jacobin-Socialism*. Evanston, Ill., 1961.

Louis, Paul. *Les étapes du socialisme*. Paris, 1903.

McDonald, Joan. *Rousseau and the French Revolution, 1762-1791*. London, 1965.

Maitron, Jean, ed. *Dictionnaire biographique du mouvement ouvrier français*. 15 vols. Paris, 1964-1977.

Martel, Wladimir. *Mes entretiens avec Granger*. Paris, 1939.

Marty, André. *Quelques aspects de l'activité de Blanqui*. Paris, 1951.

Marx, Karl. *The Civil War in France*. In *Selected Works*. New York, 1970.

Mason, Edward S. *The Paris Commune*. 1930; reprinted New York, 1967.

Mauger, Charles. *Les débuts du socialisme marxiste en France*. Paris, 1908.

Mazlish, Bruce. *The Revolutionary Ascetic*. New York, 1976.

Mermeix. See Gabriel Terrail.

Molinari, Gustave de. *Les clubs rouges pendant le siège de Paris*. Paris, 1871.

————. *Le mouvement socialiste et les réunions publiques avant la revolution du 4 septembre 1870*. Paris, 1872.

Molinier, Sylvain. *Blanqui*. Paris, 1948.

Molnar, Miklos. *Le déclin de la Première Internationale*. Geneva, 1963.

Mosse, George. *The Nationalization of the Masses: Political Symbolism and Mass Movements in Germany from the Napoleonic Wars through the Third Reich*. New York, 1975.

Museux, Ernest. *Albert Regnard et Wagner*. Paris, 1911.

Naquet, Alfred. *Socialisme collectiviste et socialisme libéral*. Paris, 1890.

Noland, Aaron. *The Founding of the French Socialist Party, 1893-1905*. Cambridge, Mass., 1956.

Nolte, Ernst. *Three Faces of Fascism*, trans. Leila Vennewitz. New York, 1966.

Nomad, Max. *The Anarchist Tradition*. In *The Revolutionary Internationals, 1864-1943*, ed. Milorad M. Drachkovitch. Stanford, 1966.

Palmer, Robert R. *The Age of the Democratic Revolution*. 2 vols. Princeton, 1964.

Paz, Maurice, ed. *Lettres familières d'Auguste Blanqui et du Docteur Louis Watteau*. Marseilles, 1976.

Pilotell, Georges. *La caricature politique*. Paris, 1871.

Place, Henri [Henri Verlet]. *1793-1869: Le peuple et la révolution; l'athéisme et l'Etre suprême*. Paris, 1869.

Plamenatz, John. *The Revolutionary Movement in France, 1815-71*. London, 1952.

Ponnat, Baron Antoine de. *La croix ou la mort*. Brussels, 1862.

──────. *Histoire des variations et contradictions de l'Eglise Romaine*. 2 vols. Paris, 1882.

Poster, Mark. *Existential Marxism in Postwar France*. Princeton, 1975.

Prélot, Marcel. *L'évolution politique du socialisme français, 1789-1934*. Paris, 1938.

Pressensé, Edmond de. *Les leçons du 18 mars*. Paris, 1871.

Prolès, Charles. *Les hommes de la révolution de 1871: Gustave Flourens*. Paris, 1898.

──────. *Les hommes de la révolution de 1871: Raoul Rigault*. Paris, 1898.

Protot, Eugène. *Chauvins et réacteurs*. Paris, 1892.

Ranc, Arthur. *Souvenirs, correspondance, 1831-1908*. Paris, 1913.

Regnard, Albert. *Aryens et Sémites: Le bilan du Judaïsme et du Christianisme*. Vol. I. Paris, 1890.

──────. *Le calendrier de l'ère révolutionnaire et sociale*. Paris, 1892.

──────. *Chaumette et la Commune de 93*. Paris, 1889.

──────. *Essais d'histoire et de critique scientifiques à propos des conférences de la Faculté de Médecine*. Paris, 1865.

──────. *Etude de politique scientifique: L'état*. Paris, 1885.

──────. *Etude de politique scientifique: La révolution sociale, ses origines, son développement et son but*. London, 1876.

──────. Preface to Ludwig Büchner, *Force et matière*, ed. and trans. Albert Regnard. 6th ed. Paris, 1884.

Rémond, René. *La Droite en France de la première restauration à la Ve République*. Paris, 1963.

Ridley, Frederick F. *Revolutionary Syndicalism in France*. Cambridge, England, 1970.

Rihs, Charles. *La Commune de Paris, 1871: Sa structure et ses doctrines*. Paris, 1973.

Rochefort, Henri. *The Adventures of My Life*. 2 vols. London, 1896.

Rose, R.B. *Gracchus Babeuf: The First Revolutionary Communist*. Stanford, 1978.

Rougerie, Jacques. *Paris libre, 1871*. Paris, 1971.

──────. *Procès des Communards*. Paris, 1964.

Scheurer-Kestner, Auguste. *Souvenirs de jeunesse*. Paris, 1905.

Seilhac, Léon de. *Les congrès ouvriers en France de 1876 à 1897*. 2 vols. Paris, 1899.

──────. *Le monde socialiste*. Paris, 1904.

Siegfried, André. *Tableau des partis en France*. Paris, 1930.

Sorel, Georges. *The Decomposition of Marxism*. In *Radicalism and the Revolt against Reason*, ed. Irving Horowitz. Carbondale, Ill., 1961.

Soria, Georges. *Grande histoire de la Commune*. 5 vols. Paris, 1970.

Spitzer, Alan. *The Revolutionary Theories of Louis-Auguste Blanqui*. New York, 1951.

Sternhell, Zeev. *La Droite révolutionnaire, 1885-1914: Les origines françaises du fascisme*. Paris, 1978.

Tchernoff, Iouda. *Le parti républicain au coup d'état et sous le Second Empire*. Paris, 1906.

Tenot, Eugène. *Paris in December 1851*, trans. S.W. Adams and A.H. Brandon. New York, 1870.

Terrail, Gabriel [Mermeix]. *Les coulisses du Boulangisme*. Paris, 1890.

———. *La France socialiste*. Paris, 1886.

Testut, Oscar. *L'Internationale et le Jacobinisme au ban de l'Europe*. 2 vols. Paris, 1872.

Thomas, Edith. *Les "Pétroleuses"*. Paris, 1963.

Thomson, David. *The Babeuf Plot: The Making of a Republican Legend*. London, 1947.

———. *Democracy in France since 1870*. 5th ed. Oxford, 1969.

Tillich, Paul. *The Courage To Be*. New Haven, 1952.

Tocqueville, Alexis de. *Recollections*, trans. George Lawrence, ed. J.P. Mayer and A.P. Kerr. 1893; reprinted Garden City, N.Y., 1971.

Touchard, Jean. *La Gauche en France depuis 1900*. Paris, 1977.

Tridon, Gustave. *Gironde et Girondins: La Gironde en 1869 et en 1793*. Paris, 1869.

———. *Les Hébertistes*. 2d ed. Paris, 1871.

———. *Du Molochisme juif: Études critiques et philosophiques*. Brussels, 1884.

———. *Oeuvres diverses*, ed. Louis Watteau. Paris, 1891.

Tudesq, André-Jean. *La démocratie en France depuis 1815*. Paris, 1971.

Vaillant, Edouard-Marie. *Un programme*. In *Almanach de la question sociale et de la libre pensée*, ed. P. Argyriadès. Paris, 1892.

———. *Le suffrage universel et les élections municipales*. Paris, 1880.

Vallès, Jules. *L'insurgé*. 1885; reprinted Paris, 1970.

Verlet, Henri. See Henri Place.

Vitu, Auguste. *Les réunions publiques à Paris, 1868-1869*. Paris, 1869.

Vuillaume, Maxime. *Mes cahiers rouges au temps de la Commune*. 1909; reprinted Paris, 1971.

Watteau, Louis. *Préface*. In Gustave Tridon, *Oeuvres diverses*. Paris, 1891.

Weill, Georges. *Histoire de l'idée laïque en France au XIXᵉ siècle*. Paris, 1925.

———. *Histoire du mouvement social en France, 1852-1910*. 3d ed. Paris, 1924.

———. *Histoire du parti républicain en France, 1814-1870*. Paris, 1928.

Willard, Claude. *Les Guesdistes*. Paris, 1965.

———. *Socialisme et communisme français*. Paris, 1967.

Wohl, Robert. *French Communism in the Making, 1914-1924*. Stanford, 1966.

Woloch, Isser. *Jacobin Legacy: The Democratic Movement under the Directory*. Princeton, 1970.

Zévaès, Alexandre. *Auguste Blanqui*. Paris, 1920.

———. *Les Guesdistes*. Paris, 1911.

———. *Henri Rochefort: Le pamphlétaire*. Paris, 1946.

———. *De l'introduction du Marxisme en France*. Paris, 1947.

———. *Jules Guesde*. Paris, 1928.

———. *De la Semaine Sanglante au congrès de Marseille*. Paris, 1911.

———. *Le socialisme en France depuis 1871*. Paris, 1908.

C. *Articles*

Bernstein, Samuel. "Jules Guesde: Pioneer of Marxism in France." *Science and Society*, 4 (1940), 29-56.

Bruhat, Jean. "Anticléricalisme et mouvement ouvrier en France avant 1914: Esquisse d'une problématique." *Le mouvement social*, 57 (October-December 1966), 61-100.

Chauvière, Emmanuel. "Le comité révolutionnaire central." *La revue socialiste*, 4 (1886), 1104-1106; 5 (1887), 167-170.

_____. "Paris libre." *La revue socialiste*, 5 (1887), 385-394.

_____. "Société républicaine d'économie sociale." *La revue socialiste*, 3 (1886), 73-83.

Doty, C. Stewart. "Parliamentary Boulangism after 1889." *The Historian*, 32 (1970), 250-269.

Girault, Jacques. "Les Guesdistes, la deuxième *égalité* et la Commune (1880)." *International Review of Social History*, 17 (1972), 421-430.

Howorth, Jolyon. "Edouard Vaillant." *International Review of Social History*, 17 (1972), 408-420.

_____. "The French Socialists and Anti-Clericalism: The Position of Edouard Vaillant and the Parti Socialiste Révolutionnaire." *International Review of Social History*, 22 (1977), 165-183.

_____. "The Myth of Blanquism under the Third Republic, 1871-1900." *Journal of Modern History*, 48 (1976), 31 pp. (IJ-00010).

_____. "La propagande socialiste d'Edouard Vaillant pendant les années 1880-1884." *Le mouvement social*, 72 (July-September 1970), 83-119.

Hutton, Patrick H. "Popular Boulangism and the Advent of Mass Politics in France, 1886-90." *Journal of Contemporary History*, 11 (1976), 85-106.

_____. "The Role of the Blanquist Party in Left-Wing Politics in France, 1879-90." *Journal of Modern History*, 46 (1974), 277-295.

_____. "Vico's Theory of History and the French Revolutionary Tradition." *Journal of the History of Ideas*, 37 (1976), 241-256.

Kriegel, Annie. "Le parti communiste français et la question du pouvoir, 1920-1939." *Les annales: Economies, sociétiés, civilisations*, 21 (1966), 1245-1258.

Lévêque, Pierre. "Libre pensée et socialisme." *Le mouvement social*, 57 (October-December 1966), 101-141.

McInnes, Neil. "Les débuts du Marxisme théorique en France et en Italie, 1880-1897." *Cahiers de l'Institut de Science Economique Appliquée*, ser. S, 102 (June 1960), 5-51.

Maitron, Jean. "Le parti blanquiste de 1871 à 1880." *L'actualité de l'histoire*, 6 (January 1954), 5-25.

_____. "A partir des papiers du Général Eudes." *L'actualité de l'histoire*, 5 (October 1953), 4-24.

Malon, Benoît. "Blanqui socialiste." *La revue socialiste*, 2 (1885), 586-597; 9 (1889), 153-170, 288-301.

_____. "Le collectivisme en France de 1875 à 1879." *La revue socialiste*, 4, (1886), 990-1016.

_____. "Le congrès de Marseille." *La revue socialiste*, 4 (1886), 1065-1088.

_____. "La journée de huit août," *La revue socialiste*, 8 (1888). 216-218.

_____. "Nos Morts (Amouroux et Cournet)," *La revue socialiste*, 1 (1885), 515-522.

Mathiez, Albert. "Notes inédites de Blanqui sur Robespierre." *Annales historiques de la Révolution Française*, 5 (1928), 305-321.

Mauclair, Camille. "Blanqui et l'énergie présente." *Mercure de France*, 23 (September 1897), 440-449.

Mazauric, Claude. "Quelques voies nouvelles pour l'histoire politique de la Révolution Française." *Annales historiques de la Révolution Française*, 47 (1975), 149-163.

Molnar, Miklos. "A Londres: Quelques jalons." *International Review of Social History*, 17 (1972), 304-317.

Paz, Maurice. "Clemenceau, Blanqui's Heir: An Unpublished Letter from Blanqui to Clemenceau Dated 18 March 1879." *The Historical Journal* (Cambridge), 16 (1973), 604-615.

————. "Le mythe de la Commune." *Est et ouest: Bulletin de l'Association d'Etudes et d'Informations Politiques Internationales*, 476 (supplement: November 1-15, 1971), 449-460.

Perrot, Michelle. "Les Guesdistes: Controverse sur l'introduction du Marxisme en France." *Les annales: Economies, sociétés, civilisations*, 22 (1967), 701-710.

————. "Le premier journal marxiste français: 'L'égalité' de Jules Guesde, 1877-1883." *L'actualité de l'histoire*, 28 (July-September, 1959), 1-26.

Pillon, F. "Le socialisme d'Auguste Blanqui." *La critique philosophique*, 4 (1888), 61-71, 126-137.

Rougerie, Jacques. "Mil huit cent soixante et onze." *Le mouvement social*, 79 (April-June 1972), 49-77.

Soboul, Albert. "Tradition et création dans le mouvement révolutionnaire français au XIXe siècle." *Le mouvement social*, 79 (April-June 1972), 15-31.

Tridon, Gustave, "La Force." *La revue socialiste*, 9 (1889), 41-53.

Verdès, Jeannine. "Les délégués français aux conférences et congrès de l'Association Internationale des Travailleurs," *Cahiers de l'Institut de Science Economique Appliquée*, ser. S, 8 (August 1964), 163.

Wolfe, Robert. "The Parisian Club de la Révolution of the 18th Arrondissement, 1870-1871." *Past and Present*, 39 (April 1968), 99.

Index